Emotions and Understanding

Emotions and Understanding

Wittgensteinian Perspectives

Edited by

Ylva Gustafsson
Åbo Akademi University

Camilla Kronqvist
Åbo Akademi University

Michael McEachrane
University of Massachusetts, Amherst

First published 2009 by
PALGRAVE MACMILLAN

Palgrave Macmillan in the UK is an imprint of Macmillan Publishers Limited,
registered in England, company number 785998, of Houndmills, Basingstoke,
Hampshire RG21 6XS.

Palgrave Macmillan in the US is a division of St Martin's Press LLC,
175 Fifth Avenue, New York, NY 10010.

Palgrave Macmillan is the global academic imprint of the above companies
and has companies and representatives throughout the world.

Palgrave® and Macmillan® are registered trademarks in the United States,
the United Kingdom, Europe and other countries.

ISBN 978-1-349-29958-4   ISBN 978-0-230-58446-4 (eBook)
DOI 10.1057/9780230584464

A catalogue record for this book is available from the British Library.

Library of Congress Cataloging-in-Publication Data

Emotions and understanding : Wittgensteinian perspectives / [edited by]
Ylva Gustafsson, Camilla Kronqvist, Michael McEachrane.
    p. cm.
Includes bibliographical references and index.

1. Wittgenstein, Ludwig, 1889–1951. 2. Emotions (Philosophy)
3. Philosophy of mind. I. Gustafsson, Ylva, 1971– II. Kronqvist, Camilla,
1976– III. McEachrane, Michael.

B3376.W564E48 2009
128'.37092—dc22   2008034756

10 9 8 7 6 5 4 3 2 1
18 17 16 15 14 13 12 11 10 09

Transferred to Digital Printing in 2014

Contents

Acknowledgements

The idea of collecting these articles by philosophers working within the tradition after Ludwig Wittgenstein (1889–1951), grew out of the project Emotion and Understanding, which received funding from the Academy of Finland during the years 2002–2005. During this time, we, the editors, were able to write on our doctoral dissertations. In August 2005 we arranged an international conference, called 'Emotions, Others and the Self', with speakers such as Robert C. Solomon, Robert C. Roberts and psychologist Brian Parkinson, alongside some of the contributors to this anthology such as John V. Canfield, David Cockburn and Phil Hutchinson. It was in the wake of this conference that the idea of this anthology was developed.

During the past few years of bringing this idea into fruition our supervisor Lars Hertzberg has been a consistent source of support. We would like to express our gratitude to him. We would also like to thank the contributors of this volume for taking part, and for having patience with our comments on their papers.

The editors and publisher are grateful for the permission to republish Peter Hacker's article, 'The Conceptual Framework for the Investigation of the Emotions', which originally appeared in *International Review of Psychiatry*, Vol. 16, No. 3 (August 2004), pp. 199–208.

Contributors

John V. Canfield is Professor Emeritus, University of Toronto. He is the author of *Wittgenstein: Language and World* (1981), *The Looking-Glass Self* (1990), and *Becoming Human: The Development of Language, Self, and Self-Consciousness* (2007). He has edited *The Philosophy of Wittgenstein* (1986, in fifteen volumes) and *Philosophy of Meaning, Knowledge and Value in the Twentieth Century* (1997).

David Cockburn is Professor of Philosophy at University of Wales Lampeter. He has taught at the University of Wales Swansea, the Open University and Åbo Akademi University, and held a British Academy Readership from 1994–96. He is the author of *Hume* (1983), *Other Human Beings* (1990), *Other Times: Philosophical perspectives on past, present and future* (1997), and *An Introduction to the Philosophy of Mind* (2001), and editor of *Human Beings* (1991).

Alice Crary is associate professor in philosophy at the New School for Social Research. She is the author of *Beyond Moral Judgment* (2007), the editor of *Wittgenstein and the Moral Life: Essays in Honor of Cora Diamond* (2007) and the co-editor of *The New Wittgenstein* (2000) and *Reading Cavell* (2006). She has written articles on ethical theory, meta-ethics, moral psychology, philosophy and literature, and feminist theory, as well as on figures such as Wittgenstein and Austin. She is currently writing a book on animals and ethics, provisionally entitled *Minding Our Fellow Creatures: Humans, Animals, Right and Wrong*.

Ylva Gustafsson is a PhD student at the Department of Philosophy at Åbo Akademi University, Finland. She is currently working on her doctoral dissertation in which she discusses questions concerning emotion, language, body and understanding. Her interests in philosophy are moral philosophy, philosophy of psychology and philosophy of anthropology.

Peter M.S. Hacker is an Emeritus Research Fellow at St John's College, Oxford, where he was a Tutorial Fellow in philosophy from 1966 to 2006. He was an undergraduate at the Queen's College Oxford, a graduate student at St Anthony's College, Oxford, and a Junior Research Fellow at Balliol College, Oxford. He is the author of eighteen books and over hundred papers. His main interests lie in the philosophy of Wittgenstein, the history of analytic philosophy, philosophy of mind, and philosophy and cognitive neuroscience. Among his recent books are *Wittgenstein's Place in Twentieth-Century Analytic Philosophy* (1996); *Wittgenstein: Connections and Controversies* (2001); *Philosophical Foundations of Neuroscience* (co-authored with M.R. Bennett, 2003); *Neuroscience and Philosophy - Brain, Mind and Language* (co-authored with M.R. Bennett, D. Dennett, and J.R. Searle, 2007), and *Human Nature: the Categorical Framework* (2007), which is the first volume of a projected trilogy on human nature.

Lars Hertzberg is professor emeritus of philosophy at Åbo Akademi University, Finland. He received his master's degree at the University of Helsinki and his doctorate at Cornell University. He has written *The Limits of Experience* (1994), as well as a number of essays on the philosophy of mind, language, ethics and Wittgenstein. His current research concerns ethics, the will, and the philosophy of language. Home page: http://web.abo.fi/fak/hf/filosofi/Staff/lhertzbe/.

Phil Hutchinson is Senior Lecturer in Philosophy at Manchester Metropolitan University, UK. His philosophical interests include questions of philosophical method, with particular focus on Wittgenstein; philosophy of the emotions and moral psychology; political philosophy, with particular focus on ecologism; the philosophy of social science; film taken as philosophy; and theories of rhetoric. Phil has two books appearing in 2008: *Shame and Philosophy: An Investigation in the Philosophy of the Emotions and Ethics* and *There Is no Such Thing as a Social Science: In Defence of Peter Winch* (the latter co-authored with Wes Sharrock and Rupert Read). To relax Phil listens to a lot of Jazz, sees a lot of films and gets very animated when discussing politics (and very irritated when listening to politicians).

Camilla Kronqvist is a researcher and teacher at Åbo Akademi University. She wrote her doctoral dissertation, *What We Talk About when We Talk About Love* (2008), on the concept of love, examining its interrelations with discussions on emotions, personal identity and morality and meaning. Her research interests include moral philosophy, the philosophy of psychology and feminist philosophy.

Michael McEachrane grew up in Sweden, received his PhD in Philosophy from Åbo Akademi University in Finland, and is currently a Visiting Lecturer of Philosophy, Afro-American Studies, and German and Scandinavian Studies, at the University of Massachusetts, Amherst. From 2006 to 2008 he was a Visiting Assistant Professor of Philosophy at Baruch College, City University of New York. He has published a number of articles on the philosophy of psychology and the philosophy of race and has previously edited the Swedish anthology *Sverige och de Andra: Postkoloniala Perspektiv* (2001) [Sweden and the Other: Postcolonial Perspectives]. At the moment he is working on two more anthologies, Across Camps: Debating Philosophical Methods and Nordic Darkness: Engaging Blackness in Sweden.

Danièle Moyal-Sharrock is a Lecturer at the University of Hertfordshire. Her research interests are Wittgenstein, Philosophy of Psychology, Philosophy of Literature and Aesthetics. Her focus has been on defining and highlighting the importance of the post-*Investigations* corpus of the 'third' Wittgenstein. She is the author of *Understanding Wittgenstein's On Certainty* (2004), and the editor of *The Third Wittgenstein: The Post-Investigations Works* (2004), *Readings of Wittgenstein's On Certainty* (2005), and *Perspicuous Presentations: Essays on Wittgenstein's Philosophy of Psychology* (2007). She is presently preparing a book on the philosophy of literature: *Get the Plot!*

Rupert Read is a Reader in Philosophy at the University of East Anglia, Norwich. His research interests include the Philosophy of Language, Wittgenstein, Kuhn, Philosophy of Literature and Film and the Philosophy of Psychology, Rupert has published widely on all these subjects including his most recent books *Philosophy for Life* (2007) and *Applying Wittgenstein* (2007).

Duncan Richter is Professor of Philosophy at the Virginia Military Institute in Lexington, Virginia, USA. He is the author of the following books: *Why Be Good?: A Historical Introduction to Ethics* (2007), *Wittgenstein At His Word* (2004), *Historical Dictionary of Wittgenstein's Philosophy* (2004), and *Ethics After Anscombe: Post "Modern Moral Philosophy"* (2000).

Joachim Schulte has published a number of articles and four books on the philosophy of Wittgenstein: *Experience and Expression* (1993), *Wittgenstein: An Introduction* (1992), *Chor und Gesetz: Wittgenstein im Kontext* (1990) and *Wittgenstein: Leben Werk Wirkung* (2005). He is co-editor of critical editions of *Wittgenstein's Tractatus Logico-Philosophicus* (1989) and *Philosophical Investigations* (2001). In recent years, he has chiefly worked on Wittgenstein's middle period. Schulte teaches at the University of Zürich.

Introduction

Ylva Gustafsson, Camilla Kronqvist and
Michael McEachrane

The familiar picture on the front cover of this book might almost strike us as *the* true representation of a smiling, human face. So immediate is our normal reaction to it – feeling happy, perhaps smiling back – that one might think that *that* would be the natural thing to do. Nurses at Finnish health-care centres presumably have such a reaction in the backs of their minds as they hand out a picture similar to this one to parents and their newborns, along with the suggestion that babies like looking at it. The accompanying text tells us that babies enjoy warm colours and rounded shapes and that they like to look at human beings and *what resembles human beings*. This was what originally inspired us to use the picture on the front cover. Not that the image, abstract as it is, really gives anyone a good idea of what it may mean to take a Wittgensteinian approach to the expressions of emotion. Quite the contrary, it is suggestive of a temptation that a Wittgensteinian approach might help us dissolve. It is the tendency to neglect the particular case, or to think that a generalizing image gives us a better idea of what a smile means than what can be gained from reflecting on concrete situations, the contexts in which we talk about smiles and where we smile to each other or pretend to do so.

The picture illustrates some problems within the two approaches to the emotions which are currently most influential within analytic philosophy. These can be broadly divided into (1) reductionist, (naturalist, physicalist) explanations of the emotions, describing emotions in terms of subpersonal mechanisms, and (2) different forms of cognitivism, regarding emotions as judgements, thoughts, construals, or appraisals of situations, seeking to make sense of the intentional aspect of emotions. While philosophers of the first group align their research programmes with those of the natural sciences, those of the latter would, instead, attempt to bring out the rationality of emotions. Within the latter approach emotions are often regarded, in line with Aristotle, as a form of practical reasoning with important connections with ethical issues.[1]

1

First consider the *spontaneity* of our response to the front cover picture. This kind of immediacy is typically neglected in the cognitive accounts. Our reaction in this case does not appear to be mediated by thought or judgement, nor to rely on our linguistic abilities. Even a newborn may respond to the picture.[2] Emphasis on cognitive content thus leaves out the spontaneity and the bodily aspects of our emotional reactions. On the other hand, consider different situations in which we would talk about smiling and joy in human life. Now it seems, instead, that the mere registering of our reactions to a schematic drawing, and taking them as proof that our emotions can be explained in terms of physiology, constitutes another form of reductionism. Even if we in some sense can feel happy as we see the picture, this is true in a limited sense only. We would, for instance, not take the smile to indicate that *the picture,* too, *likes* us. Nor would we ask the picture if it has had a good day, or what has occasioned its cheery appearance. We would not wonder whether its smile was genuine or mere pretence to hide its true feelings. All these things, we might say, are central to understanding the roles that the words 'smile' and 'joy' have in our lives.

Undoubtedly, the two central strands of thought within analytic philosophy of emotions attend to important aspects of emotion. The first one emphasizes the bodily, physiological, character of emotion: the fact that, as John Deigh (2004) puts it, 'emotions are common to both humans and beasts' (p. 9).[3] The second one, in emphasizing intentionality, or the fact that emotions take objects and are directed at happenings in the world, brings out their sensitivity to various forms of reasoning. Such duality is a characteristic of many of our emotion words. We may speak of, say, *fear* when someone jumps at a loud noise, in which case we might think of fear as a purely primitive, bodily reaction. But we may also speak of someone's fear of a rapid decline in the stock market due to the instabilities of the economy of a leading nation. If attribution of fear is to be intelligible in this case, a far-reaching understanding of social, international and economic relations must be presupposed. Deigh claims that neither of the two parties of the debate has managed to accommodate both aspects of emotion in their theories.

The existing philosophical debates on emotions have largely centred on the classical dualism between body and mind, with its respective counterparts in dichotomies between nature and culture, biology and social convention, affect and cognition. Suggestions have been made about how one might bridge the gap between the two or reduce the one to the other. Hence the tendency by naturalist and physicalist approaches to embrace reductivist materialism, reducing questions of mind to those of body, and also to present reductionist accounts of the body by describing bodily feelings in terms of physiological and neurological changes and responses.

The Wittgensteinian perspectives on emotions offered in this work provide significant insights into the background assumptions of these debates. Rather than entrenching themselves on either side of the dichotomies, the contributors suggest that the dichotomies are themselves based on problematic philosophical perspectives on emotion, on the human body as well as on language and thinking.

In the following outline of the contributions to this anthology, we will sketch some of the possible implications of this new perspective for the way we should frame our questions about emotion. We will suggest that the prevailing tendency in philosophy of emotion to look for *definitions* of what emotions really are will necessarily lead to undue neglect of the various roles that our talk of individual emotions may have in our lives. In contrast, the present contributors raise questions such as: What is the relation of our emotions to questions about who we are? What is the role of emotion in revealing reality to us? How are emotions related to moral understanding? What is the importance of language for making sense of emotions?

The first two chapters, by Alice Crary and Joachim Schulte, both address issues arising from Wittgenstein's philosophy of mind: discussing Wittgenstein's philosophy of mind in general (Crary), and his remarks on emotions in particular (Schulte).

In her chapter 'Wittgenstein's Commonsense Realism about the Mind', Alice Crary describes Wittgenstein as an early critic of still prevailing trends in the philosophy of mind, trends that seem to disqualify our ordinary understanding of psychological discourse. Our ordinary discourse, she argues, is psychologically transparent in the sense that we do not arrive at a better grasp of its subject by replacing that discourse with a physical or otherwise non-psychological vocabulary. She argues that Wittgenstein advocated 'commonsense realism about the mind', making a clean break with reductive materialisms of all stripes, including the form of logical behaviourism with which he has often been associated. Wittgenstein was also hostile to a range of non-reductive materialisms where psychological discourse is reconstrued in ways that supposedly admit translation into the terms of the special sciences. By weaving together remarks from Wittgenstein's later work, such as the ones on rule-following and privacy, aspect seeing, and the psychological qualities of gestures, bodily postures and actions in humans and animals, Crary shows how Wittgenstein defends an attractive but currently marginalized conception of mind, still directly relevant to research into the nature of mindedness.

The scrutiny of the logic of psychological thought can shed light on what being minded is like. Taking her cue from this observation, available from within commonsense realism about the mind, Crary concludes her chapter by arguing that minded beings are, as such, *historical* in a sense that merely physical things are not. According to her striking suggestion, it follows from Wittgenstein's reflections on the mind that, in representing a given human or non-human creature as the subject of psychological predicates, we effectively treat that creature as irreplaceable.

In his chapter 'Wittgenstein on Emotion' Joachim Schulte addresses a tension between Wittgenstein's earlier and later remarks on emotion, made between 1946 and 1949. Wittgenstein's earlier emphasis on the unity of the concept of an emotion, epitomized in his second attempt to delineate a general classification of psychological concepts, contrasts with his later emphasis on differences between our concepts of individual emotions. The first part of Schulte's discussion puts particular weight on the role that Wittgenstein assigned to the 'course' of emotions, whereas Wittgenstein's modified approach rather focused on those complicated patterns of life in which our emotions are embedded.

Wittgenstein was, at first, tempted to generalize, thinking that the concept of emotion corresponds to definite psychological phenomena (experiences). Later he came to show more interest in the context-dependence of the relevant concepts and their uses. Viewed in that light, it may appear doomed from the start to look for sharp and definitive accounts of emotion terms. But our confusions in the philosophy of emotion may, in many cases, be traced to our inability or disinclination to acknowledge the multifarious character of our uses of these expressions.

The following chapters, by Peter Hacker, Phil Hutchinson and Michael McEachrane, criticize reductionist tendencies in accounts of emotion within neuroscience, psychology and philosophy.

In his chapter 'The Conceptual Framework for the Investigation of Emotions', Peter Hacker argues that the experimental study of the emotions is flawed as a consequence of an inadequate conceptual framework originally inherited from William James. Hacker draws careful distinctions between appetites, feelings, agitations, and moods, and between those and different species of emotion. He argues that the very diversity of the supposedly unitary phenomenon of emotion has given rise to the difficulties and conceptual confusions that, according to him, mark the work of cognitive neuroscientists such as LeDoux and Damasio. Emotions cannot be understood as *one* thing or as one sort of experience. By contrast, Hacker distinguishes between emotional perturbations and emotional attitudes, and he differentiates between attributing an object and a cause to an emotion. He explores the links between an emotion and reasons for the emotion, reasons for associated beliefs and for action, and he looks at the connections between emotion and care or concern, and between emotion and fantasy. He also clarifies the behavioural criteria for the ascription of emotion. In the light of this conceptual network, Damasio's theory of the emotions is subjected to critical scrutiny and found wanting.

In the chapter 'Emotion–Philosophy–Science', Phil Hutchinson addresses the debate between thinkers described as cognitivists and 'neo-Jamesians'.

The two parties of the debate supposedly face the problem of reconciling bodily and intentional aspects of emotion. Hutchinson examines the attempts by Paul Griffiths and Jesse Prinz, among others, to solve the dilemma and finds them to embrace forms of reductive materialism. Hutchinson suggests that the original dichotomy between the bodily and the intentional is based on mistaken presuppositions about what it means to think, as well as what we mean when we say that a person is afraid, angry, or the like. Hutchinson's criticism of Griffiths and Prinz has similarities with Hacker's criticism of Damasio, where Hacker argues that Damasio has neglected the difference between the cause and the object of an emotion.

Hutchinson's chapter highlights the tendency, in cognitive science and cognitive theories of emotions, to equate emotions with having beliefs and, in turn, to equate beliefs with having propositional attitudes. Much of the supposedly unbridgeable dichotomy between the bodily and spontaneous character of our emotions and, on the other hand, emotions as expressive of judgements, is based on a misconception about language. In his article 'Capturing Emotional Thoughts: The Philosophy of Cognitive-Behavioral Therapy' Michael McEachrane points to a similar tendency in cognitive-behavioural psychotherapies. It involves a narrow understanding of emotional reactions as caused by words or images running through our minds, and of beliefs as propositions lodged in our minds. McEachrane argues that misleading ideas of emotions as caused by beliefs, and of beliefs and thoughts as mental representations in the form of words or images, lead to misleading diagnoses and treatment methods. McEachrane points to the possibility of a broader understanding of emotions, beliefs and thoughts. How we *take* something to *be*, he claims, is more fundamental to both emotions and beliefs than are linguistic expressions; all of which, as he points out, is of consequence to therapeutic practice.

In the light of this point, there appears to be a flaw in the way John Deigh (2004, p. 9) characterizes the debate between cognitivist and reductionist accounts of emotion. He argues that the fact that we attribute emotions to *animals* is incompatible with any account of emotion that makes intentionality its central feature. True, it would certainly be problematic to describe an animal as, say, 'thinking', 'believing', 'fearing', and 'hoping', if that is taken to imply the attribution of propositional thoughts and the related linguistic capacities. But we do not need to buy into this narrow picture of intentionality. We may also see the idea of intentionality as expressive of the ways in which we see the behaviour and reactions of both animals and human beings in a context of meaning. Speaking of intentionality here is a reminder of how what we say is connected with other things we might go on to say. We might say, for instance, 'The cat is afraid of the dog' when it is running up a tree at the sight of a barking dog, without committing ourselves to saying that it entertains the thought, 'The dog is dangerous'. Furthermore, we may say, 'It thinks that the dog will return' when the cat is still anxiously sitting in the tree half an hour later. Again, describing the cat as anxious is, of course, also to see its behaviour in the light of a certain emotional understanding.

John V. Canfield's chapter, 'The Self and the Emotions', considers the different contexts in which we speak of the self (or rather of *ourselves*) and of the emotions. The utterance, 'I am afraid', is used as a point of departure, and Canfield argues that there are lessons to be learned from the recognition that, in many cases, neither the word 'I' nor 'afraid' have any clear referent. In contrast with a view common in philosophical discussions on personal identity, Canfield argues it would be an illusion to think that there is some such thing as a definable self. After a brief summary of his recent work on the topic, involving distinctions between the empirical self, the 'I' as grammatical fiction, and the narrative 'I', Canfield addresses the concept of fear in connection with several remarks by Wittgenstein. He, then, sets out to show the implications that his views about the self have for understanding the emotion of fear and, conversely, what his interpretation of fear tells us about the 'I'.

The emphasis on the need to understand bodily as well as linguistic expressions in their proper context is a significant theme in the articles by Lars Hertzberg and David Cockburn. They criticize the assumption that bodily expressions can be described in isolation from the contexts in which they occur, since that view would oversimplify the role of those expressions in human life. Their discussions demonstrate that the dualistic tendencies to distinguish between the body and the mind, or between nature and culture, are expressive of insufficient attention to the *conceptual connections* between bodily expressions and speech. In relation to this, they show how our spontaneous, embodied reactions and demeanour are constitutive of our understanding of ourselves and other people. This is true both of the bodily expressions of the other, which provide a background against which we understand her words, actions and responses, and of our own responses to those words, actions and responses.

In his chapter 'What's in a Smile?', Lars Hertzberg questions whether it is intelligible to understand smiles as natural or conventional signs. On one side of this debate he positions Charles Darwin, who in *The Expression of Emotion in Man and Animals* wished to establish that smiles are a natural expression of pleasant feelings by showing that the connection between pleasure and smiling is causal and universal. Nelson Goodman, on the other side of the debate, argued that what smiles mean is a matter of convention, since it varies between different societies. Hertzberg argues that neither view can tenably be upheld: the connection between smiling and pleasure cannot be a law of nature since normally smiles are not involuntary movements. The connection is not independent of the smiling person's will. But the connection is not conventional either, since genuine smiles, while not involuntary, are not voluntary actions either. The voluntary–involuntary distinction does not apply to most expressions of emotion.

According to Hertzberg it is central for our understanding of bodily expressions that they are usually uncontrolled and sometimes uncontrollable. This, on the other hand, does *not* mean that they are some kind of 'natural signs' in Paul Grice's sense, since genuine smiles are expressive of a person; a person may, for instance, be held accountable for smiling. Whether we consider an expression a smile is bound up with its significance in a context. This is connected with the fact that a person's coming to understand what smiles are importantly involves the fact that these expressions will sometimes move him in particular ways.

David Cockburn's discussion could be seen as a continued argument in the same line as Hertzberg's, only it gives more emphasis to the roles of language and conversation for the understanding of emotions. Language itself cannot be understood in abstraction from our bodily expressions and from the roles of conversation in our life. The stress on intentionality usually places language *in opposition to* the spontaneity typical of bodily expressions. By discussing the different roles that bodily expressions may have in personal conversation, Cockburn wants to dissolve the dichotomy. He argues that a spontaneous character is central to our talking and that this is internally related to what we mean by our words. Through the tone of their conversations, people express different perspectives on life. These different attitudes tell us much about who the speakers are, but they may also throw light on the real character of the situation.

Cockburn's chapter contains several reminders of how emotions and embodied reactions allow us to make sense of others, of ourselves and of the world. As opposed to the idea that clarity about the way things really are presupposes abstracting ourselves from personal involvement in our situation (cf. Crary), he points out that someone's emotional reaction in a conversation may reveal the true character of human reality to us. I may come to realize that the only proper way to understand a situation is precisely one that demands my emotional involvement. Furthermore, the chapter alludes to the fundamental role that Wittgenstein assigned to primitive reactions in making sense of our words.

Ylva Gustafsson's, Danièle Moyal-Sharrock's, Duncan Richter's and Camilla Kronqvist's chapters can be read as offering additional illumination of this idea, pointing out its implications for psychology, aesthetics and ethics.

In her chapter, 'Illusions of Empathy', Ylva Gustafsson identifies a problematic tendency in many current discussions of empathy. Empathy is typically construed as an epistemological and cognitive tool that may be used for understanding other minds. According to Gustafsson, the idea of empathy as a neutral imaginative technique is expressive of a conception of human understanding as a private, inner ability. However, what it means to understand another person cannot be described in isolation from our conversations with others and from what it is to have personal relationship with other people. The question of the *truth* about someone else's emotions is not a neutral question about facts, but is inseparable from our being responsible to others.

The idea that our understanding of others is based on a neutral ability to imagine other minds also tempts philosophers to accept certain images of cruelty as an expression of a sophisticated understanding of other people. According to Gustafsson this intellectualizing picture of cruelty is rather expressive of a moral blindness.

Danièle Moyal-Sharrock's chapter, 'The Fiction of Paradox: *Really* Feeling for Anna Karenina', is a response to the question how it is that we can be moved by what we know does not exist. She examines the so-called 'paradox of fiction', which states that our emotional response to fictional characters or situations is irrational – in the same way as it would be irrational for someone to feel glad that she won the lottery if she did not. Narrow cognitive theories would claim that we cannot experience genuine emotional responses to fictional characters as we do not believe that they exist, nor act upon them as if they did. Broader cognitive theories claim that our emotional responses while reading are directed not at the fictional characters, but at the thought of what happens to them. In contrast to these ideas, Moyal-Sharrock demonstrates how our emotional engagement in literature, and its ability to invoke emotional responses in us, are essential aspects of what it means, in the first place, to understand what one is told. Literature may, in effect, have a concept formative role in that it allows us to see and reflect on aspects of life that we would not experience without it, giving us the right words to appreciate the breadth and depth of our experience.

The discussions by Moyal-Sharrock and Cockburn both remind us of the fact that we learn about human reality through the eyes of others. Together with Gustafsson, they explore the essential role of linguistic expression in making sense of emotions. This is not merely in the sense that language is essential for (at least certain kinds of) logical and cognitive reasoning. The meaning of our words cannot be grasped in isolation from the contexts in which they are uttered, from our ways of saying things, from the tone of our voices, or, as in Moyal-Sharrock's case, the literary depiction, from 'the *inseparable* conjunction of form and content' (p. 171).

Duncan Richter's chapter, 'On the Pursuit of Happiness', follows up on the various remarks on joy and happiness that Wittgenstein makes in his earlier and later writings. It is a demonstration of the multifarious roles of the concept of happiness. As Richter brings out, happiness can be thought of as a kind of mood, in which nothing is observably different and yet in some, perhaps inexpressible, sense *everything* is different. Happiness can also be understood as a morally desirable state or life: either naturalistically, as in Aristotle's ethics and some contemporary virtue theory, or in more otherworldly terms, as in the Christian conception of blessedness. And, of course, happiness can be described as an emotion (joy) or a feeling (pleasure), importantly connected with, but not identical with, certain bodily sensations. Sketching the connections between these different uses of 'happiness', Richter remains critical of the idea that one could present objective criteria for determining whether someone is happy. In the same manner as Schulte comments on the impossibility of attaining a unitary concept of emotion on the basis of Wittgenstein's later remarks, Richter insists that any general description of happiness will remain vague. Different answers to the question whether or not something should count as (genuine) happiness will, by definition, reveal something about the values of the person who does the judging. The same predicament will face anyone who tries to advance a philosophical theory of happiness.

In her chapter, 'Our Struggles with Reality', Camilla Kronqvist criticizes the tendency to describe the perspective of love as a subjective response – a fantasy which does not attend to the way things are. This notion gives undue attention to the different concerns we express when we distinguish between what is 'real' and what is an 'ideal' in the contexts of our lives. It also fails to acknowledge what it may mean to speak about truth in the context of love. She contrasts the suggestion that the perspective of love inevitably constitutes an idealization of the beloved, or of life itself, with a view suggested by philosophers such as Iris Murdoch and Simone Weil. Those thinkers claimed, on the contrary, that love involves precisely a confrontation with the *reality* of other people. Thus there may be something important to learn about the concept of *reality*, as well as that of *philosophy*, if one tries to make sense of such formulations. Like Gustafsson, Kronqvist suggests that one's problems with understanding others often involve a *moral* difficulty that one may experience in being touched by others, or about letting them enter one's life. This may also be seen as a failure in loving and being loved.

In their respective discussions, Richter and Kronqvist bring out the importance of a certain sense of attunement to the world, or emotional engagement with it, in happiness and love. Both quote Wittgenstein's dictum in the *Tractatus*, 'The world of the happy is a different one from that of the unhappy' (Wittgenstein 1993, § 6.43). Relating that idea to Wittgenstein's later discussion, where emotions are likened to patterns in the weave of life (see e.g., Wittgenstein 1967, p. 174) discussed in the papers by Schulte and Cockburn, we may also read the remarks by Richter and Kronqvist in the light of an observation by Cockburn: 'we learn about another, not only through the propositions to which she is prepared to sign up, but also through the patterns in her speech' (p. 133). That is, we learn about the other through the things she is prone to remark upon, the kinds of judgement she tends to make, the tone of voice in which she makes them, and through her receptiveness and preparedness to see situations in particular ways.

The reference to the world of the happy and the unhappy also figures in the background of Rupert Read's article on extreme aversive emotions in psychotic psychopathology. Read hopes to establish a 'deep-grammatical' difference between 'fear' and, on the other hand, the 'dread' characteristic of these extreme emotions. However, he does not stop at depicting the world inhabited by the person experiencing dread, or at characterizing the object of this dread, or at describing dread as an objectless emotion. (The existence of objectless emotions is usually seen as constituting a threat to accounts of emotions in terms of intentionality.) Read suggests a 'more useful verbal object of comparison' (p. 229). He treats these drastic and difficult experiences as a form of *loss or absence of world*. This move brings out the oversimplification involved in any generalizing attempt either to identify objects for a given emotion or to call it objectless, as well as their ignorance of the vast effects of such conditions on the lives of those concerned.

Read comments not only on the experience of de-realization in dread, but also on the connected sense of depersonalization, unravelling the extreme difficulty we may feel in understanding someone who is in the grip of dread. Faced with the sufferer of a profound psychic disturbance, 'our conceptual faculties reach a limit, a limit *of sense*' (p. 226–227). Read does not explicitly make the connection, but against the backdrop of the previous introductory discussion, it is instructive to read his remarks about how our language in this sense 'gives out' p. 223 as another testimony to the fundamental role of our (emotional) reactions to another. The difficulty of describing the sufferer of profound psychic disturbances is not simply a psychological difficulty, nor merely a moral one, to make use of a distinction that Kronqvist uses in her article. As Read says, it is a difficulty in making *sense*.

However, as Wittgenstein has taught us, and as a lesson that finds resonance in most of the contributions to this anthology, our language makes sense only insofar as *we* are able to make sense of it *together*. Our language giving out in the context that Read describes marks the stage where our sense, our feeling, of togetherness is lost. To introduce yet another verbal object of comparison, we no longer share a world.[4]

Notes

1. In his contribution to this anthology, Phil Hutchinson elaborates on the differences between these two approaches.
2. This kind of criticism of cognitive accounts is in line with those often advanced by naturalist, physicalist accounts, frequently appealing to results from neurological research. Cf. Jenefer Robinson (2004) on LeDoux's work which shows that 'the auditory thalamus' – activated by stimuli connected with fear – not only sends signals to the *auditory cortex*, where the sound is 'cognitively processed' but 'also sends signals *directly* to the amygdala, *bypassing the cortex* altogether' (p. 36).
3. For further discussion of this quote, see Hutchinson, this volume.
4. Our colleagues at the Department of Philosophy at Åbo Akademi University are gratefully acknowledged for many helpful comments to this Introduction. Hugo Strandberg is acknowledged for insightful discussions about the front cover and the meaning of a smile. Olli Lagerspetz was of great help in giving the text its final form.

Bibliography

Deigh, J. (2004), 'Primitive Emotions'. in Solomon, R.C. (ed.) *Thinking About Feeling: Contemporary Philosophers on Emotions* (Oxford: Oxford University Press).

Robinson, J. (2004), 'Emotion: Biological Fact or Social Construction?' in Solomon, R.C. (ed.) *Thinking About Feeling: Contemporary Philosophers on Emotions* (Oxford: Oxford University Press).

Wittgenstein, L. (1967), *Philosophical Investigations* (Oxford: Blackwell).

———. (1993), *Tractatus Logico-Philosophicos* (London: Routledge & Kegan Paul).

1

Wittgenstein's Commonsense Realism about the Mind

Alice Crary

1.

Our ordinary modes of thought and speech encode an understanding of our practices with psychological concepts as philosophically unproblematic in the sense that there is no question of arriving at a better grasp of what justifies them by shifting to, say, physical or other natural scientific modes of description. Although it is not unheard of for philosophers to defend this ordinary understanding of psychological discourse, the stance is only modestly represented within contemporary philosophy of mind. At the most basic level, this is because there is an important sense in which this sort of *commonsense realism about the mind* offends against the materialist zeitgeist: it does so insofar as it not only treats psychological descriptions and explanations as resisting any sort of relevant reduction to physical (or other natural scientific) terms but moreover asks us to regard psychological qualities as elements of the 'fabric of the universe' that possess the effective or causal powers attributed to them within such descriptions and explanations. Admittedly, there are additional senses in which commonsense realism about the mind is consistent with materialist commitments. There is no good reason to think that acceptance, in accordance with such realism, of our ordinary understanding of psychological discourse obliges us to embrace an antimaterialism on which minds introduce 'gaps' into physical causal chains and on which we are therefore called on to talk about physical events that cannot be fully accounted for in the terms of physical science. Nor is there good reason to think that acceptance of this understanding obliges us to embrace an antimaterialism that denies claims about what is called *global mind-body supervenience*. Nevertheless, despite being hospitable to materialism in these two respects, commonsense realism opposes materialism in the respect already mentioned, and this opposition plays a central role in accounting for its modest profile in recent philosophical conversations.

This chapter is intended as a contribution to the project of showing that commonsense realism about the mind is tenable and that it deserves more philosophical attention than it currently receives. In the pages that follow, I start by identifying one significant elaboration of such realism. I argue that Wittgenstein is rightly read, not as sympathizing with the kinds of behaviorist positions with which he is more frequently associated, but rather as making a case for a commonsense realism about psychological qualities. The case Wittgenstein makes is the work of a number of interrelated lines of thought in his later writings, and what I offer here is simply a sketch of the main contours of these lines of thought. I first briefly describe several that are helpfully conceived as starting from an attack on basic presuppositions of traditional debates between dualists and reductive materialists and culminating in a criticism of the idea of an a priori justification for reductionism (Section 2). I then turn to further lines of thought that, building on this criticism, defend commonsense realism about the mind by inviting us to understand psychological qualities as both directly open to view perceptually and unrecognizable when described in physical or other natural scientific terms (Section 3). This defense will seem unpersuasive to those who, for one reason or another, are skeptical about the kind of departure from materialism that commonsense realism represents, and, although I do not try to fully address such skepticism, I say something about grounds for confidence that one fundamental expression of it can be answered (Section 4). Finally, after thus following up on a Wittgensteinian case for commonsense realism about the mind, I conclude my attempt to motivate such realism with a comment about its interest (Section 5).

2.

A good way to approach an account of Wittgenstein's opposition to dualist and reductive materialist views of mind is by first observing that debates between advocates of these views are often framed as referendums on the prospects for accommodating consciousness within the context of materialism reductively conceived and, further, that these debates accordingly often take for granted the idea, internal to reductive outlooks, that legitimate modes of discourse about the world must be in some sense reducible to physical vocabulary. Against the backdrop of this idea, it seems reasonable to ask whether it is possible to fully capture the mental life of, say, a living human being in physical terms, and, once this question has arisen, it may seem as though there are insurmountable obstacles to returning an affirmative answer.

Certain fundamental obstacles seem to crop up if we try to incorporate the very natural belief that there are facts about our mental lives that are by their very nature perspectival – facts about how things appear from the perspective of our individual conscious experience or, in other words, facts

about 'what it's like' to be us – while also assuming that physical modes of
description involve an epistemology that abstracts as far as possible from
perspectives afforded by any of our subjective endowments. The problem is
that it is not clear how minimally perspectival, physical modes of description, however useful for capturing other aspects of our lives, can do justice
to facts of the sort in question. This is significant in part because, within the
context of the kinds of reductionist commitments that originally seem to
suggest a problem, it appears that any facts that cannot be formulated in
physical terms are as such beyond the reach not merely of physical discourse
but of discourse *tout court*. It may for this reason seem compulsory to conclude that there are certain discursively inaccessible facts about us, and this
conclusion, while it is not without some outspoken materialist opponents,
has enough advocates to sustain a lively dispute about whether it is possible
to accommodate properties constitutive of the supposedly discursively inaccessible facts (i.e., 'qualia' or 'phenomenal qualities') within a reductive
materialist outlook. One thing that is noteworthy about this dispute is that,
insofar as it turns for its interest on the assumption that clarifying the
nature of certain putative logically private properties is equivalent to illuminating conscious mental experience, it invites us to understand conscious
mental experience as at home within a logically private domain.

It is widely recognized that Wittgenstein criticizes the relevant notion of
logical privacy in portions of the *Investigations* (1967) that are sometimes
referred to as the 'privacy sections', and in a moment I say a few words about
this part of his work. But first I want to briefly consider a larger line of
thought in the *Investigations* into which Wittgenstein's remarks on privacy
are integrated – a line of thought that is aptly understood as having an
antireductionist tendency insofar as it brings into question a set of classic
approaches to defending materialism that have straightforwardly reductive
ramifications.

The particular defenses I have in mind start from an initially seemingly
plausible idea: namely, that any subjective endowments we draw on in discoursing about the world have an essential tendency to obstruct our view of
the objective world and that it is therefore only insofar as we eliminate the
contributions made by such endowments that we are entitled to regard ourselves as having gotten our minds around the way things really are. Given
that what is at issue here is an idea about how an abstract or maximally
nonsubjective vantage point is objectively compulsory, it is noteworthy that
philosophers sometimes take a commitment to approaching such a vantage
point to be a mark of the physical sciences. In light of this assumption, it
appears that we are justified both in representing our physical discourses as
having a uniquely authoritative claim to be revealing the layout of objective
reality and in drawing the materialist conclusion that the – physical or
material – features of the world with which these discourses deal represent
the most basic constituents of reality. Moreover, it is easy to see that this

basic strategy for defending materialism has reductive implications. It follows from it that we are justified in questioning the cognitive credentials of any mode of thought that resists reduction to physical terms.

The strategy depends for whatever interest it is taken to have on the idea of an abstract epistemological requirement, and a central line of thought in Wittgenstein's *Investigations* is designed to get us to ask ourselves whether we have an intelligible notion of what it would be for a conceptual practice to be governed by such a requirement or, in other words, what it would be for a conceptual practice to be such that the regularities that compose it are in principle accessible independently of any subjective responses characteristic of us as participants in the practice. In his most widely discussed engagement with this question, Wittgenstein invites us to consider conceptual practices that involve the development of mathematical series. One of Wittgenstein's goals here – and this point is interpretatively relatively uncontroversial – is getting us to see that we ourselves are unclear about what it would be for a person's mastery of even the simplest series (e.g., '2, 2, 2, 2...') to be independent of a *sense* of the importance of similarities uniting its members. A further goal – and this additional point, while interpretatively much more controversial than the last one noted, is made persuasively in writings of Stanley Cavell and John McDowell – is getting us to see that if we now abandon as confused the idea of an abstract epistemological requirement we do not thereby relinquish our claim to the ideal of objectivity. After all, if we reject this idea in a rigorously consistent manner, we cannot continue to allow it to shape our view of what access to the objective world is like. On the contrary, now we are obliged to refashion our image of what epistemic contact with objective reality is like so that an abstraction from everything subjective is no longer its touchstone.

To be sure, Wittgenstein's remarks on simple mathematical series only appear to have these consequences insofar as mathematics is taken to represent an optimal case for satisfying the abstract epistemological requirement that is in question. Although there are features of mathematics that have led some philosophers to credit it with this optimal status, it is neither *prima facie* implausible nor uncommon for philosophers to suggest that what get called concepts of *inner* and *outer experience* represent better cases. This understanding of concepts of inner and outer experience is generally represented as licensed by a philosophically influential conception of experience as in essence a matter of awareness of contents that are merely causally produced and that are hence necessarily available apart from any conceptual activity. The idea is that, where discourse about experience is understood, in accordance with this conception, as involving the subsumption of such nonconceptual and hence ideally abstract contents under concepts, it appears to be an indefinitely rich source of illustrations of conceptual exercises that qualify as abstract in the relevant, ideal sense.

An image of our discourse about experience as a source of ideally abstract conceptual activity is an important critical preoccupation of the *Investigations*. Wittgenstein's most direct and forceful criticism of the image comes in his reflections on privacy and is concerned in particular with the bearing of the image on the case of inner experience. This criticism is pertinent to a study of Wittgenstein's basic view of mind, not only insofar as it contributes to his attack on the idea of an abstract epistemological requirement, but also insofar as it contributes to his attack on the notion of logical privacy, touched on above, that informs some central conversations between dualists and reductive materialists. Wittgenstein's critical attention is directed toward a conception of basic elements of our inner lives like sensations as merely given particulars that are available to thought apart from any conceptual activity on our part and that are accordingly not only abstractly available but also necessarily resistant to discursive formulation, and, in criticizing this conception, Wittgenstein is challenging guiding assumptions of those dualists and reductive materialists who conceive conscious mental experience as consisting in confrontations with discursively unformulable particulars.

Pivotal for Wittgenstein's criticism is the recognition that we lack a model of what it is for a belief to be rationally justified that does not involve its placement in a conceptual context, as a conceptually articulated consideration that is itself implied or to some degree supported by a further conceptually articulated consideration. Guided by this recognition, Wittgenstein observes that, if we are to preserve the intuitively attractive view that inner experience places rational constraints on belief formation, we are obliged to abandon a nonconceptualist understanding of such experience. Or, to put the point in some of his own terms, he observes that, if we are to preserve the intuitively attractive thought that any particular sensation, S, places rational constraints on our beliefs about it – if we are to avoid putting ourselves in a position in which there is no room for 'talk about "right"' in reference to our beliefs about S because 'whatever is going to seem right to [us] is right' (Wittgenstein 1967, § 258) – then we are obliged to give up an understanding of sensations as merely given particulars that are accessible to reflection apart from conceptual activity on our part and hence in a manner that renders them discursively unformulable.

In addition to raising a question about the cogency of the notion of logical privacy that dualists and some reductive materialists take for granted, this strand of Wittgenstein's thought has a direct bearing on accounts of our concepts of inner and outer experience on which their applications appear to satisfy an abstract epistemological requirement. Philosophers who represent bits of nonconceptual content as providing rational warrants for the use of concepts of inner and outer sense are attempting to combine a nonconceptualist understanding of experience with the view that experience rationally constrains belief. One important moral of Wittgenstein's remarks here is that there is something confused about attempting this feat of combination.

Having already mentioned that it follows from the kind of attack Wittgenstein launches on an abstract epistemological requirement that we should revise our conception of contact with objective reality so that such contact no longer seems to call for a blanket abstraction from subjectivity, I now turn to the antireductionist implications of the revision in question. What at a very basic level drives the revision is a view of our cognitive predicament on which all our modes of thought and talk, including those internal to the physical sciences, are essentially informed by subjective endowments. This view deprives us of the a priori grounds some philosophers have taken us to have for insisting that a comprehensive reductionist posture *must* be correct. By the same token, the view carves out a conceptual space in which to mount defenses of nonreductive accounts of particular discourses, including defenses of nonreductive accounts of psychological discourse such as the one Wittgenstein himself gives in presenting a species of commonsense realism about the mind.

3.

Central to Wittgenstein's case for commonsense realism is a set of remarks, collectively representing a significant portion of his later opus, having to do with the idea of a conceptual connection between, on the one hand, different forms of sentience and sapience and, on the other, patterns of expressive behavior. The idea of a direct tie between aspects of mind and modes of behavior is philosophically controversial, and it is more controversial in reference to sentience than in reference to sapience. So it is interesting that, while Wittgenstein has a great deal to say about necessary links between expressive behavior and different forms of sapience (e.g., different species of understanding, reading, thinking, remembering, and intending), he also emphasizes the idea of inseparable links between mental items and modes of behavior with regard to sensation.

Here we might reasonably turn to Wittgenstein's remarks on the sensation of *pain* in *Investigations*, §§ 283–284. The strategy of these remarks is to recommend the idea of a direct relationship between mind and behavior by getting us to see that we are not clear what it would be to speak of pain in reference to a bearer like a stone that doesn't act from what it feels. Can I in fact imagine myself 'having frightful pains and turning to stone while they last'? Well, I can stifle the expression of even quite terrible pain, remaining immobile and in this respect resembling a stone. Does it follow that I can imagine a stone's having pains? The trouble is that a stone isn't the type of thing that makes an effort to stay still, and it's not clear what it is for me to have pain apart from an urge to do things like attend to an affected part of my body, protect it, grimace, etc. If I lack the urge to do any such things, if

I really have turned to stone, what does it mean to say that I am in pain? Is the idea that the pain is there in my consciousness and thus available for contemplation? But to the extent that I represent my relationship to my pain as a merely contemplative one, lacking any necessary tie to behavior, I siphon off what is awful about pain and arrive at a concept of it fundamentally different from our ordinary one. It is by inviting considerations on these lines that Wittgenstein's reflections on stone and pains are intended to elicit the recognition that, as we ordinarily conceive it, pain encodes a necessary connection to behavior. Let me add that accepting the considerations in question does not commit us to denying that people sometimes conceal pain or give insincere expressions of it. The considerations are designed to get us to see that it doesn't make sense to attribute pain to a creature that doesn't act from how it feels, and the point here is that nothing prevents us from allowing that a given creature that *does* act from how it feels might also be capable of strategies of concealment and insincerity.

Wittgenstein has often been read as sympathizing with classic logical behaviorism, and commentators who read him in this way tend to focus on remarks, like those just discussed, in which he is concerned with the idea of a necessary connection between mindedness and behavior. So it is worth observing that, whereas classic logical behaviorism is a reductive doctrine (specifically, a doctrine that treats mental qualities as functions of behavior that can be fully described in physical terms), Wittgenstein himself makes it clear that he thinks that the modes of behavior to which our attention is directed when we are concerned with aspects of mind is *qualitatively* different from behavior that can be faithfully captured by means of its physical measurements and, further, that it is impossible adequately to describe such behavior apart from the use of psychologically meaningful terms. (See esp. Wittgenstein 1967, § 284. See also Wittgenstein 1980a, § 314.)

Important for Wittgenstein's case for regarding the pertinent modes of behavior as psychologically irreducibly meaningful is his account of what in Part II, § xi of the *Investigations* he calls *aspect seeing*. Wittgenstein's topic here is situations in which, while visually surveying an object, we see a new aspect of it while also seeing that the object has not changed (e.g., 1967 pp. 193 and 195–196). His emphasis is on pictures and diagrams, including the famous 'duck-rabbit' (Wittgenstein 1967, pp. 194–195 and passim), which are designed to alternately present different aspects, and he focuses in particular on how new aspects of a thing may strike us quite suddenly. A focus on the instantaneous character of aspect seeing suits his purposes because it allows him to distinguish visual cases of the sort that interest him, in which we in fact see something new, from cases in which we instead interpret something we see in a new way (e.g., Wittgenstein 1967, pp. 193–194, 204–205 and 212). He draws attention to the fact that he is concerned with visual transitions that cannot be accounted for simply by appeal to an interpretation external to what is seen – describing them at times as transitions in which a thought contributes internally to our perception of a thing so that the contributions of thought and visual experience cannot be factored out (e.g., Wittgenstein 1967, pp. 197 and 212) – because he wants to bring out how we are here dealing with perceptual experiences that it is natural to think of as involving concepts whose contents are not reducible to independently accessible perceptual information.

Notice that there can be no question of taking the phenomenon of aspect seeing, as Wittgenstein understands it, at face value within any members of a familiar class of philosophical accounts of perceptual experience on which such experience is essentially a matter of the registering within consciousness of nonconceptual, merely causally produced contents. Within the context of such accounts, the physical dimensions of an object fix what is there to be perceived so there is no room to accommodate the possibility of seeing something new while surveying an object that is itself unchanged. It is for this reason significant that, as we have seen, within the *Investigations* Wittgenstein's treatment of aspect seeing comes after his defense of an account of – inner and outer – experience as ineradicably conceptual and, further, that, unlike the accounts of perceptual experience just mentioned, this account makes room for the possibility that what a person genuinely sees in some situation may alter to reflect a new way of conceiving what is before one's eyes that, while cognitively fully legitimate, is unavailable in other terms.

Now we have before us lines of thought from Wittgenstein's writings that speak for representing ourselves as licensed to straightforwardly incorporate the phenomenon of aspect seeing. Against the backdrop of these lines of thought, it is noteworthy that Wittgenstein observes that the psychological qualities of bits of behavior are among the aspects of things that can dawn on us. In the *Investigations*, Wittgenstein takes an interest in situations in which, after being initially blind to the expression on a person's face, we suddenly see it as, say, a smile (e.g., 1967 pp. 197–198 and 210), and elsewhere he presents a rich variety of cases in which we are suddenly struck by the psychological character of the behavior or bodily disposition of a person or animal (e.g., Wittgenstein 1980a, §§ 873–874, 878, 880, 882, 1066–1068, 1072–1073 and 1106; also Wittgenstein 1980b, §§ 170 and 358–359). When Wittgenstein thus portrays us as directly seeing the psychological character of different modes of behavior and bodily dispositions, he is asking us to think of the relevant visual experiences as encoding concepts whose contents are not reducible to independently available perceptual contents. He is asking us to regard behavior expressive of aspects of mind as irreducibly psychologically meaningful, and, given that he is committed to regarding mindedness as inseparable from expressive behavior, it follows that he is rightly taken to be defending the view that our ordinary ways of talking about the mind resist both physical reduction and translation into other nonpsychological terms. *This* is what makes me say that Wittgenstein favours a species of what I am calling 'commonsense realism about the mind.'

4.

The Wittgensteinian case for commonsense realism I just presented may seem open to the objections of philosophers who repudiate the nonreductive posture such realism involves, claiming that the most perspicuous accounts of the causal relations with which psychological explanations are concerned inevitably proceed in the terms of physics and that, in representing psychological qualities (such as, e.g., perceptions and intentions of different kinds) as having real effects in the world, our ordinary psychological modes of thought of speech wrongly treat these qualities as potent or causally effective in ways that they are in fact not. But, however plausible it may at first seem, a claim on these lines is not ultimately viable. Indeed, we need not venture beyond some widely received lessons of the last decades of work in philosophy of mind to find good grounds for questioning it.

It would be possible to capture an important lesson of a large body of recent research in philosophy of mind by saying that we lose sight of the kinds of connections in our lives we trace out using psychological predicates (e.g., connections between specific kinds of perceptions and intentions, on the one hand, and specific kinds of actions, on the other) if we attempt to describe these connections in physical terms. The body of research to which I am referring is one characterized both by a widespread consensus that particular psychological qualities are physically realized in multiple ways and by a widespread consensus that the circumstances that contribute essentially to individuals' possession of particular psychological qualities include some that are external to their individual makeups. A good case can be made for thinking that if, following up on this body of research, we embrace both multiple realizability and psychological externalism, we thereby represent psychological qualities as lacking the sort of unity at the level of physical description that would license us to insist that the patterns among them that interest us must be recognizable at this level. This is noteworthy because it means that we also thereby deprive ourselves of grounds we may once have thought we had for doubting that psychological descriptions and explanations supply the best, most perspicuous and illuminating accounts of certain effective – or causal – relations in our lives.

The body of research in philosophy of mind to which I referred in the last paragraph won't seem to strip us of grounds for doubting that psychological descriptions and explanations supply our most perspicuous accounts of certain causal relations as long as we believe that we have *a priori* philosophical grounds for thinking that these descriptions and explanations cannot be both physically irreducible and cognitively authoritative in an unqualified sense. But the lines of thought from Wittgenstein's writings discussed above in Section 2 are designed to discredit this belief. The object of my remarks in this brief section is simply to touch on considerations in favor of thinking that one of the most significant objections to commonsense realism that may still seem pertinent even if these lines of thought are accepted as sound can be satisfactorily met.

5.

Setting aside the question of objections to the species of commonsense realism about the mind that Wittgenstein defends, I want to close with a few reflections about what's at stake in our acceptance of it. In asking us to regard ordinary psychological discourse as both resistant to translation into nonpsychological terms and cognitive fully authoritative terms, such commonsense realism implies that investigation of the logic of psychological discourse is uniquely capable of illuminating the nature of mindedness. With an eye to bringing out the interest of this point, I here discuss one lesson that investigation of this sort now appears to be capable of teaching.

The lesson that interests me emerges when we bring into relief a sense in which the logic of psychological discourse excludes constraints internal to even weak versions of what are called *individual claims about mind-body supervenience* (i.e., claims about how an individual with a particular mental quality at a given time must have a physical makeup at that time such that anything with the same physical makeup at a time also then has the same mental quality). Let me stress that I am not here concerned simply to demonstrate *that* claims about individual mind-body supervenience are untenable. Advocates of psychological externalism have already made this point forcefully. What concerns me right now is not a general conclusion about the failure of individual supervenience claims but rather a specific observation about a relatively neglected way in which these claims come into conflict with the logic of psychological predicates.

If we are to grasp the point in question – and I should mention that I am deeply indebted for the argument presented in the next several paragraphs to conversations with Cora Diamond as well as to a paper of hers entitled, 'The Interchangeability of Machines' (1969) – it is helpful to note that it is an implication of individual supervenience claims that individual physical indistinguishability entails psychological indistinguishability. We can approach an account of the significance of this entailment relationship by making some observations about the nature of our physical modes of description that shed light on what physical indistinguishability amounts to. Suppose that, adopting a venerable philosophical strategy, we take machines as models of merely physical systems and, additionally, take questions about what it is to describe the workings of machines as models for questions about what it is to describe processes constitutive of physical systems. Now it may well seem noteworthy to us that things we say about the workings of a machine do not by and large contain any reference to its history. As Diamond points out, we can always stop the workings of one machine and replace it with a machine that is in relevant respects the same, and this means that we can always describe what a machine is doing without any ineliminable reference to what it did in the past or to what it will do in the future.

To say this is not, as Diamond also observes, to deny either that a machine may in some cases be described as following a self-modified program or that, in such cases, the machine will invite the use of present tense predicates that a replacement does not. But in these cases we could analyze the present tense predicate applying exclusively to our original machine (viz. a predicate that describes it as following a self-modified program) into a past tense component applying only to it (viz., a predicate describing it as having generated the program it is currently following) and a present tense component applying also to the machine replacing it (viz., a predicate describing whichever machine is in question as following the relevant program). So, while there are present tense predicates supported by our original machine that its replacement doesn't support, there are no such predicates that cannot be analyzed into present and past tense predicates such that all of the present tense predicates apply to the original machine as well to its replacement. Given that an exactly analogous point can be made about how it is invariably possible to describe a machine in terms free from any ineliminable references to what it will do in the future, it follows that we are justified in asserting that things we say about the operations of a machine are not essentially dependent on its history.

This assertion has as its corollary an assertion about the character of the events that compose the operations of a machine. What are in question are events that are temporally self-contained in that they bring about or are brought about by conditions of things that can in theory be reproduced without their occurrence, and, insofar as the workings of machines are apt models for the processes constitutive of other physical systems in this respect, it follows that these systems are also rightly conceived as composed of temporally self-contained events. This conclusion is significant because it follows from it that, if individual physical indistinguishability entails psychological indistinguishability, it must in theory be possible to describe the psychology of an individual in a way that doesn't depend on the individual's history. Now it appears that attempts to evaluate claims about individual mind-body supervenience bring us face to face with a question about whether we can capture an individual's psychology in exclusively ahistorical terms – or whether we instead require the use of certain irredeemably historical predicates.

Consider what it would be for a predicate to be historical in the relevant sense. Here we might focus, for the sake of convenience, on predicates with an ineliminable reference to the past. A predicate that had such a reference would be one that was concerned with some item that necessarily depends for its status as the kind of thing it is on the existence of a certain temporal background. We could credit ourselves with discovering items integrated into this kind of temporal pattern if, to use terms of Diamond's, we encountered qualities or activities of an individual that *bring in* something that the individual did (or that happened to her) in the past in such a way that, without the relevant past item, the individual could not be said to possess the quality or to be engaged in the activity at issue. For the sake of convenience, let me describe predicates for such past-oriented features, together with predicates for similarly future-oriented features, as *historical predicates.*

Are our ordinary psychological predicates historical predicates? In the next few paragraphs, I sketch a strategy for answering this question affirmatively. Although this strategy is not specifically Wittgenstein's, it draws significantly on elements of Wittgenstein's thought. Further, although Diamond does not describe the strategy in question, it is compatible with things she does say. The strategy involves situating Wittgenstein's remarks about a conceptual connection between aspects of mind and modes of behavior against the backdrop of an observation about the temporal logic of voluntary action.

While voluntary actions are anything but homogeneous – differing from each other in, for example, their durations and in the forms of cognitive sophistication they require – we can without distortion or inaccuracy say that *no* voluntary action is essentially composed of the kinds of temporally self-contained events that make up the operations of machines. When we describe a subject as acting voluntarily, we describe her as producing behavior that is ascribable to her in a sense in which merely reflexive behavior is not. We imply that, in acting in the manner in question, she is responding to her situation in a way that is in an important sense her own. It follows that it is possible to talk about earlier and later stages of any voluntary action such that some of the later stages – specifically, those involving movements that are in themselves indistinguishable from reflexive behavior – depend essentially for their voluntary character on or, in Diamond's terms, *bring in* earlier stages. One result is that it seems clear that there can be no question of capturing the distinctive character of voluntary action without using historical predicates.

This conclusion has implications for how we understand the significance of things Wittgenstein says about a necessary link between different forms of sapience and sentience, on the one hand, and behavior, on the other. This is because, in the relevant portions of his work, Wittgenstein is specifically concerned with *voluntary* behavior. He is – to put it in terms that I employed earlier in discussing his remarks about pain in *Investigations*, §§ 283–284 – making a point about how it would be a sign of confusion to ascribe emotions, sensations, or modes of cognition to creatures that do not act from what they feel, or respond to what they perceive or think in acting, in ways that merely reflexively behaving creatures do not. He is inviting us to understand ordinary psychological predicates as concerned with patterns of voluntary behavior, and it follows from things I have been saying about the temporal logic of such behavior that, if we accept this understanding of ordinary psychological predicates, we commit ourselves to conceiving them as historical predicates.

For the purposes of illustration, we might turn to emotional predicates such as 'feels deep grief.' The set of Wittgenstein's remarks that have to do with conceptual connections between aspects of mind and modes of behavior include remarks on grief and other emotions. (Thus, e.g., in the *Investigations*, he observes that ' "grief" describes a pattern which recurs, with different variations, in the weave of our life' (1967, p. 174).) These remarks may seem philosophically unremarkable in light of the emphasis within contemporary philosophical conversations about the emotions on claims about how emotions are cognitive in the sense of involving attitudes or behavioral responses to objects. But the point here does not depend for its force on the details of any particular account of the patterns of voluntary behavior to which individual emotions are conceptually tied. The point is simply *that* individual emotions are conceptually tied to patterns of voluntary behavior. Given an understanding of voluntary behavior as having a temporal logic such that later stages bring in earlier ones, it follows from this point that the predicates we use to pick out different emotions must be historical.

It is not difficult to see that, if we follow up on lines of thought from Wittgenstein's work that thus support a conception of psychological predicates as historical, we at the same time commit ourselves to a conception of these predicates as having a logic that excludes claims about individual mind-body supervenience. For it follows from even weaker versions of such a claim that individual physical indistinguishability entails psychological indistinguishability, and accommodating an entailment relationship on these lines means construing any cognitively respectable psychological predicates as having the same nonhistorical character of predicates we use in physical descriptions. Of course, if we took ourselves to have grounds for thinking that psychological discourse depended for its authority on the availability of a reduction to nonhistorical, physical terms, then a conclusion about how psychological predicates are historical would simply seem to cast doubt on the predicates' cognitive credentials. But against the backdrop of Wittgenstein's efforts to show that psychological discourse is both physically irreducible and characterized by an authority that is fully firsthand this conclusion can be seen as presenting us with a lesson about what mindedness is like.

At issue is a lesson about how a minded being is as such not interchangeable like a machine but rather historical in a sense that makes it *irreplaceable*. Notice that the kind of irreplaceability in question is not a matter of a merely subjective attitude that we may or may not adopt toward particular minded life forms. Although we may value a thing of any kind as the particular thing it is, refusing to be consoled for its loss by a replacement just like it, the kind of irreplaceability in question here concerns an attitude toward minded beings that, far from being thus idiosyncratic, is internal to certain fully objective, cognitively respectable ways of discoursing about such beings.

Since the idea of an attitude internal to certain fully objective modes of discourse is anathema to many philosophers, it is important to observe that philosophical resistance to this idea can be traced to an assumption – an assumption that Wittgenstein specifically targets for critical attention in the course of attacking sources of philosophical insistence on reductionism – about how discourse about the world is governed by an abstract epistemological requirement. If, in accordance with the idea of such a requirement, we assume that bringing the world into view is essentially a matter of abstracting as far as possible from subjective endowments, then it will be unclear how an undistorted mode of discourse might as such embody an attitude. By the same token, if, following in Wittgenstein's footsteps, we abandon the idea of an abstract epistemological requirement, we thereby remove the grounds we may have seemed to have for rejecting the suggestion that undistorted discourse can encode attitudes and, at the same time, also the grounds we may have seemed to have for rejecting the more specific suggestion that our psychological discourse encodes an attitude toward minded beings as irreplaceable.

What follows from our willingness to embrace the idea that this attitude is internal to fully objective, psychological modes of discourse? Now we are obliged to regard the recognition that what stands before us is a minded being of some kind as by itself giving us a reason to treat it in ways that reflect its irreplaceability. Moreover, although it is undoubtedly possible to overstate the significance of this lesson – although many different ways of treating minded beings may well reflect their irreplaceability – at the very least it follows from it that the recognition that something before us is even a very primitive minded being by itself gives us grounds to avoid killing it that we don't have for avoiding the destruction of even the most delicate machine. Given the prevalence within contemporary ethics of disagreements about whether minded living beings as such place claims on us, this conclusion is anything but insignificant, and it is an important part of the interest of the sort of commonsense realism about the mind Wittgenstein advocates that it brings within reach this kind of conclusion about the significance of mindedness.[*]

Note

[*] This chapter is the diminutive counterpart of a longer manuscript on Wittgenstein's philosophy of mind that covers similar ground in greater detail. I presented earlier

versions of this material at the philosophy departments of Tel Aviv University, Michigan State University, Cornell University, University of Wisconsin-Milwaukee, Guelph University, and at a symposium on Wittgenstein's Philosophy of Mind at the 2008 Pacific Division Meeting of the APA, and I am grateful for the constructive feedback I received on these occasions. I would especially like to thank, for their helpful comments, Carla Bagnoli, Andrew Bailey, Jason Bridges, Don Dedrick, Luca Ferrero, Eli Friedlander, Menachem Fisch, Marylin Frye, John Hacker-Wright, Harold Hodes, John Koethe, Stephen Leeds, Hilde Lindemann, Stefan Linquist, Tori McGeer, Stephen Mulhall, Jim Nelson, Philip Pettit, Naomi Scheman, Nicholas Silins, David Stern, Meredith Williams, and Crispin Wright. I owe special debts to Jay Bernstein, Cora Diamond, Jonathan Ellis, Nathaniel Hupert, and Elijah Millgram for constructive conversation and correspondence.

Bibliography

Diamond, C. (1969), 'The Interchangeability of Machines', in Macintosh, J.J. and Coval, S. (eds), *The Business of Reason* (London: Routledge & Kegan Paul), pp. 50–72.

Wittgenstein, L. (1967), *Philosophical Investigations* (Oxford: Blackwell).

——. (1980a), *Remarks on the Philosophy of Psychology, Vol. I,* Anscombe, G.E.M. and von Wright, G.H. (eds) (Oxford: Blackwell).

——. (1980b), *Remarks on the Philosophy of Psychology, Vol. II,* von Wright, G.H. and Nyman, H. (eds.) (Oxford: Blackwell).

2
Wittgenstein on Emotion

Joachim Schulte

In this chapter I try to argue that in Wittgenstein's writings between 1946 and 1949 and, in particular, in the context of his remarks on emotions a tension can be seen between his emphasis on the unity of the concept of an emotion and a conflicting emphasis on differences between our concepts of individual emotions. This tension is at the same time one between earlier and later remarks.[1] Accordingly, in the first section I shall give a brief account of the earlier thought on emotion (1946–1948) as epitomized in Wittgenstein's second attempt at delineating a general classification of psychological concepts (RPP II, § 148[2]), while in the second section I try to sketch Wittgenstein's modified approach (1948–1949) as indicated by a number of subsequent remarks. I do not want to suggest that the modified approach can be fully and clearly stated, but I do think that it is informed by a peculiar metaphor which suggests that Wittgenstein was moving in a direction which he had not seen in earlier writings.

1. Early remarks

If one wishes to discuss Wittgenstein's remarks on emotion, the first problem one faces is that of translation. As far as I can see, the German word *'Emotion'* occurs only once in Wittgenstein's writings, and in the relevant passage it is used to refer to William James's theory of the emotions. The word usually translated as 'emotion' is *'Gemütsbewegung'*. Nowadays this word may sound a little old-fashioned, but it is the word Wittgenstein uses throughout. An obvious difficulty is posed by the fact that *Gemütsbewegung* seems to cover a different range of cases from the English word 'emotion'. Still, I see no way of avoiding the word 'emotion' as a rendering of Wittgenstein's *Gemütsbewegung*. Readers will simply have to bear in mind that in certain cases Wittgenstein's notion of an emotion (*Gemütsbewegung*) is different from what an English speaker might expect.[3]

According to Wittgenstein, it is a general characteristic of emotions[4] that they have genuine duration. He explicitly says that this is a feature that all emotions have in common. This is an important claim; it emphasizes the unity of the concept of an emotion. The expression 'genuine duration' not only serves to say that the continuing item has, or may have, beginning and end. Even though Wittgenstein does not say so in so many words, the suggestion seems to be that genuine duration excludes the possibility of interruption.

Is it really justified to attribute genuine duration to all emotions? It is an essential feature of Wittgenstein's kind of conceptual investigation that there is no easy way of answering such questions. It will be necessary to examine individual concepts. In the case of concepts like 'anger' or 'delight' the matter is fairly obvious. It happens at a certain moment, and often very suddenly, that one gets angry; and as soon as the anger has passed, one has stopped being angry. Similarly with delight. My delight (say, over a bunch of flowers) may last more or less long. So, one may say 'I am still delighted by these flowers', but after some time it will be ridiculous to speak of continued delight.

The matter is more difficult when we are dealing with emotions that are connected with or related to moods. Think of sadness. It is quite possible to say that someone has been sad for weeks, or even months. And in such cases it may be problematic to mention a clear end of this sadness. Similar considerations apply to worry and grief, joy and gladness.

Another problem turns up when one discusses emotions that do not last long enough, as it were, to speak of 'genuine duration'. Examples are 'surprise' and 'fright'. True, they *can* be said to last for a bit, but in most cases it is a matter of seconds. Good examples of genuine duration are those cases where it is appropriate to say things like 'He was scared stiff' or 'He was paralysed with fright'. One reason why these are good examples is that this sort of paralysis does not tend to last very long. Similarly, it would be extremely strange to say that someone was startled for a couple of hours.

These considerations suggest that not to all, but only some typical emotions the feature of genuine duration can be attributed without qualification and hesitation. There are other kinds of cases – especially when we are dealing with moods or diffuse or momentary emotions – where talk about genuine duration seems less clearly appropriate.

Wittgenstein notes that emotions take a characteristic course. Evidently, this statement is closely connected with the feature of genuine duration, for only a continuing process can exhibit a certain course. But duration and course are by no means the same thing. What Wittgenstein means by 'a course' is the typical way in which things develop while an emotion lasts. Wittgenstein's own example is the typical course of anger: it flares up, later it will abate and finally vanish. Similar cases, Wittgenstein says, are those of joy, depression and fear. But here one may spot a number of difficulties. Even in the case of anger it is by no means obvious that this emotion will always run its course in accordance with the pattern described. There are examples where anger passes just as quickly as it flared up. In other words, it is not necessary that anger subsides gradually. It may disappear all at once. Joy and fear, too, are emotions that may develop in accordance with various types of pattern.

A further characteristic of emotions is their lack of localization. Here it is necessary to make a clear distinction between the emotion itself and sensations (or other types of feeling) typically or accidentally accompanying it. These feelings can often be accorded a place, even though not always in the same sense of 'place'. A lump in my throat is localized in a different way from a heavy heart. But in the case of all these feelings or sensations it will be possible to speak of a certain place, whereas this will not work when we are discussing anxiety, embarrassment or dejection. Sometimes, however, one wonders whether it is always possible to make a clear-cut distinction between an emotion as such and the feelings or sensations accompanying it. Is oppression an emotion or a feeling which accompanies an emotion? Does a person who is too embarrassed to speak have sensations of embarrassment in addition to his emotion? In view of such questions one may easily think that such attempts at separating feelings or sensations from emotions are rather artificial. Moreover, what may suggest itself here is the idea that the degree of separability may help to characterize certain emotions.

An important connection between (not localized) emotions and their accompanying (localized) sensations is established through the fact that, corresponding to our various emotions, there are characteristic kinds of expressive behaviour. Here, primarily but not exclusively, one will think of facial expressions; and one may also remember that facial expressions have to 'fit' their emotions. At this point there loom many questions concerning the connection between emotions and expressive behaviour. The basic type of situation, however, is obvious: a person looks sad, and you may ask him why he is sad; a person looks surprised, and you may ask him why he is surprised; a person looks scared, and you may ask him why he is scared.

This type of situation raises various questions. Perhaps the other person will reply that he is not sad, or surprised. He may claim to feel absolutely normal and to have thought of nothing in particular. If the other person is sincere, we have either made a mistake in 'reading' his face or he did look sad without really being sad. Neither possibility can be excluded without further ado, and in either case we might judge the situation differently if we knew more about the relevant context, that is, if we had a more reliable picture of the person and his circumstances or if we had more time to observe the situation more closely.

As Wittgenstein points out, context is equally important when we are dealing with a case of pretending. Suppose someone simulates surprise or pretends to be scared. In such a case the other person may look scared, and if he is asked why, he will answer by giving an invented reason. But if we become suspicious, the context will reveal clues that may help us answer the question whether or not the person had been sincere. The possibility of pretending needs to be explored for the reason that those features of which one believes that they require simulation tend to be the same ones that appear crucial to finding out whether or not the emotion in question is present. That is, there is a conceptual connection between 'being sad' and 'pretending to be sad' – a connection that can be exploited to identify the essential characteristics of sadness.

Here we notice another connection which was of great importance to Wittgenstein. That is a connection with William James's famous theory according to which physical processes, bodily sensations and so on are immediate triggers of our (felt) emotions. This theory can be summarized by saying that we do not cry because we are sad, but are sad because we cry. It is not easy to refute this idea, for we do after all know from experience that a deliberate smile can help to improve one's mood or that it may be easier to imitate a certain (type of) person if one assumes a certain posture. These are examples to which Wittgenstein gave a lot of thought, and it would surely be important to discover why he did not agree with James.[5] Most of his implicit or explicit criticisms depend on the fact that his view of the relation between conceptual and empirical, or causal, matters is different from James's.

By no means, however, does Wittgenstein want to deny that there is an important connection between physical processes and felt emotions. What he is interested in is the conceptual aspect of this connection. This, however, is not easy to get hold of. At any rate, he says that from the mere existence of characteristic expressive behaviour it follows that there are feelings which are characteristic of the emotion in question. 'Thus sorrow often goes with weeping, and characteristic sensations with the latter. (The voice heavy with tears.) But the sensations are not the emotions. (In the sense in which the numeral 2 is not the number 2.)' (RPP II, § 148.) The comparison with the difference between numeral and number emphasizes the conceptual difference between an emotion and the sensations accompanying it. On the other hand, the fact that we talk of *characteristic* sensations suffices to show that we may invoke a kind of 'logical' connection between expressive behaviour, emotion and sensation.

Wittgenstein's account of emotions involves drawing a distinction between directed and undirected emotions. Directed emotions refer or pertain to an object: for example, the joy one feels at the news of having received a medal pertains to the medal (or the honour connected with it). In some cases the object of an emotion coincides with its cause. In other cases, however, the two are to be distinguished. Thus, it may be that I am annoyed about my meal – but not because the food tastes bad but because it interferes with my diet plans. It is in this context that Wittgenstein declares: 'The language-game "I am afraid" already contains the object' (RPP II, § 148). Owing to its brevity this statement can be misleading, and has misled some readers. Thus, Malcolm Budd thinks that it alludes to the process of learning expressions like 'I am afraid' as well as to a consequence following from this, namely that, if the speaker is using language correctly, he has the authority of determining the object of his fear while others have no right to dispute his claim. According to Budd, one result of this is that a felt emotion which does not enable the relevant speaker to discern an object is an undirected emotion.[6]

But it is difficult to see why this should be the point of Wittgenstein's remark. True, as regards the identification of the object of his fear, the speaker is in a position of especial authority, but the relevance of this fact remains unclear. In particular, it should not be invoked by way of referring to a process of learning words, for without further qualification that process is a purely accidental matter of no conceptual relevance. The result mentioned by Budd ('The speaker is not able to recognize an object, so his emotion is undirected') is trivial at best. In any event, its formulation is misleading: it suggests that the speaker wishes to find out something about his emotion by means of examining it in an attempt to discover whether it has, or fails to have, an object. Even if one does not find this account bizarre, it cannot be reconciled with Wittgenstein's ideas. After all, this type of introspective examination is of a kind whose absurdity he keeps trying to point out.

In this context, Wittgenstein presumably wishes to make a simpler point. His statement that the object is already contained in the language-game emphasizes that this language-game (with 'I am afraid') differs from other ones in this respect, for instance: that even if the speaker does not mention an object, we may ask him and expect him to be able to specify the object in one way or another. (To be sure, this aspect of the matter can be gleaned from Budd's reading too.) From this it is possible to derive various consequences, for instance that if the speaker does not mention an object, he may be concealing something. Moreover, if a speaker insists on having the right to claim to be unable to specify the object of his fear, we may correct his use of language. If he says he does not know what he is afraid of, we are allowed to reply that in reality he is not talking about fear at all but at most about some indeterminate kind of anxiety. And in that case our behaviour towards him may be quite different from a case in which we do have a reason to suppose that there is something which he is afraid of.

In many cases we find it appropriate to talk about the *content* of an emotion. In this regard, Wittgenstein tends to express himself very carefully, since in his view using the word 'content' can easily mislead us.[7] There are several contexts where he discusses the word as it occurs in combinations such as 'experiential content' or 'content of consciousness', and more often than not the tenor of his remarks is critical. One example is a popular way of talking about experiential content which claims to speak in a direct way of certain qualitative aspects of our experiences ('I know what toothache is like', etc.). It is in connection with such claims that Wittgenstein points out that this kind of content is not communicable, and unintelligible even from the perspective of the speaker himself, unless he makes essential reference to objects or events, ways of behaving or public situations that are intersubjectively accessible (cf. RPP I, § 91).

In other passages the doubtful character of the notion of 'a content' is stressed by identifying content with an alleged 'private object' which, as Wittgenstein says at one point, is something we should always eliminate (see RPP I, §§ 109, 694, 985). In Wittgenstein's eyes, we are tempted to speak of content in terms of pictures. But the picture is supposed to be one 'in the subjective sense' of this word (RPP I, § 694), that is, something to which we can gain absolutely no intersubjective access. While it is quite possible to communicate imagined pictures by means of physical sketches or other public illustrations, talk about essentially 'inner' pictures is nothing but 'a myth'. To be sure, Wittgenstein has no intention to proscribe this sort of use of the word 'content' in general. Thus we may for example say that the experiential content of seeing something is the same as imagining it, but this is permissible only to the extent 'a painted picture can reproduce what is seen and what is imagined' (RPP II, § 109).

Addressing the topic of emotions, Wittgenstein writes: 'The content of an emotion – here one imagines something like a picture, or something of which a picture can be made. (The darkness of depression which descends on a man, the flames of anger.)' (RPP II, § 148.) What is emphasized here is evidently that aspect of pictures which can be rendered objective, and is hence intersubjectively accessible. According to Wittgenstein, in speaking of the content of an emotion one does not mean an essentially inner picture, which would be entirely otiose, but one which can be reproduced and symbolized.

But that is not the whole story. The examples mentioned by Wittgenstein (darkness, flames) suggest that the word 'picture' is to be taken, not only in the literal sense of a sketch or a drawing, but also in a figurative sense. The darkness of depression need not be an imagined kind of darkness, but depression – or talking about depression – may involve images which can satisfactorily be rendered as something dark. And in this context, 'satisfactorily' means that the rendering is intelligible to myself and other people. Something similar applies to the flames of anger, and here the point may be even clearer. In this case we are dealing with a conventional, an almost trite metaphor; and that is exactly why the picture works so well. One straightforwardly understands what it means, just as if its meaning had been spelled out in so many words.

But Wittgenstein goes one step further. Basically, he indicates, the content of an emotion could directly be rendered by a human face, or by a picture of a human face. The face of an angry man is a picture of anger – though not a picture of his angry inner life. One could take a photograph of an angry man and use it to illustrate the meaning of 'anger'. What Wittgenstein has in mind here is probably one of the following three possibilities, or all three of them. Emotions can be represented by means of (1) schematic images (2) a movie, or (3) an actor. All three ways of proceeding are mentioned in Wittgenstein's writings:

(1) Primitive schematic pictures (of the 'smiley' type) can be used, without additional comment, to prompt responses like 'cheerful' or 'sad'. What is interesting is that these identical pictures can be embedded in different contexts to produce more finely differentiated kinds of responses. Instead of 'cheerful' we may then, according to the suggested situation, get responses like 'merry', 'light-hearted', 'happy', 'jolly', and instead of 'sad' we may get 'dejected', 'gloomy', 'grief-stricken' and so on. This shows, on the one hand, the importance of context to the interpretation of expressive behaviour; on the other hand, it shows that in some cases talking about the 'content' of an emotion involves a rather primitive picture.

(2) Cuts from movies can be used to represent various forms of change of facial expression. By this means it would not only be possible to illustrate a typical course of an emotion but also transitions from one emotion to another. Even if one is ignorant of the plot, such cuts will be sufficient to give a varied description of the emotions to be illustrated.

(3) An actor can be employed in a similar way as the movie-cuts mentioned in the previous paragraph. Such an actor can, on demand, illustrate typical courses of an emotion or changes from one emotion to another one. Thinking about and comparing these various possibilities of illustration may then raise the interesting question whether a complex performance is more apt than a primitive picture to deserve to be called 'the content' of a given emotion. Another point that should be taken into account is the fact that a primitive picture of type (1) is reminiscent of a (hieroglyphic) script and can in this way throw light on the possibility of using conventional signs to express and allude to certain emotions.

We started our account of Wittgenstein's views on the topic of emotion (*Gemütsbewegung*) by observing that, in his view, emotions are characterized by having genuine duration. At the same time, we noted that the supposed generality of this claim can hardly be sustained. For one thing, there are enduring, mood-like *Gemütsbewegungen* without a clear end. For another, there are *Gemütsbewegungen* that pass so quickly that speaking of 'duration' seems inappropriate. Occasionally Wittgenstein himself appears to have had doubts about the general validity of his criterion of genuine duration. In one manuscript passage he says: 'Does a man feel his sadness all the time while his sadness lasts? – He does for example have sad thoughts' (MS 133,

p. 63r). Presumably this means that there are cases where one does *not* feel sadness all the time; but sadness 'colours' the whole inner life of a sad person, his thoughts as well as his feelings.

This remark is also instructive for the reason that it highlights a question which often lurks in the background of Wittgenstein's remarks, namely whether in a given case it is appropriate to speak of a psychological *state* or *process* (cf. PI § 308). For if we are really dealing with a state (or a process), its duration cannot be identified with the relevant emotion's capacity to 'colour' thoughts and feelings.

This is not the place to unravel this complex set of questions. But what should give us pause is the following observation: 'Love and hate might be called mental dispositions, and so might fear in one sense' (RPP II, § 148). Now one may well wonder what remains of the criterion of *genuine* duration. According to Wittgenstein, the difference between (psychological) states and dispositions consist in this, that a state does not continue when it is interrupted whereas of a disposition it cannot meaningfully be said that it has or has not been interrupted.

> ...then an important difference between dispositions and states of consciousness consists in the fact that a disposition is not interrupted by a break in consciousness or a shift in attention. (And that of course is not a causal remark.) (RPP II, § 45)
>
> The general difference between all states of consciousness and dispositions seems to me to be that one need not find out by spot-check whether they are still going on. (RPP II, § 57)

Now, Wittgenstein says clearly that love and hate have no *genuine* duration. But this means that, in his view, love and hate are not emotions – *if* the criterion of genuine duration remains valid. And in fact, this is a conclusion that Wittgenstein does draw for a different, but perhaps related reason. He writes that certain 'attitudes (e.g., love) can be put to the test, but not emotions' (RPP II, § 152). This may mean that, in cases like love or hate, a test *conducted by the subject himself* is possible, in a case like anger, however, impossible.[8] (Here as in many other cases, 'impossible' means that it would be absurd to say that through testing oneself one has found that one really continues to be angry.)

This is a remarkable conclusion, a conclusion which should make us think about the unity of the concept of an emotion. For one must remember that love and hate are normally counted among our paradigmatic emotions. They figure on numerous lists of the emotions which have been drawn up since Aristotle and which are sometimes cited to show by way of example what is meant by 'an emotion'. If Wittgenstein is right in concluding that in reality love and hate should not be included in such lists, then this is a result worth pondering.

2. Later remarks

In June 1948 (that is, shortly before completing the material collected in RPP II) a new metaphor emerges from Wittgenstein's manuscript notes. While it is connected with various ideas developed in his earlier writings, it changes the overall physiognomy of his considerations. This metaphor unfolds only gradually and, in line with its possibilities of application, takes different kinds of shape. Here I shall try to give a brief account of this development, focussing on our concepts of emotions.

In the context of a general discussion of questions of concept formation Wittgenstein emphasizes that, in the realm of human action, certain phenomena require a specific background to count as phenomena of this or that kind. The background of acting, he says, is variegated, not monochrome: it forms 'a very complicated filigree pattern' (RPP II, § 624; the original manuscript entry has 'ornament' instead of 'pattern'). This pattern is too complicated to produce a copy, but it is possible to recognize it 'from the general impression it makes'. This background with its filigree pattern is called 'the bustle of life' (RPP II, §§ 625–626). A little later, Wittgenstein speaks of 'the whole hurly-burly' which forms 'the background against which we see an action' (§ 629). And in his manuscript he says: 'The background of life is, as it were, *pointillé*' (MS 137, p. 54b). One purpose all these different formulations can be seen to serve is to render plausible that in this area our concepts have no clear boundaries. The language which we use to talk about human actions contains blurred concepts which, however, especially in virtue of their indistinctness are serviceable instruments for us human beings (cf. RPP II, § 637).

This idea of indistinctness or blurred concepts plays an important part in Wittgenstein's subsequent considerations. What he wants to get clear about is the relation between conceptual fuzziness and recognizable form. At the same time he tries to make us see the many ways in which our concepts are rooted in the primitive needs and reactions of human life. Again and again he finds new formulations to get it across that language springs from instinct, not from reasoning (see e.g., RPP II, § 632; cf. MS 137, p. 64b).

What Wittgenstein tends to call 'primitive' kinds of action and reaction, which can be found to characterize the way of life of our remote ancestors as well as that of sophisticated moderns, offer particularly impressive examples of forms of behaviour that exhibit clearly circumscribed and (re-)identifiable patterns. These 'patterns of life' form contexts whose existence is a precondition which must be satisfied for our concepts to be applicable to human actions and types of behaviour. In other words, such concepts hinge on the existence of such patterns of life. These patterns are not rigid, and that is, as Wittgenstein points out (RPP II, § 652), one reason why those concepts that depend on them can become indeterminate. In this area, determinateness would be possible only if life proceeded in an extremely regular fashion. The question 'What would happen with our concepts if our life displayed this sort of regularity?' is one which Wittgenstein raises (see LW I, § 406 = PI II, p. 174, quoted below). Another question, which poses itself as a matter of course, is: How much indeterminateness can our concepts tolerate without losing their applicability?

The notion of a background emerges in the context of Wittgenstein's discussion of the concept 'lying'. Further considerations that centre on this idea can be found where he talks about our notions of 'pretending' (RPP II, § 672) and 'simulation' (LW I, § 862). It is in this connection that the metaphor of life as a carpet[9] in which pretending, for example, occurs as one pattern (or type of pattern) among many is used for the first time[10]: individual patterns of pretending are not always complete, nor always the same, but when examining cases of pretending we 'in our conceptual world' do not perceive scores of disparate phenomena but always the same kinds of things in slightly modified shapes. Here, Wittgenstein tends to use the word 'variation', and this use is reminiscent of his morphological idea of unfolding a concept's potentialities by means of indicating a series of variations.[11] (This idea is obviously connected with the notion of family resemblance, cf. PI §§ 65ff.)

The image of patterns recurring in varied shapes in the carpet of life serves to illustrate a complex series of insights. An important point is that in spite of their recognizability such patterns can be blurred, not only at their edges, but in all kinds of respects. And this reflection helps us to get away from our practice of focussing on conceptual *boundaries* – the idea that it is natural to compare concepts with more or less well-delimited areas.[12] Wittgenstein also wants to underline the varieties of ways in which these patterns are connected: there are manifold respects in which they are linked together, and in addition they have to harmonize with each other if they are to figure as patterns of one and the same carpet. Analogous considerations go for the relations between relevant concepts. Besides, the image of a carpet serves to explain a characteristic type of correspondence between patterns and concepts used to describe them: these patterns are parts of a fabric whose threads go in many different directions and thus help to stabilize the fabric. Here we are evidently meant to understand the way the relevant concepts work in an analogous fashion (cf. the related thought in PI § 67).

In Wittgenstein's view, the notion of a pattern plays a key role also because it involves useful ways of illustration or representation by means of exemplifying patterns. This is important because exemplification can help to elucidate concepts. Thus one can for example explain the concept of pretence by means of exemplifying its patterns on the stage (MS 137, p. 64a). In this way it is possible to illustrate that – and in which respect – pretending presupposes a motive and carries with it the risk of discovery.

In subsequent remarks the notion of a pattern is mentioned again and again, several times by using the composite expression 'pattern of life'. In

November 1948, however, Wittgenstein varies or modifies his metaphor. He explicitly refers to the idea that a concept dependent on a pattern of life must contain a degree of indeterminacy (RPP II, § 652), but now he uses the expression 'a stencil' or 'a stereotype of life' (*Lebensschablone*, LW I, § 206). At the same time he tries to explain his metaphor. We are asked to imagine a strip of some kind bearing a pattern of regular lines. This pattern is overlaid by irregular and multicoloured drawings that can be described by specifying the location of their elements on top of the pattern. But if there turn up anomalies in the pattern, its application becomes problematic. Now there are several possibilities: there could be explicit rules for deviating cases; but it could also be that this particular pattern (including its irregularities) was used and accepted in teaching without raising questions about the anomalies.

The decisive point is that the pattern (or stencil or stereotype) will always involve irregularities if it really is a pattern of *life*. This becomes clear if we look at the following passage from Wittgenstein's manuscript:

> A pattern of life is the basis of a use of words. The pattern changes. The language-game begins to totter. | The pattern of life, after all, is not one of exact regularity. (MS 167, p. 16r = draft of LW I, § 211.)

To be sure, the different metaphors that Wittgenstein uses in this connection may serve to bring out different aspects of his thought. But what remains stable is his interest in the relations between life as background, the indefinite or irregular patterns of this life and the correspondingly indefinite concepts that we have to make do with in the context of our language-games.

This perspective is closely connected with Wittgenstein's general reflections on the relation between concept formation and facts of nature (PI II, p. 230). This is an aspect of the matter which I shall have to leave out of account. Here I am concerned to shed some light on a more specific connection which Wittgenstein begins to discuss by considering the notion of hope:

> Can only those hope who can talk? Only those who have mastered the use of a language. That is to say, the phenomena of hope are modifications [variations] of this complicated form of life. (If a concept aims at a character of human handwriting, it has no application to beings that do not write.) (PI II, p. 174)

In a manuscript draft of this passage (MS 137, p. 115a) Wittgenstein speaks of modifications 'of a more complicated pattern of life' or 'of that very complicated pattern'. So it is probable that in this passage the expression 'form of life' is also to be understood in the sense of 'pattern of life'. By the 'phenomena of hope' Wittgenstein presumably means those expressions of hope which can be discovered by observing human behaviour (if one has mastered our use of the concept 'hope'). These expressions can be regarded as variations of one and the same pattern, but at the same time one must not overlook that these are phenomena that cannot be captured by means of a completely regular pattern.

One reason why the notion of hope is of particular interest to Wittgenstein is the fact that he feels tempted to treat it the same way as our concepts of paradigmatic emotions. Examination of the notion of hope, however, shows that while there are reasons for treating it that way, there are other reasons for denying it the status of an emotion. One result of these reflections is that several concepts that seem to belong to our standard concepts of emotions reveal themselves as equally dubious candidates for that category. Still, there are several supposed emotions that continue to fulfil all our standard criteria for falling under the concept of an emotion, and with respect to some of these paradigmatic cases Wittgenstein writes:

> For us, 'grief' describes a pattern which recurs, with different variations, in the carpet of life. If a man's bodily expression of sorrow and of joy alternated, say with the ticking of a clock, here we would not have the characteristic course of the pattern of sorrow or of the pattern of joy. (PI II, p. 174)

In this passage, Wittgenstein not only assigns grief, sorrow and joy their respective places in the explanatory structure formed by our central notions of 'pattern', 'carpet of life' and 'variation'; he also emphasizes how important it is for such patterns that the course of their occurrence is *not* a regular one.

From the complex metaphor forming the basis of the last two quotations and their drafts there emerges a view which is remarkably different from the ideas on which Wittgenstein's attempted classifications of psychological concepts and their respective explanations of concepts rested. The earlier conception assumed a model in terms of which we have psychological phenomena (experiences) on the one hand and corresponding concepts on the other; the latter will be true of the former if they satisfy certain criteria.

This admittedly fairly natural model is one from which Wittgenstein now wants to keep at least some distance by not focussing on individual criteria or characteristics but, rather, on more complex structures which in their turn are always to be seen in the context of other complex structures. These structures are what he calls *patterns*, whose function, formation and context dependence he attempts to clarify in some of the passages quoted above as well as on many further pages of the manuscripts written in 1948 and 1949.

By making this attempt Wittgenstein moves away from all traditional ways of explaining psychological concepts. In particular, the idea of focussing, not on specified objects or phenomena and the properties attributed or denied them, but on patterns – that is, complex but at the same time firmly interconnected structures – falls foul of all common forms of analysis.[13] This is not the place to give a detailed account of that idea and all its ramifications; here I merely wish to look at the bearing it may be seen to have on the concept of an emotion and what explanatory value it may turn out to have in this connection. This discussion may then serve as a first step towards clarifying Wittgenstein's idea in a more general way.

Of course, from the changes in Wittgenstein's way of looking at things that have here been characterized by emphasizing the metaphor of varying patterns in the carpet of life it does not follow that all the insights gained in the context of his earlier attempts at classifying psychological concepts will have to be jettisoned. But these insights will now have to be employed within a different framework implying new emphases. In particular, what changes is the relation between unity and variety. Attempts at classification of the kind on which explanations like those described on the first pages of this chapter tend to be based stress the unity of the more general concept. In our case, this means that the concepts of individual emotions look like small conceptual domains encircled by the comprehensive concept of an emotion. Emphasizing the unity of this concept guides our investigation of emotion concepts and directs our attention to similarities and connecting links.

If, on the other hand, we conceive of individual emotions as varying patterns in the carpet of life, we need to notice slight variations and are hence inclined to focus on the distinguishing features of these emotions. That sharpens one's eye for dissimilarities between various forms of what is usually called the same emotion and between different emotions. Particular stress is laid on the context of life where different emotions are expressed, and this way of orienting one's investigation has a tendency to lead to conceptual differences that depend on the degree of complexity and complicatedness of the life under consideration.

Two points are of particular importance. First, emotions have a certain place in our lives. That is to say, there are specific occasions that may lead up to a given emotion. If the situation were different, attributing this emotion would be bizarre. In other words, an emotion involves certain antecedents, motives, circumstances, characteristic forms of response, and so on, and this dependency is reflected by its concept. Here it is immediately obvious that the typical occasions on which different emotions tend to arise require descriptions of varying complexity – descriptions which also vary according to the degree of complicatedness of the life concerned. Emotions that may be attributed to non-human animals – such as anger, fear, joy, sadness and fright – admit of relatively primitive characterizations. Grief, on the other hand, is surely more complicated than those:

> As an example think of the description of 'occasions'. Is it really clear that one has to understand the description of an 'occasion of grief'? For the

occasions of grief are interwoven with 1000 other patterns. Is it clear that someone must be able to learn the technique of naming this kind of pattern? That he be able to pick an occasion of grief out of the other patterns the way we do? | But here there are simple and more complicated cases; and that is important for the concept. ... (LW I, § 966–967)

Matters are yet more complicated if an emotion presupposes language as well as highly developed social conditions. It is not only hope that cannot be attributed to a dog, but remorse too cannot be fitted into the life of languageless creatures (RPP II, § 308). And this is the second point I wanted to mention, for in accordance with various possibilities of embedding different emotions in different language-games, these emotions will form distinct patterns which allow us to make corresponding distinctions between them.

In this connection a perspective concentrating on the formation of patterns implies notable consequences. In the case of certain paradigmatic emotions (fear, joy, anger, etc.) it is possible to illustrate them satisfactorily by means of schematic pictures or simple pantomime without paying attention to context. This method becomes increasingly difficult and eventually impossible to apply when one deals with more finely discriminated emotions or with emotions that can only be attributed to language-users.

The first way of complicating matters is easy to explain by drawing up lists reaching from paradigmatic emotions to ever more finely discriminated ones, for example: angry, furious, enraged, wrathful, piqued, nettled, ..., or sad, grief-stricken, dejected, gloomy, sombre, wistful, ... It is interesting that some of the earlier items on these lists can be illustrated by graphic descriptions like 'hot under the collar', 'down in the mouth', 'hang one's head' whereas there are fewer or no such expressions available for later items.

The second way of complicating matters comes to the fore if you think of the possibility of explaining emotions by means of stage performances. Simple basic emotions can be illustrated by a competent actor without props, using only facial expressions and gestures. But as soon as things become more complicated pantomime is not enough – the actor will have to use language. For this purpose drama has conventional means like monologues or asides. These possibilities present themselves especially in those situations where we are dealing with the phenomena of lying, pretending and simulation frequently discussed by Wittgenstein. It is apropos such situations that he writes: 'We combine diverse elements into a "Gestalt" (pattern), for example, into one of deceit. | The picture of the inner completes the Gestalt' (RPP II, § 651). The pattern of deceit involves occasion, motive, opportunities and other characteristics of the situation in question. Even in fairly uncomplicated cases of deceit the pattern would be incomplete without bringing in certain aspects of the use of language. And it is through this way of complicating matters that a certain picture of the inner appears on the scene: the monologue delivered onstage is moved to a private, inner stage where the ego is apprised of hitherto unrevealed intentions. Of course, this pattern is a construction, a picture, but it is a picture which forms part of the relevant concept. Presumably, it is the same with more complicated emotions. The patterns of remorse and hope involve pictures of thoughts occupied with a deed one regrets or an object of hope. It is in this way that, in the case of our more complicated emotions, the inner is assembled in order to complete the pattern.

Notes

1. It goes without saying that 'later' does not mean 'correct'. Nor is 'earlier' equivalent to 'wrong'.
2. For abbreviations of the titles of works by Wittgenstein, see the list following this section. I use existing translations, tacitly making changes wherever I feel that a different rendering is an improvement. The sign '|' is used in quotations to indicate a new paragraph.
3. Here it may be helpful to mention examples of *Gemütsbewegungen* taken from a few particularly relevant passages: *Trauer* (sadness, sorrow), *Freude* (pleasure, delight, joy), *Gram* (grief, sorrow), *Entzücken* (delight), *Depression* (depression), *Zorn* (anger, wrath), *Furcht* (fear, fright). The following items appear to be on Wittgenstein's list of *Gemütsbewegungen*, but one may want to argue that it is not completely clear that they belong there: *Überraschung* (surprise), *Schreck* (fright, shock), *Bewunderung* (admiration), *Genuß* (pleasure, enjoyment), *Liebe* (love), *Haß* (hatred), *Hoffnung* (hope).
4. It has been pointed out to me by Peter Hacker as well as Michael McEachrane that Wittgenstein must have meant something like 'occurrently felt emotions'. Well, he may have meant this, and perhaps the German word *Gemütsbewegung* (as opposed to the English word 'emotion') tends to imply this. At any rate, what Wittgenstein does say in RPP II, § 148 is that genuine duration is something that all *Gemütsbewegungen* have in common. As I point out below, Wittgenstein himself became dissatisfied with this view and with the whole approach that was meant to give this view bite. I wish to thank both Peter Hacker and Michael McEachrane for their helpful comments. Unfortunately, I have not been able to accommodate all their observations. In particular, I am not as sure as they are that Wittgenstein cannot have said, or meant, certain things that tend to strike most readers as peculiar.
5. See Schulte (1993), chapter 8.
6. Budd (1989), pp. 153–154.
7. See Schulte (1993), pp. 102–106, 145–146, 154–156.
8. It is, for example, quite normal to say that one tries to find out whether one is really in love with a certain person, whereas it does not normally make much sense to say that one tries to find out whether one is really angry, pleased, sad, etc.
9. Peter Hacker has suggested that 'tapestry of life' might be a better translation. In view of the fact that one tends to associate different images with these metaphorical expressions I prefer to use the more literal rendering 'carpet of life'. As far as I can see, the title of Stefan George's poems (referred to in my next note) is usually translated as 'The Carpet of Life'. This may be regarded as counting as an additional reason for using 'carpet' rather than 'tapestry'.

10. MS 169, p. 68v [LW II, p. 42]. Cf. LW I, § 406 [PI II, p. 174] and § 862. Wittgenstein's unusual expression *'Lebensteppich'* is reminiscent of the title of one of Stefan George's cycles of poems (*Der Teppich des Lebens*, 1899). There is a reference to George in the manuscript draft of RPP I, 1087 (MS 135, p. 53v, 28 July 1947).
11. For Wittgenstein's morphological ideas, see Schulte (1990), pp. 11–42; cf. the shorter account in Schulte (2002).
12. Cf. Wittgenstein's remarks on Frege's notion of a concept as a *Bezirk*, PI § 71.
13. Certain elements of Wittgenstein's conception may put readers in mind of Hilary Putnam's idea of 'stereotypes'. Possibly, one path by which Wittgenstein arrived at his notion of a pattern was delineated by his grappling with the ideas of gestalt psychologists like Wolfgang Köhler.

Abbreviations of works by Wittgenstein

LW I   *Last Writings on the Philosophy of Psychology* (Vol. I), edited by von Wright, G.H. and Nyman, H., translated by Luckhardt, C.G. and Aue, M.A.E. (Oxford: Blackwell, 1982).

LW II   *Last Writings on the Philosophy of Psychology: The Inner and the Outer* (Vol. II), edited by von Wright, G.H. and Nyman, H., translated by Luckhardt, C.G. and Aue, M.A.E. (Oxford: Blackwell, 1992).

MS   Manuscript – numbers are given in accordance with the von Wright catalogue of Wittgenstein's Nachlass.

PI   *Philosophical Investigations*, translated by Anscombe, G.E.M.. 3rd edn (Oxford: Blackwell, 1967).

RPP I   *Remarks on the Philosophy of Psychology*, Vol. I, edited by Anscombe, G.E.M. and von Wright, G.H., translated by Anscombe, G.E.M. (Oxford: Blackwell, 1980).

RPP II   *Remarks on the Philosophy of Psychology*, Vol. II, edited by von Wright, G.H. and Nyman, H., translated by Luckhardt, C.G. and Aue, M.A.E. (Oxford: Blackwell, 1980).

Bibliography

Budd, M. (1989), *Wittgenstein's Philosophy of Psychology* (London: Routledge).
Schulte, J. (1990), *Chor und Gesetz: Wittgenstein im Kontext* (Frankfurt am Main: Suhrkamp).
——. (1993), *Experience and Expression* (Oxford: Clarendon Press).
——. (2002), 'Goethe and Wittgenstein on Morphology', *Wittgenstein Studien* 5, 55–72.

3
The Conceptual Framework for the Investigation of Emotions*

P.M.S. Hacker

1. Conceptual elucidation and experimental investigation

For a long period the experimental study of the emotions was out of bounds for neuro-psychologists and neuro-psychiatrists. Now, 'thanks to the work of Ledoux [(1996)] and Damasio [(1994)], emotions are once again a legitimate topic for research' (David and Halligan 2000, p. 508). However, as I shall argue, the conceptual structures with which they operate (partly inherited from William James) are misconceived.[1] Mary Phillips has recently observed that 'there is at present no generally accepted theoretical framework for human emotion' (Phillips et al. 2003). Philosophical analysis, properly conducted, can assist in filling this lacuna.

Philosophy cannot make empirical discoveries, and it is not its task to produce empirical theories. Its task is to describe the conceptual structures in terms of which we articulate our experience and its objects. So while it should not propose *empirical theories* of the emotions, it can elucidate the *conceptual* framework for experimental investigation. Hence too, it can prevent conceptual confusions that vitiate the design of, and the conclusions inferred from, experiments.

Fruitful experimental work requires a correct conceptual framework characterizing the concepts of the phenomena investigated. Unless one is clear what precisely counts as an emotion, one may find oneself investigating phenomena, for example appetites, that are only tangentially related to the emotions (cf. Roles 2000). Unless one is aware of the conceptual distinction between the neural states and processes which make it possible for an animal to feel an emotion and the emotion it feels, one will be prone to confuse an emotion with a brain state (cf. LeDoux). Unless one distinguishes between the feelings that are sensations and the feelings that are emotions, one may confuse sensations engendered by thoughts with emotions (cf. Damasio). And unless one distinguishes between the causes and the objects of emotions, and between feeling an emotion and realizing what emotion one feels, one may think that identifying the cause of an emotion plays a role in emotion-perception (cf. Phillips 2003), whereas in fact there is no such thing as *perception* of one's own emotion, and the ability to say what emotion one is feeling need not depend on identifying its causes but does depend on identifying its object.

2. Feelings

The word 'feeling' is multivalent. It is important not to confuse its different meanings (Figure 3.1).

We must distinguish the feelings that are perceptions from the feelings that are sensations. To feel the heat, solidity, elasticity or dampness of an object with one's hand, elbow or cheek are forms of tactile perception. To do so is to exercise a cognitive faculty. To feel a pain, tingle or tickle, however, is not a form of perception. To feel a pain is no different from having a pain. Such sensations are localized *in* the body (it always *makes sense* to ask where one feels them), but are not felt *with* any part of the body. Sensations, unlike perceptions, are not correct or incorrect, and the liability to have sensations is not a cognitive faculty. Localized bodily sensations must be distinguished from sensations of overall bodily condition, such as feelings of weariness or lassitude.

Appetites are distinct from affections. Natural appetites are feelings of hunger, thirst or blind animal lust. Non-natural (acquired) appetites are addictions. Natural appetites are blends of sensation and desire characteristic of animals (see Figure 3.2). The sensations characteristic of appetites are localized – the sensation of hunger is located in the midriff, of thirst in the parched throat. The sensations associated with appetites are forms of unease that dispose one to action to satisfy the appetite. The desire blended with

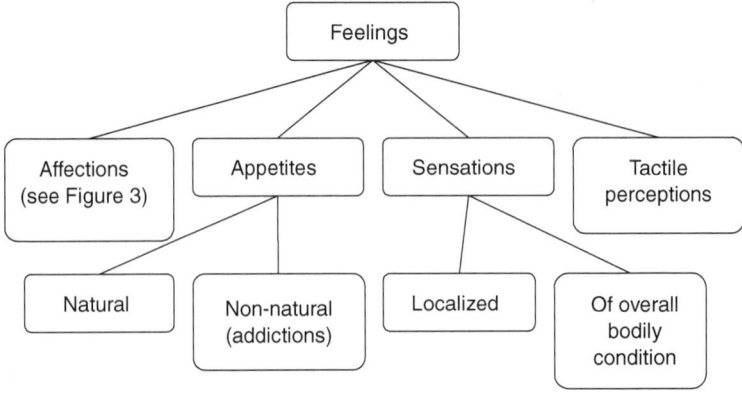

Figure 3.1   Types of feelings distinguished

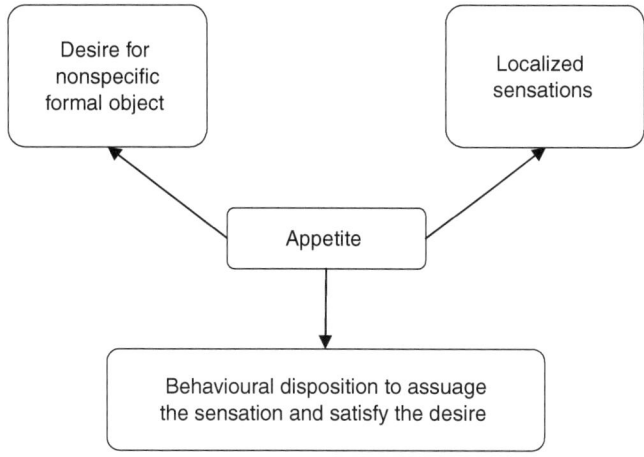

Figure 3.2 Conceptual links of appetite

sensation is characterized by its *formal* object (e.g., hunger is a desire for food, thirst for drink, lust for sexual intercourse). Distinctive of desires constitutive of appetites is their lack of a *specific* object (one cannot be hungry for dessert but not for the main course). The intensity of the desire constitutive of appetite is typically proportional to the intensity of the sensation. Fulfilling an appetite leads to its temporary satiation and so to the disappearance of the sensation. Appetites are not constant, but recurrent, typically caused by bodily needs (or hormonally determined drives) consequent upon deprivation of food, drink or sexual intercourse.

Affections, like appetites and sensations, are felt. The feelings that are affections can be divided into emotions, agitations and moods (see Figure 3.3). One feels love or hate (emotions), excited or astonished (agitations), cheerful or depressed (moods). Unlike sensations, affections do not have a bodily location and do not inform one about the state of one's body, even though they are sometimes linked with sensations. One does not feel pride in one's chest, even though one's chest may swell with pride, or fear in one's mouth, even though one's mouth may feel dry with fear. One's blush of shame does not inform one of the state of one's facial arteries, although it may inform one that one is more ashamed than one thought, and one's tears of grief do not inform one of the state of one's lachrymal glands, although they may inform one that one loved Daisy more than one thought. Unlike feelings that are perceptions, the affections do not inform one about the world.

Paradigmatic emotions are such things as love, hate, hope, fear, anger, gratitude, resentment, indignation, envy, jealousy, pity, compassion, grief, as well as emotions of self-assessment such as pride, shame, humiliation, regret,

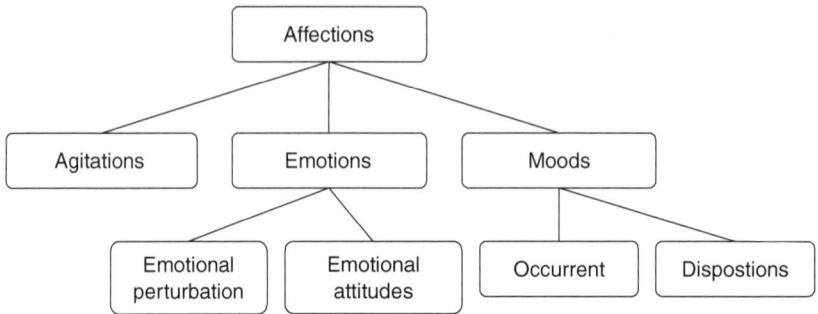

Figure 3.3 Types of affection

remorse and guilt. The conceptual structure of the emotions will be described
below.

Agitations are short-term affective disturbances, typically caused by something unexpected. They include such temporary states as being and feeling
excited, thrilled, shocked, convulsed, amazed, surprised, startled, horrified,
revolted, disgusted, delighted. They are caused by what we perceive, learn or
realize. Because they are disturbances, caused by unanticipated disruptions,
they are not motives for action as emotions may be, but temporarily *inhibit*
motivated action. One may behave in certain ways *because* one is excited,
thrilled or shocked. But one does not act *out of* excitement, thrill or shock in
the sense in which one acts out of love, compassion or gratitude. Agitations
are modes of reaction: one cries out *in* horror or amazement, recoils *with*
revulsion or disgust, is convulsed *with* laughter or paralysed *with* shock.
Occurrently felt emotions, by contrast with longer-standing emotional attitudes, often bear a kinship to agitations in the perturbations of, for example, the throbbing temples of rage, the trembling, sweating and shallow
breathing of fear, the tears and cries of grief.

Moods are such things as feeling cheerful, euphoric, contented, irritable,
melancholic or depressed; they are states or frames of mind, as when one is
in a state of melancholia, or in a jovial or relaxed frame of mind. They may
be occurrent or longer-term dispositional states. One may feel depressed for
an afternoon, or one may be suffering from a depression that lasts for
months. As disposition, a mood is a proneness to feel, during one's waking
hours, joyful, depressed, cheerful, etc. Moods are less closely tied to objects
than emotions, for one may feel cheerful or depressed without one's mood
being directed at any specific object, whereas one cannot feel love without
feeling love for someone or something or feel angry without feeling angry
with anyone or about anything. Equally, moods are linked not to specific
patterns of intentional action, but to manners of behaviour. Cheerfulness,

melancholia and depression, unlike love, envy or compassion, do not provide motives for action, but they are exhibited in the manner in which one does whatever one does, in one's demeanour and tone of voice. This is a corollary of the fact that moods colour one's thoughts and pervade one's reflections.

It is, therefore, unwarranted to characterize moods, as Damasio does, as emotional states that are frequent or continuous over long periods of time (Damasio 1999, p. 341). One may fear war for a long period, but that does not imply that one is in any particular mood, although, to be sure, one's fear may contribute to one's melancholic mood. Othello's jealousy was persistent and continuous, but unlike his consequent depression, it was not a mood. And frequently to fear things may be to be timorous by nature, but it is not to be in any mood.

The difference between affections in general and emotions in particular, on the one hand, and appetites, on the other, should be evident. Recent work on appetites has been mischaracterized as a result of failure to note it. E.T. Roles (2000) purports to investigate the neural substrate of the emotions. But he takes as paradigmatic examples of emotions, and as the object of his research, thirst, hunger and animal lust. Despite the interest of these investigations, they are not about, and do not obviously have any bearing on, the emotions, for hunger, thirst and lust are appetites, not emotions.

First, emotions are not linked to localized sensations in the same way as appetites are. Some emotions are associated with sensations (fear, rage), others are not (pride, remorse, envy). One does not have a feeling of pride in one's stomach or in one's chest; although there are sensations characteristic of occurrent anger, such as throbbing temples and tension, one does not feel anger in one's temples or stomach muscles as one feels hunger in one's belly. Secondly, emotions have not only formal objects – in the sense that what one fears is what is thought to be frightening or harmful and what one feels remorseful about is a misdemeanour one has committed – but also *specific* objects, as when one fears tomorrow's examination or feels remorse for lying to Daisy. Thirdly, the intensity of emotions is not proportional to the intensity of whatever sensations may accompany their occurrent manifestation. How proud I am of my children's achievements cannot be measured by reference to sensations. But it may be exhibited in my behaviour, for example in the way I praise them, and in the manner in which I talk about them. Similarly, how much I fear heights may be manifest not in the intensity of perturbations I feel on rock-faces (which I assiduously avoid), but rather in the lengths I go to avoid heights. Fourthly, emotions do not display the pattern of occurrence, satiation and recurrence characteristic of appetites for they do not have the same kind of physiological and hormonal basis as the appetites. Fifthly, the emotions have a cognitive dimension absent from the appetites. The hungry animal wants food, the thirsty animal wants drink, the animal on heat wants sexual intercourse, but no particular knowledge or beliefs are essentially associated with these appetites. By contrast, the frightened animal is afraid of something it knows or thinks is dangerous, a mother is proud of her offspring believing them to be meritorious, the repentant sinner is remorseful, knowing himself to have sinned. Finally, many emotions are exhibited by characteristic facial expression and manifested in typical tones of voice – as in the case of fear, anger, love and affection. Hunger and thirst are not.

The boundaries between emotion, agitation and mood are not sharp. Emotional perturbations (as I shall refer to the typical somatic, expressive and behavioural manifestations of many occurrent emotions) have, as remarked, an affinity with agitations. Emotions may fade into moods, as when terror that abates leaves behind a mood of objectless anxiety. And conversely, a feeling of undirected anxiety may crystallize into a specific fear. The psychological category of the affections displays both conceptual complexity and diversity, the conceptual patterns to be discerned are irregular, and the variations from type to type are considerable. Consequently most generalizations concerning the concepts within the three sub-categories need to be qualified with a 'for the most part' or a 'typically'.

3. Emotions

Emotion words function as names of character traits (loving, affectionate, proud), of motives (acting *out of* or *from* hatred, envy, jealousy) and of felt emotions. The notion of felt emotion does not discriminate between *episodic emotional perturbations* and longer-standing *emotional attitudes*. Emotional perturbations (see Figure 3.4) resemble agitations in certain respects. Some, for example fear or anger, have characteristic somatic accompaniments, both sensations that are felt and physiological reactions that are measurable. Others do not, for example feelings of pride, humility, compassion, gratitude and respect. They are manifested in *expressive* behaviour which may take various forms. It may be behaviour that is not action at all, as in the case of blushes of embarrassment or love, and perspiration and pallor of fear. It may be voluntary (the utterances of love and affection, of hope or pride), partly voluntary (raised voice of anger, that can be inhibited) or involuntary action (cry of terror). And it may be exhibited merely in the manner of acting (e.g., *tone* of voice, *impatient* actions of anger). Some emotional perturbations are closely associated with relatively specific forms of intentional and instrumental action or inclinations to act, as in the case of fear of imminent danger (inclination to avoid or flee) or pity (inclination to help). Others, such as regret or hope, are not. Some, in the case of human beings, are directly linked to reasons for acting and to motivated action, for example fear of a dangerous object is linked to acting out of fear for the reason that the object is dangerous, and pity is linked to acting to ameliorate the condition of another for the reason that they are suffering. Others have no such direct (but only

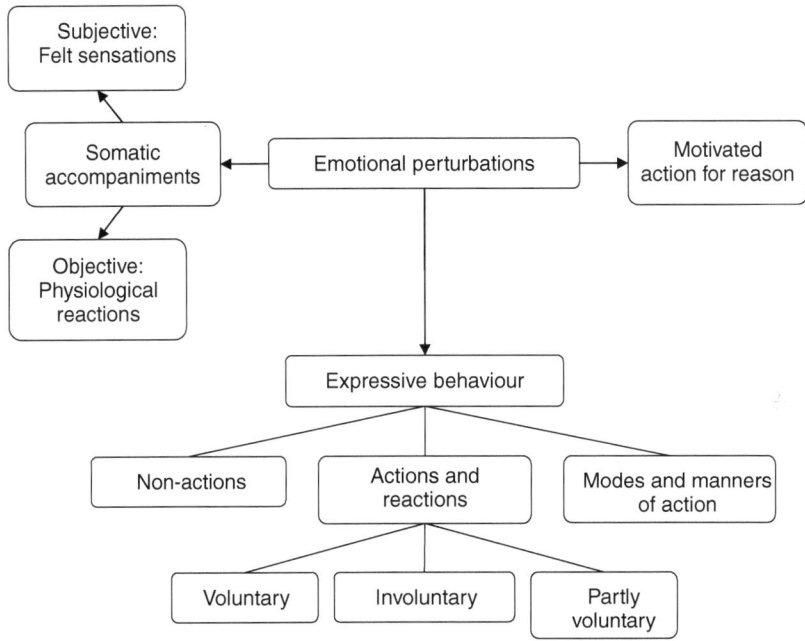

Figure 3.4   Conceptual links of emotional perturbations

indirect) links to motivated action. In characterizing someone as 'being emotional', we typically mean that he is prone to emotional perturbations, given to outbursts of feeling, which he expresses freely, perhaps to excess, and tends to allow his emotions to cloud his judgement.

Emotional perturbations have further attributes which they share with emotional attitudes, for example causes, objects, agential reasons for the feelings and for their constitutive beliefs, reasons for acting, appraisal and evaluation. These will be examined below.

It is important not to allow the perturbational aspect of the emotions to occlude their attitudinal aspect, or to think that research on the perturbations characteristic of an emotion can provide an adequate account of that emotion. Neuroscientific work, influenced by the misconceived Jamesian theory of the emotions, has screened out the attitudinal, as well as the motivational, cogitative and fantasy aspects of the emotions. One may love or hate a person, an activity, a cause, or a place for the whole of one's life. One may be proud of the achievements of one's youth for the rest of one's days, and one may respect or detest, be envious or jealous of a person for years. One may be ashamed or guilty of one's misconduct for decades, and one's regret for one's follies may never cease. One's judgement may be clouded not only by emotional agitation and distress (perturbation), but also by one's long-standing resentments, envies or jealousies (emotional attitudes). Love may be felt as a perturbation to which those who are falling in love are susceptible, or as a standing attitude of conjugal, parental, filial or fraternal feeling. The emotional attitude of love is not a disposition to corresponding episodes of loving perturbation, but a lasting concern for the object of love, a standing motive for action beneficial to the beloved, a desire for shared experience, and a persistent colouring of thought, imagination and fantasy. The standing emotion of anger with a person is not a proneness to episodic outbursts of anger, but persistent ill-will and absence of amiability resting on the agent's reasons for his anger. The emotions of love, hate or envy, for example, consist above all in the manner in which the object of the emotion *matters* to one and the reasons for which it is important (one cannot feel indifferent about the object of one's feelings); hence also in the motives that move one to action – for one will act *out of* love, hate or envy. One's emotions are then evident in the reasons that weigh with one in one's deliberations, in the desires one harbours and in the thoughts that cross one's mind in connection with the objects of one's feelings. One's emotions are inseparable from one's fantasy life and imagination, one's wishes and longings (see Figure 3.5).

It should be obvious that one cannot measure a person's emotion simply by the frequency or intensity of the emotional perturbations he feels. Fear may be manifest in the lengths one goes to avoid the situations that terrify one. Its motivating force cannot be quantified as rises in pulse-, breathing- or perspiration-rates can be. Rather, its strength is evaluated by the extent to which the emotion determines behaviour over time and the kind of behaviour it determines. The depth of a person's remorse is exhibited less in episodic outbursts of remorse, more in the endeavours to make amends and

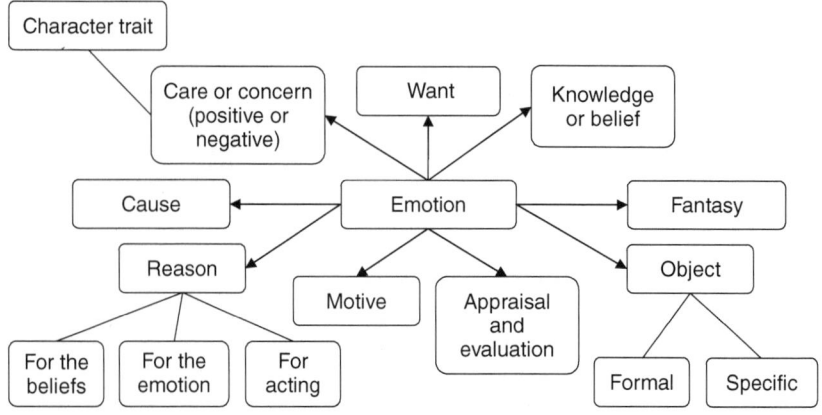

Figure 3.5   Conceptual links of emotion

in the obsessive thoughts about his wrongdoing. The strength of a person's love is manifest not just in felt perturbations, but also in his concern for the welfare of the object of his love and in the sacrifices he is willing to make for the sake of what or whom he loves. One may concede that a long-standing emotional attitude *may*, given appropriate circumstances, imply a lower threshold for the onset of corresponding emotional perturbation (e.g., in the case of anger or hatred). But that is, at best, only part of the story, since appropriate circumstances may not obtain (given assiduous avoidance behaviour, as in the case of fear of heights), the agent may exercise self-control, and the relevant perturbational behaviour may not be that of the emotion in question (as in the case of love, which is exhibited in the wide variety of forms of care and concern).

It should be equally evident that the ways in which emotional attitudes are manifest in behaviour over time are highly conditioned by social conventions that partly determine within a social group what may *count* as an expression of love or hatred, gratitude or resentment, affection or contempt. Although there may be a natural foundation of expressive behaviour on which such conventions are built, they vary greatly from society to society, from one historical period to another, and, within a given society, from one social class to another. Similar variability is exhibited by the grounds for an emotion, since what counts as *a good reason* for pride, resentment, indignation, contempt, and so on is a partial function of the culture and conventions of the society to which the person belongs. So too, the motivational character of an emotion; what forms of behaviour may be warranted by a given emotional attitude, is typically culturally conditioned.

Any experimental investigation of the emotions must take into account the complexity of the concept of an emotion, the conceptual diversity of the emotions, and cultural variability of the reasons for and the motivating character of the emotions to which human beings are susceptible. There is no single paradigm of an emotion that can serve as a conceptual prototype from which to generalize. Equally, one must beware of experiments on non-human animals as a basis for generalizations concerning human emotion. For the horizon of actual emotions as well as the horizon of possible emotions in animals is far narrower than with human beings. It is determined by the fact that animals are not language-using, concept-exercising creatures. They can fear something here and now, but they cannot now fear something elsewhere tomorrow, as we can. And they cannot feel such emotions as remorse, which requires a knowledge of good and evil, an awareness of having done wrong, and a determination to make amends. Animal emotion is neither reasonable nor unreasonable, whereas human emotion may be, since human beings may have reasons and justifications for feeling as they do, and the feelings they have may afford them reasons for acting. The study of human *emotions* is a study of *human* emotions. And the study of *human emotions* presupposes the background of specific cultural forms of human life.

Emotions generally have objects. If one is afraid, one is afraid *of* someone, or *that* something is going to happen; if one feels remorse, guilt or regret, it is *for* doing something; if one feels envy, it is envy *of* someone *for* his good fortune. It is important to distinguish the object of an emotion from its cause, since neuroscientists commonly confuse and conflate them. What *makes* one jealous is not the same as what one is jealous *of*; your indignant tirade may *make* me feel ashamed, but what I am ashamed *of* is my own mis-behaviour. What one is frightened *by* is the cause of one's fear, what one is frightened *of* is its object. These can coincide in certain cases, but in others they cannot. For when the object of fear, hope or excitement lies in the future or if it is non-existent (fear of ghosts), what one is afraid *of*, hopes *for*, or is excited *about* cannot be the cause of the emotion. What causes an emotion may be what sparks it off – a sudden thought, a casual remark or a reminder. What is crucial for the identification of an emotion is not its cause (of which the subject, e.g., an acrophobe, may be ignorant), but its object.

Emotions are linked in complex ways to what the agent knows or believes. For in so far as an emotion must have a proper object in order to qualify as the emotion it is, the agent must take the object of his emotion to satisfy the formal characteristics which determine the object as appropriate. If he fears A or A's action, he must believe that A and A's action are a threat. If he feels pity for another, he must believe that person to have suffered a misfortune. If he feels regret, remorse or guilt, he must believe that he has done something unfortunate or wrong.

This cognitive component in emotions has important ramifications. First, a person cannot ordinarily feel a certain emotion and fail to know what its object is. He cannot feel grateful and yet know neither to whom he is grate-ful nor what he is grateful for; he cannot feel ashamed and not know what he is ashamed of doing; he cannot feel pity yet know neither for whom nor for what. In *limiting cases*, one may feel objectless fear (*Angst*) or guilt; but these are necessarily exceptions to the rule.

Secondly, one usually has reasons for feeling as one does. If one fears A, it is because one knows or believes that A threatens an interest one has. One will normally have reasons for thinking that this is so, reasons one may adduce to explain or justify one's fear. Hence one's emotions can be reason-able or unreasonable. As already remarked, what counts as a good reason for a given emotion, *a fortiori* for a given form of behaviour motivated by that emotional attitude, is typically historically conditioned and (depending on the emotion in question) a partial function of social norms. So, despite the fact that one cannot feel an emotion at will, it makes sense to say of some-one that he *ought* to feel proud or ashamed of himself because of what he did, or that he *should not* feel resentful of A since A could not help doing what he did. If a person's emotional reaction to a circumstance is not war-ranted, either at all or to the degree to which he feels it, we criticize him for the unreasonableness of his emotional response. It is unreasonable, we may say, to be jealous about something as trivial as *that*; or, while conceding that A's spouse's behaviour *is* an intelligible ground for jealousy, we may criticize A for the intensity of his jealousy, that is for his excessive reaction. A person may feel an emotion as a result of a false belief. Normally discovery of the falsity of the belief eliminates the emotion. If the grounds for one's fear evaporate, the fear will normally evaporate with it. Conversely, things being thus-and-so may be a reason for feeling a given emotion – and those who come to know or to believe that things are so, and *who care*, will normally feel that emotion. They have a reason for so feeling. The reasonableness of emotions lies in such forms of sensitivity to reasons in a given social and cultural context, and it is here that the responsibility a person has for his emotions resides. The emotions we feel are reasonable (within the framework of the culture and times to which we belong) to the extent that they are directed towards an object that warrants the feeling, and to the extent that the intensity of the emotion felt is proportional to its object. Of course, the knowledge of the facts that constitute a reason for feeling such-and-such an emotion do not necessitate any such feeling. But if one does not respond appropriately to the tragic or joyful circumstance, one is deficient in sensibility, and lacks the feeling proper to the circumstance – which is a mark of *not caring* about things which, in general, we think we should care about.

4. Misconceptions: Damasio

Damasio's work on emotionally incapacitating brain damage is renowned, and his insistence on a link between the capacity for rational decision-making and consequent rational action in pursuit of goals, on the one hand, and the capacity for feeling emotions, on the other, is thought-provoking.

Damasio's conception of the emotions is influenced by James, who held that emotions are the feelings of somatic disturbances consequent on the perception of an 'exciting fact'. An emotion, according to James, is not the somatic change, but the agent's perception of it. Every one of these bodily changes is allegedly perceived as soon as it occurs. One cannot abstract from an emotion 'all the feelings of its bodily symptoms' and find anything left behind other than a cold and neutral state of intellectual perception (James 1950, pp. 449–451). Damasio himself sees 'the essence of emotion as the collection of changes in body state that are induced in myriad organs by nerve cell terminals, under the control of a dedicated brain system, which is responding to the content of thoughts relative to a particular entity or event' (Damasio 1994, p. 139). The somatic changes are held to be caused by thoughts. Damasio's conception of thoughts is firmly rooted in the eighteenth-century empiricist tradition. Thoughts, he claims, consist of mental images (Damasio 1994, pp. 107f). The images constituting thoughts are comparable to the images of which perception allegedly consists, differing from them in being fainter or less lively. In this respect

Damasio self-consciously but misguidedly follows the footsteps of Hume, thinking that if thought were not exhibited to us in the form of images of things and of words signifying things, then we would not be able to say what we think. But to say what one thinks is to *express* one's thoughts, not to *describe* them or *read them off* something else.

Damasio, unlike James, distinguishes *an emotion*, that is 'a collection of changes in body state connected to particular mental images that have activated a specific brain system' from the *feeling of an emotion*. 'The essence of feeling an emotion is the experience of such changes in juxtaposition to the mental images that initiated the cycle. In other words, a feeling depends on the juxtaposition of an image of the body proper to an image of something else, such as the visual image of a face or the auditory image of a melody' (Damasio 1994, p. 145). So, an emotion is a bodily response to a mental image, and the feeling of an emotion is a cognitive response to that bodily condition, a cognitive response 'in connection to the object that excited it, the realization of the nexus between object and emotional body state' (Damasio 1994, pp. 130, 132). Feelings of emotion, Damasio avers, *'are just as cognitive as any other perceptual image*, and just as dependent on cerebral-cortex processing as any other image'. However,

> feelings are about something different. But what makes them different is that they are first and foremost about the body, they offer us *the cognition of our visceral and musculoskeletal state* as it becomes affected by preorganized mechanisms and by the cognitive structures we have developed under their influence. Feelings let us *mind the body* ... Feelings offer us a glimpse of what goes on in our flesh, as a momentary image of that flesh is juxtaposed to the images of other objects and situations; in so doing, feelings modify our comprehensive notion of those other objects and situations. By dint of juxtaposition, body images give other images a *quality* of goodness or badness, of pleasure or pain. (Damasio 1994, p. 159)

Accordingly, Damasio proposes the somatic marker hypothesis. The hypothesis is that somatic responses to 'images' (i.e., perceptions and thoughts) serve to increase the accuracy and efficiency of decision processes, screening out a range of alternatives and allowing the agent to choose from among fewer (Damasio 1994, p. 173). 'When a negative somatic marker is juxtaposed to a particular future outcome the combination functions as an alarm bell. When a positive somatic marker is juxtaposed instead, it becomes a beacon of incentive' (Damasio 1994, p. 174). So somatic markers, constituted by the somatic response to situations confronting us, assist deliberation by highlighting some options and eliminating them. These somatic responses which we allegedly use for decision-making 'probably were created in our brains during the process of education and socialization, by connecting specific classes of stimuli with specific classes of somatic state' (Damasio 1994, p. 177).

Culturally inculcated 'gut reactions' provide the basis for rational decision-making. This leads Damasio to conjecture that the decision-making and executive deficiencies in patients suffering from lesions in the prefrontal cortices is explained by lack of somatic markers to guide them.

This idea is conceptually questionable.

(1) An emotion is not an ensemble of somatic changes caused by a 'thought' about (i.e., mental image of) an object or event.

First, even if a given emotional perturbation does involve a range of somatic changes, what makes the sensations sensations of fear as opposed to anger, and what makes the blushes blushes of shame rather than of embarrassment or of love is not the 'thought' or mental image, *if any*, that causes them, but the circumstances and the object of the emotion.

Secondly, if emotions were essentially ensembles of somatic changes caused by mental images, that is, if that is what the term 'emotion' means, then learning the meaning of emotion words and hence learning how to use them would be a matter of learning the names of complexes of bodily changes with specific causes (hence akin to learning the meaning of an expression like 'giddiness' or 'seasickness'). But we do not learn the use of emotion words by learning sensation-names or names of overall bodily condition, but rather by learning what are appropriate objects of the relevant emotions, for example, of fear (what is dangerous or threatening), of anger (what is annoying, offensive or wrong), of pride (worthy achievement or possessions), of guilt (one's misdemeanours), and so forth, and learning how to use these terms ('afraid', 'angry', etc.) in the expression of one's feelings towards the appropriate objects, in the description of the feelings (but not the sensations) of others, and in the giving of explanatory and justifying reasons for one's reactions and actions.

Thirdly, if emotions were ensembles of somatic changes caused by mental images, then one could not have good reasons for feeling a certain emotion, and would not be answerable for one's emotions in the manner in which we are. For although there may *be* a reason (i.e., an explanation) why one has a headache, or why one's breathing-rate or heart-beat rises, one cannot *have* a reason (i.e., a ground or warrant) for such things. Given appropriate circumstances, we can say that someone ought to, and has good reason to, feel proud or ashamed, but we cannot say that he ought to raise his pulse-rate or increase his psychogalvanic reflex reactions.

Fourthly, one can feel an emotion E without any E-type perturbation. One can love a person, object (a piece of music, a book or painting, a landscape) or a value (justice, honour) without undergoing any somatic changes distinctive of love when one thinks about them. There need be no somatic changes accompanying the thought that the rate of inflation is likely to rise – but one may well fear that it will. If A did one an important favour in one's youth, one may remain forever grateful – but one need not break out in a sweat whenever one thinks of it. There are no distinctive somatic changes characteristic of pride in something – or of many other types of emotion and many other emotions with certain kinds of object. One might argue that *by definition* to feel an *intense* occurrent emotion does require *some* somatic changes. But even in such cases, the somatic changes do not *identify* the emotion.

To insist on these points is not to deny that there is a link between *certain* emotions and emotions directed to *specific objects*, on the one hand, and types of emotional agitation involving *inter alia* somatic changes, on the other. The emotional agitation may be *characteristic* of that emotion or of that emotion with that type of object, given appropriate circumstances. Nevertheless, the emotion *is* not the somatic change that might be caused by the thought (or mental image) of the object of such an emotion. Moreover, it would be misguided to suppose that by studying the neural concomitants of artificially induced emotional perturbations (e.g., by pictures or music) and the effects on cognitive performance, one is actually studying the emotion in all its complexity (the kinds of reasons for the emotion, both perturbation and attitude, the kinds of motivation it affords and why, the kinds of behaviour it motivates, its dependency upon social and cultural norms, the kinds of unreasonableness or irrationality that may be manifest and the reasons and causes of them).

(2) Perceiving an object or perceiving that things are thus-and-so does not involve *having images* of anything – to perceive Paris is not to perceive or have an image of Paris; and, conversely, to have an image of Paris (as when one dreams or daydreams) is not to perceive Paris. It is equally misguided to suppose that in order to think something or think of something it is either necessary or sufficient to have an image of anything, let alone an image of what one thinks or thinks of or of words that would, if uttered, express what one thinks or refer to what one thinks of. Moreover, it is mistaken to suppose that one thinks *in* images or that in order to speak with thought one must first say to oneself in one's imagination what one is going to say out loud. One can talk to oneself in the imagination (which involves auditory images) without thinking (as when one counts sheep in the imagination in order to *prevent* oneself from thinking), and one can think without talking to oneself in the imagination (as when one speaks thoughtfully to another).

Since neither thinking nor perceiving need involve images, the somatic changes that *may* be part of a given emotional agitation and which *may* (but need not) be caused by a thought (in the proper sense of the term) or by perceiving something need not be caused by mental images.

(3) While there is a difference between feeling an emotion (e.g., jealousy) and realizing what emotion one feels (e.g., realizing that one is jealous), there is no difference between having an emotion and feeling an emotion (being jealous and feeling jealous), any more than there is a difference

between having a pain and feeling a pain. Damasio's stipulated distinction between emotion and feeling an emotion has nothing to recommend it, since an emotion is not an ensemble of somatic changes and feeling an emotion is not the experience of such changes in juxtaposition to mental images that caused them.

(4) It is mistaken to suppose that feeling an emotion is a cognitive response to a bodily condition caused by mental images. If, when frightened by a noise at night, I feel frightened that there is a thief in the house, and my pulses race, my (felt) fear is not a response to my racing pulses. What I was frightened *by* was the noise (not an image of a noise), what I was frightened *of* was a burglar's having broken in. I may or may not notice my racing pulses – but whether I do or do not, my fear of a burglary is not a response to them.

(5) Feelings of emotion are not *about the body* at all. What they are 'about' or 'of' is the object of the emotion. What a person is proud of may be his achievements, lineage, children, possessions, and so forth – but not any somatic changes that may occur when he thinks of them. What a person feels guilty about are his wrong-doings, not any bodily perturbations that may occur when he thinks about them.

(6) An emotional response need not be cognitively linked to the cause of the emotion or the cause of the somatic changes that may accompany an emotional perturbation. We are often ignorant of the causes of our emotional feelings. I may not know (and may be mistaken about) what *caused* me to feel love for Maisie or to hate injustice – but what I must know, what *is* 'cognitively linked' to these feelings, is *what their objects are*. If the connection of a feeling of emotion to what it is 'about', that is its object, were a causal one, then unless such causal knowledge is non-inductive, knowing what one is frightened of, angry with or about, proud or ashamed of would be a hypothesis. But I don't discover the object of my feelings by tracing the causes of the perturbations (if any) that I feel.

(7) One's 'feelings of emotion', one's love, hope, or pride, are not ways of finding out facts about 'our visceral and muscoskeletal state'. Indeed, one's emotions do not inform one either of the state of one's body or of the state of the world around one. But one's emotional perturbations may inform one of one's emotional attitudes. A pang of jealousy may indicate that I am in the process of falling in love with Maizie, a blush of embarrassment may bring home to me that I am ashamed of having lied, my tears of grief may make me realize how much I loved Daisy. Far from one's emotions informing one about the state of one's body, the state of one's body informs one about one's emotions.

(8) Damasio's somatic marker hypothesis is misconceived. The emotions are not somatic images that tell one what is good and bad. Bodily reactions

are not Ersatz guides to action, and do not inform us about good and evil. If one is indignant at a perceived injustice, what tells one that the object of one's indignation is an evil is not that one feels flushed in association with the thought of the act in question. On the contrary, one is indignant at A's action because it is unjust, not because one flushes in anger when one hears of it. One knows it to be unjust because it rides roughshod over someone's rights, not because one flushes in anger. Indeed, the flush is only a flush of anger in so far as one is thus indignant. And one will feel indignant only to the extent that one cares about the protection of the rights of human beings (or of *this* human being).

One might conjecture that although Damasio may be perfectly correct in associating the capacity for rationality in practical reasoning and in pursuit of goals with the ability to feel emotions, the linkage lies in a common feature underlying both. Since the emotions do not let us 'mind the body', and since feeling the somatic reactions to circumstances is not a litmus-paper test for good and evil, or for the beneficial and harmful, it is implausible to suppose that what is wrong with patients who have suffered damage to the ventromedial sector of the prefrontal cortex is that their somatic responses are awry or uninformative for them (as it were, a Pavlovian deficiency). But what might be investigated is whether the brain damage in the kinds of patient Damasio investigated affects the capacity to care or to persist in caring about goals and objectives. For such a deficiency would affect both their emotions and their ability to pursue goals over time. One feels no emotions about things concerning which one is indifferent, and one does not pursue goals efficiently unless one cares, for one reason or another, about achieving them.

Contrary to what Damasio claims, there need be nothing 'hidden' about the emotions of others. It is mistaken to say that 'you cannot observe a feeling in someone else' (Damasio, 1999, p. 42). It is equally mistaken to think that 'you can observe a feeling in yourself'. We are prone to confuse the fact that we often do not show our feelings and sometimes indeed make an effort to conceal them, with the misguided idea that the emotions are in some deep sense 'private' and 'hidden'. But this is confused. We can often see delight and rage in a person's face, joy, anguish or horror in his eyes, contempt or amusement in his smile. We can hear the love and tenderness, the grief and sorrow, the anger and contempt in a person's voice. We can observe their tears of joy or grief, cries of terror, joy or amazement, and blushes of embarrassment or shame. On the other hand, to feel an emotion oneself, for example, to feel proud or ashamed, is not to observe anything. This has multiple ramifying consequences for psychiatric theories that seek to explain such phenomena as autism in terms of children's deficiencies in formulating theories about the psychology of others. But that is a tale for another occasion.

Notes

I am grateful to Dr Maria Alvarez and to Dr Matthew Broome for their comments on an earlier draft of this paper, and to Professor Max Bennett for his comments, advice and encouragement.

* The article was originally published in *International Review of Psychiatry*, Vol. 16, No. 3 (August 2004), 199–208. The editors and publisher are grateful for the permission to republish it.

1. The following discussion is based upon chapter 7 of *The Philosophical Foundations of Neuroscience* (Bennett and Hacker 2003) which contains a more comprehensive survey of these matters. I am grateful to my co-author for permission to condense our argument for this paper.

Bibliography

Bennett, M.R. and Hacker, P.M.S. (2003), *The Philosophical Foundations of Neuroscience* (Oxford: Blackwell).

Damasio, A.R. (1994), *Descartes's Error: Emotion, Reason and the Human Brain* (London: Macmillan).

——. (1999), *The Feeling of What Happens* (London: Heinemann).

David, A.S. and Halligan, P.W. (2000), 'Cognitive Neuropsychiatry: Potential for Progress', *Journal of Neuropsychiatry and Clinical Neuroscience*, 12 (4) (Fall 2000), 506–510.

James, W. (1950), *The Principles of Psychology* (New York: Dover).

LeDoux, J.E. (1996), *The Emotional Brain* (New York: Simon and Schuster).

Phillips, M.L. (2003), 'Understanding the Neurobiology of Emotion Perception: Implications for Psychiatry', *British Journal of Psychiatry*, 182, 190–192.

——, Drevets, M.D., Rauch, S.L. and Lane, R. (2003), 'The Neurobiology of Emotion Perception I: The Neural Basis of Normal Emotion Perception', *Biological Psychiatry*, 54 (5), 504–514.

Roles, E.T. (2000), *The Brain and Emotion* (Oxford: Oxford University Press).

4

Emotion–Philosophy–Science*

Phil Hutchinson

Contemporary analytic philosophy of emotions is currently dominated by two seemingly opposing camps.[1] In one camp we have those generally labelled cognitivists and in the other those who favour a Jamesian approach, the neo-Jamesians.[2] The term 'cognitivism' brings together writers on emotions, some of whom might be termed *pure* cognitivists, for example Solomon (1976 and 2003c), Taylor (1985) and Nussbaum (2004), and those who might be termed *hybrid* cognitivists, for example Goldie (2000) Greenspan (1995) Nash (1989) and Stocker (1987). In the other camp we have the neo-Jamesians, which as the name suggests comprises those philosophers and psychologists who advance a contemporary variant of William James's account of emotion and in doing so often align themselves with the research program initiated by Darwin ([1872] 1999) and later Ekman (1972); those Darwinian claims are often buttressed by theoretical claims drawn from neuroscience and cognate theories of mind, for example Damasio (1994), Prinz (2004) and Robinson (1995).

In short, cognitivists take emotions to be centrally, and explain them in terms of, appraisals, judgements or evaluative beliefs; neo-Jamesians explain emotions in terms of awareness of bodily changes, usually patterned changes in the Autonomic Nervous System (ANS). How the debate is polarized can be captured by returning to a passage from William James's paper in *Mind*, published in 1884, a passage frequently quoted and/or referred to by those on either side of the debate.[3]

> Our natural way of thinking about... emotions is that the mental perception of some fact excites the mental affection called the emotion, and that this latter state of mind gives rise to the bodily expression. My thesis on the contrary is that *the bodily changes follow directly the* PERCEPTION *of the exciting fact, and that our feeling of the same changes as they occur* IS *the emotion.*[4] (James 1884, pp. 190–191; emphasis in original)

The cognitivist philosophers of emotion favour analysis of the thoughts that constitute the emotion, in its social setting or embedded in a narrative: the 'natural way of thinking about...emotions', as James puts it. Neo-Jamesians, in following James's claim that the *'bodily changes follow directly the* PERCEPTION *of the exciting fact'* eschew the talk of thoughts and favour a cognitive neuroscience approach, *sometimes* drawing on or appealing to evolutionary psychology/socio-biology.

I believe the dispute to be misconceived, the misconception having its roots in a certain reading of the famous passage from James. The misconception frames the discussions coming from both camps. What I hope to do in what follows is provide a reframing. If I am correct in what follows, it might be that the only thing to change is the landscape of emotion research not the character of each of those who live there. I'll first draw out the differences between the two camps and then look at some recent statements from a number of philosophers about the character of the dispute between the camps and how one might resolve the dispute as they have characterized it.

1. Cognitivism versus neo-Jamesianism

First let us look at how the dispute has been played out in recent work in the philosophy of the emotions; we can do this by showing how these philosophers disagree on a number of points.

So, cognitivists depict emotional episodes as fundamentally outward-facing and Jamesians as fundamentally introspective.

Cognitivists argue that emotions are rational. Jamesians argue that they are non-rational or rationally inert irruptions in an otherwise rational life; more recently, neo-Jamesians have sought to give an account of emotions which can accommodate the rationality of emotion, while retaining the central Jamesian commitment, for example Prinz.

In cognitive theories intentionality is at centre stage, our thoughts are directed at something in the world; in neo-Jamesian theories passivity is at centre stage, we are struck by or afflicted by something.

In its most extreme manifestation, cognitivism takes emotions to be under our control, to be chosen by us (see Solomon 2003c). In its most extreme manifestation neo-Jamesianism takes emotions to be essentially reflex-like, to happen to us sub-personally, in a manner akin to a reflex (see Robinson 1995).

Sometimes the debate can appear as if it were about whether our emotional responses to our environment are conscious or unconscious; that is for cognitivists our emotions are essentially, are explained and constituted by, propositional beliefs: the person consciously believing or judging that X; and for neo-Jamesians our emotions are essentially patterned bodily changes: non-cognitive sub-personal reflex-like responses to X. Though one would not be mistaken in thinking the debate *might* correctly be characterized this way (for this is sometimes the impression given, see D'arms and Jacobson 2003), it is not an accurate characterization of what is at stake. Cognitivists are not of necessity (even those who often proceed as if they are so) committed to a propositional attitude theory of mental content: that is to have a thought is to have a propositional attitude.[5]

One further aspect of the debate is the issue as to whose or what's emotions we are explaining. Are we providing an account of emotions in human beings (or even just some human beings having a particular culture) or human beings and beasts? Cognitive theories, it is sometimes claimed (see Deigh 2004), cannot explain emotions in non-human animals on account of the centrality of intentionality to that approach. Jamesian theories, in being amenable to the explanation of emotion in non-human animals, cannot adequately account for the apparent centrality of intentionality in human emotional experience.

Finally, we might note that cognitivists treat an emotional utterance as an *expression*, akin to a smile or a grimace and hence partially constitutive of the emotion, or as an *avowal* as to one's beliefs or judgements which *are* the emotion; Jamesians treat emotional utterances as *descriptions* or *reports* of inner states.

These differences can be summarized in a table:

Cognitivism	Jamesianism
Emotions are centrally appraisals/judgements/evaluations of a certain class or family	Emotions are centrally feelings of bodily changes as those changes occur
Emotions are rational	Emotions are irrational or simply not rationality-apt. More recently, emotions might be rational but their rationality is anomalous and/or extraneous
Emotions are intentional	Emotions are brute
Emotional episodes are centrally outward-facing	Emotional episodes are centrally introspective
Emotional utterance = expression (functionally analogous to a smile, a frown, a grimace or a cry of anguish). The utterance is part of the emotion.	Emotional utterance = description (a report of an inner event). The utterance and emotion are discrete; the latter is merely a label we attach to our emotions.
Study of emotion is undertaken by the analysis of thoughts in a social setting and/or embedded in a narrative: Meaning of emotion is central	Study of emotion is undertaken by cognitive neuroscience and a study of bodily changes that theorizes their evolutionary purpose: Cause of emotion is central
We are answerable for our emotions	We are subject to our emotions

Continued

Continued

Cognitivism	Jamesianism
Chief influences are philosophers and certain schools of philosophy: Aristotle and the Stoics; Nietzsche, Sartre and Existentialism; and, it is claimed, Wittgenstein.	Chief influences are neuroscience and evolutionary biology: Darwin's work on emotional expression in 'man and animals' and work on the Autonomic Nervous System
Cognitivism's 'chain of events': (1) object – (2) perception/judgement/ belief – (3) outward behavioural manifestation (1) we lose a loved one – (2) we are sad – (3) we cry [because we are sad] (1) we meet a snake – (2) we are frightened – (3) we tremble and run [because we are frightened] (1) we are betrayed by a colleague – (2) we are angry – (3) our hands shake, we flush and shout [because we are angry]	Jamesian chain of events: (1) object – (2) bodily change – (3) awareness of bodily change (1) we lose a loved one – (2) we cry – (3) we are sad [because we cry] (1) we meet a snake – (2) we tremble and run – (3) we are frightened [because we tremble] (1) we are betrayed by a colleague – (2) our hands shake, we flush and shout – (3) we are angry [because we are shaking, flushing and raising our voice]

2. Problems of emotion

John Deigh (2004) has identified that the problem facing theories of emotions advanced by theorists in both camps is their inability to cover both of two facts about emotions.

- *Fact one* is the intentionality of emotion.
- *Fact two* is that, as Deigh puts it, 'emotions are common to both humans and beasts' (p. 9) (with the caveats that (1) humans have a broader set of emotions, and (2) we are not committed to all beasts having emotions).

Deigh's claim is that philosophers of emotion are a little like the man whose blanket only reaches his chest, thus leaving him cold in his bed at night; if he pulls the blanket up to cover his chest his feet become exposed and thus cold. So, the goal is to find someway of covering the chest (acknowledging the centrality of intentionality) while also covering the feet (explaining emotion in man and beasts). We'll have uncomfortable and sleepless nights unless we do. Whenever theorists of emotion try to cover intentionality adequately, they do so, according to Deigh, by forgoing the ability to explain emotion in non-human animals. Of course, cognitivists are historically seen as strong on fact one, while Jamesians/Darwinians are taken to be strong on fact two. We might equally observe that it is often taken to be the case that cognitivists face substantial difficulty in acknowledging fact two just as Jamesians, at least appear to, deny fact one. We might say that cognitivists are good at keeping their chests warm, while (neo-)Jamesians are known for their toasty-warm feet.

Deigh continues:

> A successful theory of emotions must account for both of these facts [Facts one and two]. It cannot skirt them. Yet accounting for both has proven to be surprisingly difficult. Some theories, particularly the cognitivist theories that have been so influential in philosophy and psychology over the last thirty years, use the first fact as their point of departure and leading idea, but they then have trouble accommodating the second. Other theories, particularly those that have developed under the influence of Darwin's seminal work *The Expression of the Emotions in Man and Animals* (1998), take the second fact as their springboard, but then they have trouble accommodating the first. The reason in either case, is the way intentional states of mind are typically understood and the way primitive emotions are typically understood. The problem of closing this gap seems to outstrip the resources of these theories. The point is not generally recognised, however. It tends to lie beyond the theories' horizons. (Deigh 2004, p. 10)

So what answers might one essay to the problem, which is here identified by Deigh? Well recent literature has seen a few different attempts. I'll here briefly discuss some prominent ones.

2.1. Paul Griffiths: the eliminativist's response

Paul Griffiths (1997) has suggested that the problem is the very thought that one can, indeed, provide an account of emotion, for 'emotion' does not pick out a natural kind, but rather two (plus, possibly, one pseudo-kind of 'displaced action "emotions"'). The vernacular concept 'emotion' should be, according to Griffiths, eliminated in favour of two new kind terms. The first kind of 'emotions' are the 'basic emotions', best explained by Paul Ekman's 'affect program research' and complemented by the work of Damasio (1994). These 'basic emotions' are said to correspond roughly to the vernacular 'emotion' concepts of anger, surprise, joy and disgust. The second kind of 'emotions' are the 'higher cognitive emotions' or 'complex emotions', best explained by evolutionary psychological explanation. These 'complex emotions' are said to correspond roughly to the vernacular 'emotion' concepts of guilt, remorse, loyalty and shame.

Griffiths' response to the problem as identified by Deigh, therefore, is to simply say that providing one theory which covers both facts can't be done, thus, trying to provide one is ill-conceived. For any likeness between the 'basic emotions' and the 'complex emotions' is purely analogous (a correspondence only in purpose or function) and not homologous (correspondence in terms of essential structural form).[6] Therefore, these emotions, basic and complex, are *really* different and only *superficially* similar or of the same kind. Analogous correspondence is superficial correspondence and homologous correspondence is real correspondence, hence the title of Griffiths' book: *What Emotions Really Are.* Griffiths, therefore, directly counters Deigh's claim that 'a successful theory of emotions must account for both of these facts. It cannot skirt them', by denying that there is such a thing as 'emotion' that we should wish to theorize.

Griffiths' response has been hugely influential; I am yet to be influenced. His importing of the analogue/homologue distinction from comparative biology seems to me to come close to simply begging the question in any debate between cognitivists and Jamesians, because for the distinction to be pertinent one must already have in place a prior commitment to what one takes to be essential to emotion or a prior commitment to a particular form of explanation. For, in Griffiths' case what is claimed to be essential is evolutionary heritage rather than, say, functional role. Griffiths merely assumes the priority of homologous correspondence over analogous correspondence when that is precisely where the debate is to be located. For, one might merely respond and ask why, in terms of the explanation of emotion, we should privilege one form of correspondence, likeness or identity over another? That the homologue/analogue distinction serves a crucial explanatory role in certain areas of biology is undoubted. However, this does not mean that the distinction automatically carries over to other areas, nor that it has authority in those areas in virtue of its success in comparative biology. Any capacity for settling disputes in these new areas (emotion research) that the distinction might have needs to be established independently of its success in its original area (comparative biology). What, one might ask, warrants according this distinction sovereignty beyond the domain in which it has established that sovereignty?

Griffiths' prioritization of homologous correspondence over analogous is driven in part by the underlying theory of language advanced in his book. I will not address this here, as I have done so in detail elsewhere (Hutchinson 2008, ch. 1, sections 2 and 3). However, Griffiths (2004) also provides us with a snappy defence of his prioritization of homologous correspondence.

Suppose that two animals have homologous psychological traits such as the basic emotion of fear in humans and fear in chimpanzees. We can predict that, even if the function of fear has been subtly altered by the different 'meaning' of danger for humans and for chimps, the computational methods used to process danger-related information will be *very similar* and the neural structures that implement them *very similar* indeed. ... Now, suppose that two animals have psychological traits that are analogous – fear in the rat and fear in the octopus, for example. It is a truism in comparative biology that similarities due to analogy (shared adaptive function) are 'shallow'. ... In contrast, similarities due to homology (shared ancestry) are notoriously 'deep': even when function has been transformed, the deeper you dig, the more similarity there is in the underlying mechanisms. (Griffiths 2004, p. 238)

One should be cautious, hereabouts; it would be easy to allow oneself to be led astray by the use of 'shallow' and 'deep'. Each and every use of 'deep' is not synonymous with 'profound', much less 'real', no more than each and every use of 'shallow' is synonymous with 'superficial', though this seems to be the thought that Griffiths wants to suggest with the help of the authority he assumes for distinctions privileged in comparative biology. Furthermore, pay close attention to precisely what is said here, in the opening few lines: Griffiths writes that even if the function of fear in humans and chimps is 'subtly altered' because of the different meaning of 'danger' for the two animals 'the computational methods used to process danger-related information will be *very similar* and the neural structures that implement them *very similar* indeed'. Close scrutiny shows us that this tells us at best little. Even were we to accept – for now, and only for now – the invocation of 'computational methods' as unproblematic,[7] Griffiths tells us that these are 'very similar' in humans and chimps and that the neural structures are 'very similar indeed'. It seems that all are merely *similar* then: function (because of the different, though similar, meaning of 'danger'), computational methods (because explained by different, though similar, computational theories), and neural structures (because of their being members of different species but the same phyla, thus having biologically different, though similar, brains). The only reason for favouring explanation in terms of the latter two and not in favour of the former is methodological predilection: the *a priori* methodological commitment to the priority of homologous correspondence, which has been imported from biology.

It should be noted, however, that the difference Griffiths notes in function is only active if we ignore the distinction between the particular object of a particular emotion and the formal object of the emotion; this is a distinction employed by all cognitivists. An example of the distinction between formal and particular object is as follows: The *particular* object of my fear is the dog before me now aggressively pulling at its fraying harness while growling at me. The *formal* object of my fear might be something like 'that which I perceive poses a threat to my well-being'. In a formal analysis of emotion, as undertaken by philosophers, one is concerned with formal objects. That is to say the analysis of the meaning of emotion terms indexes their meaning to their formal objects. Once this distinction is active, once we are clear that our account of emotion is in terms of *formal* objects, we can see that the emotion of (say) fear in humans and chimps might have the *same formal* analysis and thus the same meaning, while their computational methods and neural structures are different (for they are merely very similar). So, on Griffiths' own terms – recall the phrases I emboldened in the quote, above – our substitution of formal for particular object means that what is the *same* is function, while what is different are the computational methods and neural structures; for as we noted above, the computational methods and the neural structures are claimed only to be 'very similar'; and two things being similar = two things being different; two things being similar ≠ two things being the same.

In terms of Deigh's two facts (that emotions are intentional (fact one) and that emotions are common to humans and beasts (fact two)), we can see from the passage, quoted above, that it is fact two which is centrally important for Griffiths. However, as we have seen, if it is so, then he has no reason to forego the analysis in terms of formal object in favour of a theoretical explanation in terms of cognitive neuroscience. The problem Griffiths faces is that in pursuing his project he still wants to explain 'fear' (and sadness, and remorse, etc.). First and foremost, then, in wanting to explain any emotion one must *identify* the emotion. Griffiths writes of rats fearing, chimps fearing, humans fearing and octopuses fearing, he then suggests that the 'fear' we predicate of the three mammals on the list is homologous and thus shares 'deep' correspondence, while their (mammal-) 'fear' shares only 'shallow' analogous correspondence with the 'fear' of the octopus. But, as we have seen, this claim rests on a prior methodological commitment to the priority of homologous correspondence. For in each case, one must first of all identify 'fear', if we don't then we are simply not explaining what we set out to explain: *fear*. We identify 'fear' in terms of its formal object, which, in the case of fear, we might say is that which the creature takes to be a threat to it (no conscious 'believing that' need be invoked here), or that which elicits, under normal conditions, a certain pattern of behavioural response, and so on. The difference Griffiths has emphasized is not between different meanings of fear but different biological structures of (in the case of his examples) species belonging to different phyla.

Griffiths has provided an example of how species differ in accordance with the classification, while telling us nothing about 'fear'. Octopuses and chimps do not share the same evolutionary ancestry (unless one goes very far back, of course), and one of the ways in which this can be demonstrated is that the biological mechanisms that are involved in certain patterns of behaviour (interaction with environment), such as fear behaviour, are significantly different in structure to each other while similar in structure to species with shared ancestry (species from the same phylum, for example). Griffiths' point is a reiteration of the evolutionary account of species masquerading as a claim about the reality of emotion.

If, irrespective of my considerations you are wont to follow Griffiths, consider the following: two beings share the same attributes, let's say they both look like healthy human beings; they react to pain in the same way, though one might have a higher threshold to pain than the other; they respond to loss and bereavement in the same way, though one has experienced much and is now more 'hardened'. All things considered, they are the same sort of being in terms of their lives in the world, their interactions and transactions with others in their shared world. More to the point, they understand each other as on occasion being afraid and on having lost a loved one, being grief-stricken. One comforts the other and reports their grief in a certain tone of voice to friends and relatives. In this way they acknowledge one another, through acknowledgement of one another's fears, grief, joy and and so forth. Now, what changes about this story if one finds that one of these two beings has radically different biological mechanisms that physically facilitate certain of their typical fear behaviour or grief behaviour? Well, just like Griffiths in his discussion of the octopus and the chimp, nothing changes; we continue to talk of the two beings as being afraid and being grief-stricken.

The last sentence of the previous paragraph suggests something that might strike us as interesting. In contrast to Griffiths, we might argue that what is interesting is that which licenses our predicating fear of both the octopus *and* of the chimp. Why, we might ask, while we might harbour reservations about talking of an octopus being afraid, our reservations in respect of talking of octopus-fear are not of the same magnitude as the reservations we might have in saying of an octopus that it is grief-stricken (the employment of 'it' in this sentence might be informative here, too). This might tell us something about emotions, how certain basic emotions differ from more complex emotions, such as shame. I'll leave this suggestion here.[8] I will now progress to an examination of another, recent and influential, attempt to meet the difficulties as specified by Deigh.

2.2. Jesse Prinz: the emotion problem?

Jesse Prinz provides his own version of Deigh's dilemma, what Prinz calls 'the Emotion Problem':

> So we have a serious puzzle. The fact that emotions are meaningful, reason sensitive, and intentional suggests that they must be cognitive. The fact that some emotions arise without intervention of the neocortex suggests that emotions cannot *all* be cognitive. The emotions that arise in this way seem to be meaningful. This seems to suggest that being meaningful does not require being cognitive. Noncognitive states are explanatorily anaemic and cognitive states are explanatorily superfluous. Noncognitive theories give us too little, and cognitive theories give us too much. Call this the Emotion Problem. (Prinz 2003a, p. 78)

Let us lay out Prinz's claim syllogistically:

1. cognition is absent; put Prinz's way: nothing is taking place in the brain which involves the intervention of the neocortex;

2. (while 'cognition' is absent), the person is in an emotional state and this suggests that something *akin* to cognition – something that fulfils the outward criteria for being cognition – is taking place, that is something akin to the perception and evaluation of an object;

3. the conclusion drawn is that something else, other than the involvement of the neocortex, must be *playing the role* of cognition; *something* non-cognitive must *give forth* meaning, and must be directed onto things in the world: must be intentional. Since cognition-as-neural-activity-involving-the-intervention-of-the-neocortex (what Prinz takes *to be* cognition) is not present, but a meaningful emotional episode is, meaning must emerge from an embodied emotion having semantic properties which enable it to refer in the absence of cognition (in the absence of neocortical intervention).

So are there any assumptions in play here? Well, Prinz certainly seems to have little issue with the assumption that cognition is a brain process involving the intervention of the neocortex. That this assumption is well founded is less clear to me. One can take such a – narrowly defined, and *a priori* – view of cognition-as-a-brain-process-necessarily-involving-the-intervention-of-the-neocortex, but one is certainly not obliged to do so.[9] We can rather take what it is to cognize to be to perceive, to think, to believe etc. If the evidence suggests cognition – that is something is meaningful for us – yet the neocortex seems to be bypassed, then only prejudice regarding the nature of (or meaning of) cognition – perceiving, thinking, believing etc.: taking in the world – leads you to conclude that no cognizing is taking place. Prinz not only assumes cognition is a process, but that it is a brain process, which involves the intervention of the neocortex. In addition, he *assumes* – at least he does not give us *reason* to believe this to be so – that neocortical-involvement in brain processes gives rise to meaning. How so?

Let me put this a little differently. It is one thing for neuroscientists and neuroanatomists to identify the intervention of the neocortex when people appear to be thinking, and so on – that is when a person is 'cognizing'. It is another thing to conclude that it is the neocortex that, through its intervention, somehow mysteriously transforms otherwise brute brain processes into meaningful and intentional ones: that cognition *is* brain-activity-involving-neocortical-intervention. However, what might give rise to some questions for those reading Prinz is what, having defined cognition as he has, he commences to do: sets up the 'Problem' for which he will provide the needed solution by saying that the mystery that needs solving is that 'something that takes place in the absence of neocortical intervention has the properties of meaning something about something'; that is it has all the attributes of cognition.[10]

There are, therefore, a number of assumptions at play in Prinz's premises. We need not accept that there is a problem such as he presents, for we are not obliged to work with the definition of cognition with which he furnishes us. If we set these assumptions aside for now – and only for now – and examine his conclusion/solution to 'the Emotion Problem', we might find further problems.

Prinz's solution invokes a computational theory of mind, involving elicitation files with psychosemantic content. What this enables Prinz to claim is that emotions are essentially what James claimed them to be: perceptions of bodily states, but they can also be intentional and meaningful, for the bodily changes trigger psychosemantic representations of the object of the emotion. Prinz, therefore, provides us with a computational psychological version of Richard Lazarus's 'core relational themes'; he writes:

> Emotions ... can be individuated by their reliable elicitors. This suggestion can be taken a step further. According to prevailing theories of mental representation, a mental state gets its intentional content in virtue of being reliably caused (or having the function of being reliably caused) by something (Dretske 1981, 1988; Fodor 1990). Let's assume that a theory of this kind, whatever the details, is correct.[11] There is some causal relation that confers content. If emotions are perceptions of bodily states, they are caused by changes in the body. But if those changes in the body are reliably caused by core relational themes, then our representations of the body may also represent those themes. (Prinz 2004, p. 55)

So, Prinz is determined to stick with James: emotions are perceptions of bodily states. But the changes in the body that cause these states are 'reliably caused by core relational themes'. It is these core relational themes that are represented psychosemantically and thus give our Jamesian emotions meaning, without foregoing the Jamesian commitment. However, one might feel prompted to ask why we need the concepts of psychosemantics? For, we have concepts, the ones we use in our day to day transactions in the world with others, the ones through which we read our world, through which we register, acknowledge and communicate loci of significance in our world. Why, one might ask, can these same public concepts not give rise to meaningfulness? Prinz's answer, as we saw in the first quote, above, is because sometimes we have an emotion when there is no neocortical intervention in the brain processes taking place. But this does not answer the question: how can our – theoretically postulated – 'inner' concepts located in – theoretically postulated– modules do the work denied to our public concepts? All we have done, in claiming to provide a solution to the 'problem', is theorize that we have some concepts inside a module which do the work that we are denying our (public) concepts can do. What are the relevant properties possessed by the 'inner' concepts of psychosemantics, unavailable to our public concepts? All that seems to be clear is that they are, in some sense, inner.[12]

Again, let's be clear about the 'problem' here. We are told by Prinz that cognition does not take place because the neocortex does not intervene in the brain processes; hence, we cannot make sense of our emotions having meaning when they occur in the absence of neocortical intervention. The solution is proposed that we have some inner concepts; that is the semantically endowed inner concepts of psychosemantics. But if our ordinary (public) concepts were not sufficient for meaning in the absence of neocortical intervention then why are the concepts of psychosemantics?[13] What is the telling difference between our public concepts and those of psychosemantics? The only difference seems to be that the former are outer and public, and the latter are, in some sense, inner and private; this seems far from sufficient for the latter to have any powers over and above those we might predicate of the former.

There is also, of course, the regress problem. Briefly, this goes as follows: if it is suggested that in order for our public concepts to mean anything they must be underpinned by the more basic concepts of psychosemantics, then what underpins the concepts of psychosemantics? Why do our public concepts require underpinning by another more primitive (it is the theorists of psychosemantics that claim them to be more primitive) set of concepts, yet these more primitive concepts do not themselves require underpinning? Again the concepts of psychosemantics differ – on Prinz's own account – from our public concepts only in that they are: (1) 'inner', and (2) more primitive. Is this a satisfying solution?

The bind in which Prinz finds himself can be traced to the empiricist's picture of mind and world with which he proceeds. Meaning is conveyed by the mind (brain). The world is unconceptualized, brute given, merely having causal impact upon our minds. Not only are we not obliged to accept this picture of mind and world, but there are others available to us, such as, for example, that suggested (for therapeutic purposes) by John McDowell and recently embraced by Hilary Putnam: the neo-Aristotelian picture of mind. This does not saddle us with the problems bequeathed to us by Prinz's guiding picture of mind. Ultimately Prinz offers us a sophisticated way of responding to Deigh's two-facts-problem. His is another in a long line of theories on both sides of the cognitivist–Jamesian divide that try to theorize their way to being able to account for both facts.

3. The appeal to and of sub-personal mechanisms and attributes

Let us take stock. Griffiths rejects the attempt to provide a theory of emotion by arguing that the term emotion, in reality, covers two natural kinds (plus maybe one pseudo-kind). Prinz tries to solve the problem through the marrying of Lazarus's notion of core relational themes with a computational theory of mind, which builds on those advanced by Dretske and Fodor. We have seen that we are not obliged to accept either Griffiths' or Prinz's conclusions.

Now, Prinz's 'solution' to his 'problem' was particularly indicative, for the standard way in which both sides of the Jamesian–cognitivist divide try to bridge the gap, if not initiate rapprochement, is to imbue something sub-personal with cognitive powers. So, for Jamesians this is to concede that meaning and intentionality are important, while at the same time retaining the Jamesian commitment to emotions being perceptions of patterned bodily changes. For the cognitivists this is to concede that one can perceive without having taken a propositional stance towards the world.

In the Jamesian camp Jenefer Robinson (1995, pp. 59–60 and 2004) has talked of 'subception', which is perception only sub-personally-so; that is it is perception taking place without the 'perceiver's' awareness of their (body or skin) perceiving. What Robinson's talk of 'subceptions' is designed to achieve is the thought that the bodily changes are intentional in that they are borne of, or are, sorts of 'perceptions', just not what we had hitherto understood as perceptions. They are, we are told, sub-personally perceived in that it is not the person doing the perceiving but a sub-personal mechanism doing the perceiving, unbeknownst to the person.

Cognitivists can employ similar tactics. In a late paper, Robert Solomon (2003a), the 'purest' and most 'unreconstructed' of all cognitivists, on most people's account, argued that the judgements he takes to be the emotion can be 'pre-linguistic' (p. 15) 'judgements of the body' (p. 14). He writes,

> Thus the judgements that I claim are constitutive of the emotion may be non-propositional and bodily as well as propositional and articulate, and they may further become reflective and self-conscious. What is cognition? I would still insist that it is basically judgement, both reflective and pre-reflective, both knowing how (as skills and practices) and knowing that (as propositional knowledge). A cognitive theory of emotion thus embodies what is often referred to as 'affect' and 'feeling' without dismissing these as unanalysable. (Solomon 2003a, p. 16)

This is a way of retaining his commitment to the intentionality of emotion while accommodating the challenge posed by those who hold that bodily changes are central. But the talk of such 'judgements' being pre-linguistic is not entirely clear – Solomon prefers 'pre-linguistic', while the author he draws upon, George Downing (2001), uses 'pre-cognitive'. It is just difficult to grasp what might be meant by a pre-linguistic judgement, such that it raises the question as to the role being played by the 'pre' prefix. What could it be for linguistically endowed beings' bodies to judge pre-linguistically? Do they judge a pre-conceptualized, brute, world? I think, rather, what Solomon has in mind is that there are cases when we act so as to indicate that we have judged, without our having taken up a propositional (judging) stance to the world. On this point we can (I will, here) agree with Solomon.

Solomon, in a similar manner to Robinson and Prinz, tries to resolve the problem by predicating of something sub-personal what we, ordinarily, predicate of persons: that is that they judge (appraise, evaluate). This said, Solomon is on to something important, at the end of the above quote, when he insists that cognitivists' invocation of affect does not commit them to the invocation of an unanalysable component.

In making this concession, in adapting his judgementalism in this direction, Solomon seems to be moving his version of cognitivism in the direction of those we might call the 'hybrid cognitivists', such as Goldie and Greenspan. Goldie has argued for the intentionality of feelings, both bodily – with the body or part thereof as object of the feeling – and 'outwards-directed' feelings – that is, feelings directed towards the object of the emotion (see Goldie 2004, p. 92). And Goldie's claim *seems* correct. We do *feel* the pain *in our foot*, or *in our chest*, and we do *feel* afraid *of the spider* which scuttles across the floor at our feet; these are the (particular) objects of which those feelings are about, they are the objects of those feelings. But we should like to know more than this. Goldie joins Robinson, Prinz and Solomon, in trying to resolve the problem by saying of something sub-personal what we would usually say of the person; for is it not the *person* who feels the pain in his foot or in his chest and is it not the *person* who feels – who IS – afraid of the spider. Thus, is it not the *'person'* in the sentence who is the locus of our predication of intentionality, not, that is to say, that person's 'feelings'.

In a similar manner to Goldie, Patricia Greenspan writes, 'affect evaluates! Emotional affect or feeling is itself evaluative—and the result can be summed up in a proposition' (Greenspan 2004, p. 132). Now, we can raise the same issues in response to Greenspan as we did in our discussion of Goldie. For Robinson, Prinz, Solomon, Goldie and Greenspan, in their attempts to overcome the problem posed, all submit to the temptation to predicate of a part what is a property or a capacity of the whole. Bennett and Hacker (2003 and Bennett et al. 2007) have termed such argumentative moves, the mereological fallacy.

4. The formal analysis of thought and theories of mental content

The mereological objection aside, Greenspan makes an important point (following the em-dash in the above quote), which supports that made by Solomon. Greenspan's point is important to bear in mind so as not to be misled by those critics, such as Deigh (2004), Griffiths (1997), and D'arms and Jacobson (2003), who assume predicating content equals or entails predicating the having of a propositional attitude. As Greenspan alludes to here, invoking evaluation, and thus content and intentionality, does not entail that one must hold to the stronger and more problematic claim that a propositional stance must have been taken to the world. The content can be read off the world, which can then be represented in propositional form. This is the Fregean thought; and it is something which needs to be kept in mind. Saying with Frege that a thought is expressed in a sentence with propositional form, is not to commit oneself to the view that for a person to have a thought is for them to have taken up a propositional attitude towards the world, in the robust sense of them believing or judging that *x*. It is merely to say that this is how we represent the sense of the thought for the purposes of logical analysis of *the* mind (as opposed to the study of the minds of individuals). In interpreting this stance as entailing that a thought *is* a propositional attitude one is making a move which is neither advocated nor demanded by Frege.

So why would the modifications of Solomon, Greenspan and so on not satisfy Deigh? He writes,

> Standard cognitivist theories, as I observed earlier, explain this feature [intentionality] by attributing propositional thought to emotions, for they take the emotions distinctive of human beings as the paradigm of their subject and the thought content of these emotions is propositional. (Deigh 2004, p.18)

These modifications don't satisfy Deigh because he takes cognitivists to be committed to attributing propositional thought to emotions. A cognitivist in the philosophy of the emotions, even a 'standard' or 'pure' cognitivist, does not of necessity – that is in virtue of being a cognitivist and having intentionality as central to their account – face the problems Deigh claims they do, because they are not *obliged* to attribute propositional thought to emotions, as Deigh claims they are. There are those who *seem* to so attribute, as do the early Solomon (1976), Gabriele Taylor (1985) and Martha Nussbaum (2004), but even they are not committed to do so. There is nothing in a commitment to the centrality of intentionality that entails a commitment to emotions as propositional attitudes. Deigh's criticism relies on conflating the Fregean formal analysis of thoughts, such that they are *represented* in propositional form, which is a commitment to a certain form of philosophical analysis of *the* mind – one which is concerned to resist any temptation to, or slide into, psychologism – with a theoretical position in the philosophy of mind that holds that to have a thought with content *is* to have a propositional attitude towards the world. This, latter position, is a substantive theoretical claim about the nature of the mental content of individuals, while, in contrast, Frege was concerned with the philosophical analysis of *the* mind. Fregean analysis is conducted by *representing* thoughts as propositions for the purposes of logical analysis; there is no further commitment to thoughts being propositional attitudes or the having of a thought being the having of a propositional attitude.[14]

Having rejected the conflation, there's still more work to be done. For, in resisting the identification of a certain form of analysis of thought content with the having of a propositional attitude, in some robust sense of 'having', we need to give an account of content, which can accommodate the intentional character of emotion to which we are committed. We can analyse thought in that which it is most ready-to-hand, the language with which we speak, without encoding that language in a *Begrifschrift* or as a set of propositions. It is in analysing thought in this way that we resist the postulation of propositional shadows to thought.[15]

5. Deigh's facts, James' claim

What both positions, cognitivism and neo-Jamesianism, have in common is the latent, though thought-constraining, picture of the mind and body as discrete. Talking as James does of what comes first thoughts or bodily changes and arguing in these terms with James, as do many cognitivists, buys into this picture where one might rather question the framing of the whole debate. A 'cognitivism' which eschews a commitment to this dualism of thoughts and bodily changes, one which is rather committed to thoughts being embodied, is a cognitivism which in analysing emotion in terms of formal objects (Kenny 1963) or core relational themes (Lazarus 1991) or paradigm scenario (de Sousa 1987) or through the internal relations holding between the conceptualization of a state of affairs and the concept of the emotion for an enculturated being (as in my own world-taking cognitivism, Hutchinson 2008) is a version of cognitivism which is not committed to a propositional attitude account of mental content.[16] It is a version of cognitivism that can and should (and in the case of my own account does) reject the 'chain of events' – as characterized in the table above. We reject the 'chain of events' by arguing that it is not a chain of externally related discrete events but rather one emotional event, albeit formally *analysable* into internally related 'components'. This then renders the opposition setup by James between the 'natural way' of thinking about emotions and his way of thinking about emotions as less than helpful. The cognitivism I here advocate sees the chain of events as presented by James and as represented in either side of the last row of the table (above) as no more than an artefact of analysis and not a necessary aspect of the ontology of emotion. This version of cognitivism – what we might call, so as to make this point clear, embodied world-taking cognitivism – is an account of emotion which claims that to identify the emotion is to identify its meaning. It is an account which can cover both of Deigh's facts.

Notes

*An early version of this paper was presented to the Department of Philosophy Seminar Program at Lancaster University. I thank the audience there for some fruitful discussion. Thanks to Peter Goldie, Paul Griffiths, Lars Hertzberg, Dina Mendonca, Rupert Read and the editors of this volume for reading and offering very helpful comments. I, of course, am responsible for any errors.

1. In this chapter I deal only with emotion as currently debated within the analytic tradition. I engage with emotion as discussed by continental philosophers (particularly Agamben, though touching on Heidegger and Levinas) in chapter 2 of my book, *Shame and Philosophy* (2008).

2. I use 'cognitivism' and 'neo-Jamesianism' tentatively. William James famously claimed that the emotion was the feeling of patterned bodily changes; I employ 'neo-Jamesian' to denote those philosophers that subscribe to this view and in doing so often draw and/or build upon Charles Darwin's research and/or the 'findings' of neuroscience. 'Cognitivism' is the most widely used term for those philosophers who reject William James's approach and seek to explain emotions in terms of the thoughts that constitute them (broadly speaking), though this term is neither universally employed nor accepted. Furthermore, it should not be taken to imply affiliation to or kinship with the methods or claims of cognitive science. Other terms used to denote this group of philosophers and or their theories are 'Judgement theory', 'Judgementalism', 'Appraisal Theory', 'Propositional Attitude Theory', and 'neo-Stoicism'. Deigh (1994 and 2004) employs the term 'cognitivism' in critiquing cognitivists; Peter Goldie (2004) uses 'cognitivism', (as he says) 'tendentiously' (p. 91), and writes that it is the view he favours; De Sousa (2004) also uses the term. 'Judgement theory' is the term favoured by Jenefer Robinson (2004) to denote these theorists, of whom she is critical. 'Judgementalism' is employed by Greenspan (2004, p. 128), though she does not include herself in the category picked out by the term (though her critics, cognitivist and Jamesian, often do include her in the category). 'Quasi-judgementalism' is the term favoured by D'arms and Jacobson (2003) who employ it so as to include Greenspan and Robert C. Roberts (Greenspan rejects the label, 2004, p. 133). The 'quasi' prefix might be seen to serve two roles here: (1) it allows evaluative beliefs to be captured by the term and thus can be applied to theories where the theorist does not employ the word 'judgement'; and (2) it allows that the judgements need not be manifest to the agent at the time of the emotion. D'Arms and Jacobson (2003) use it in the sense of (2). 'Appraisal Theory' is the term that Jesse Prinz (2004) employs to denote the non-or counter-Jamesian theories of emotions, which has the benefit of including cognitive psychologists but the disadvantage of also including Prinz's own 'psychosemantic appraisals', and thus becoming a too-broad church, so to speak. (Prinz invokes Lazarus's notion of 'core relational themes' at a computational level to imbue his neo-Jamesianism with intentionality. More below.) 'Propositional Attitude Theory' is the term coined by Griffiths (1997) and is simply misleading. Many of those to whom Griffiths hopes to refer in employing this term are not committed to the claim that emotions are propositional attitudes, nor even to a propositional attitude account of mental content. Nussbaum talks of 'neo-Stoic' views. However, it too is somewhat misleading, for one of the things that the Stoics held was that emotions are *mistaken* judgements or appraisals, that is that the judgements that constitute emotions are always false. That is not something to which many cognitivists subscribe.

3. See, for example, Prinz (2003b, p. 5) and Solomon (2003a, p. 12).

4. It's telling to note, given the widely held assumption that Wittgenstein was an anti-Jamesian proto-cognitivist (see, for example, Griffiths (1997) account of the emergence of cognitivism in Kenny's *Action, Emotion & Will*) that Wittgenstein

would find neither of the options presented by James to be satisfactory. Both options, as presented in the quote from James, suggest or imply a mind–body dualism.

5. Paul Griffiths did much to foster this misconception by choosing, in his influential book *What Emotions Really Are*, to refer to cognitivists as Propositional Attitude Theorists. See chapter 1 of my book (2008) for a detailed critique of Griffiths.

6. So, my arms *qua* human arms and the wings of a bat are homologous, but not analogous (in many respects, as they do not serve, by and large, the same function). The wings of the bat and the wings of the housefly are analogous (in that they serve the same function, by and large) but not homologous (in that their structures do not descend from a common evolutionary ancestor).

7. I only mean to suggest that computational theories of mind are not obligatory and that they have no distinctive status among theories of mind such that we must see them as being scientific. We can merely stay agnostic on this, here.

8. I say something about this in chapters 3 and 4 of my *Shame and Philosophy* (2008).

9. In this respect it is worth noting that it is important not to give up the term 'cognition' to cognitive neuroscience and neuroreductionists; Prinz rushes to embrace their version of cognition.

10. There is some interesting extended discussion and argument regarding many of these issues in Bennett, Dennett, Hacker and Searle (2007).

11. Prinz here employs a strategy similar to that Paul Griffiths is wont to pursue (see Hutchinson (2008, ch. 1) for a discussion of Griffiths doing the same), merely asserting the prevalence of a particular theory of mind. It is enough to note that the theory of mind here 'assumed correct' has no right to be so assumed. It has been frequently contested (e.g., the essays in section VI of Putnam 1994; Williams 1999; Button, Coulter, Lee and Sharrock 1995; Sharrock and Coulter 2007a, b; and Hutto 2008; to list a very small sample).

12. One could go into much detail on this. I shan't; at least not here. For pretty devastating critiques of such theories see Austin (1962) and Travis (2005). It is also pertinent, following Austin and Wittgenstein, to question in what sense the concepts of psychosemantics and the modules that encapsulate them are 'inner'; briefly, if I say the book is in the drawer, or the pig is in the sty, then we can be expected to be able to respond to basic questions such as, 'If we open the drawer/sty will we find the book/pig?' Can one say cognate things about thoughts and the head? It might be objected that it is another use of 'inner' that is in play here, similar to (for example) 'John is in the Army'. But John joined the Army, he left the Army after his six-year stint, his parents watched him marching with his platoon at his passing-out parade, etc. 'John being in the Army' does not imply location. Is this the use of 'in' our theoreticians of psychosemantics invoke? Does it make sense to talk of psychosemantic concepts being *in* modules in this way?

13. Calling them *bio*semantics and telling an evolutionary story doesn't help. Why do they evolve in a way that our public concepts don't? And if you feel inclined to retort that our public concepts do evolve (and I have no objection to speaking this way) then why the need for the inner concepts of biosemantics?

14. This is, of course, not to be committed to the idea that thoughts are never propositional attitudes towards the world. It is only to make the point that in representing thoughts as sentences with propositional from, for the purposes of

analysis, we are not logically committed to thoughts being propositional attitudes.

15. See Travis (2000) *Unshadowed Thought* for a critique of 'shadows' and how to avoid their postulation. While I largely endorse Travis's work in this area I have some reservations; For a good introduction to Travis's thought and for an insightful highlighting of certain problematic issues, with which I concur, see Martin Gustafsson's (2002) 'Meaning, Saying, Truth'.

16. It is important to note that some of those I list here, do, on occasion, tend to dualist characterizations, Lazarus is particularly culpable. However, none need to do so. Their accounts of emotion are such that there is no logical requirement of them to do so.

Bibliography

Austin, J.L. (1962), *Sense and Sensibilia* (Oxford: Oxford University Press).

Bennett, M., Dennett, D., Hacker, P.M.S. and Searle, J. (2007), *Neuroscience and Philosophy: Brain, Mind and Language* (New York: Columbia University Press).

——. and Hacker, P.M.S. (2003), *The Philosophical Foundations of Neuroscience* (Oxford: Blackwell).

Button, G., Coulter, J., Lee, J.R.E. and Sharrock, W. (1995), *Computers, Minds and Conduct* (Cambridge: Polity Press).

Calhoun, C. and Solomon, R. (eds) (1984), *What is an Emotion: Classic Readings in Philosophical Psychology* (New York: Oxford University Press).

D'arms, J. and Jacobson, D. (2003), 'The Significance of Recalcitrant Emotion (or anti-quasijudgementalism)', in Hatzimoysis, A. (ed.), *Philosophy and the Emotions: Royal Institute of Philosophy Supplement:* 52 (Cambridge: Cambridge University Press), pp. 127–146.

D'Sousa, Ronald (2004) 'Emotions: What I Know, What I'd Like to Think I Know, and What I'd Like to Think' in Solomon, R.C. (ed.) *Thinking About Feeling: Contemporary Philosophers on Emotions* (Oxford: Oxford University Press), pp. 61–75.

Damasio, A.R. (1994), *Descartes' Error: Emotion, Reason and the Human Brain* (London: Macmillan).

Darwin, Charles (1872 [1999]), *The Expression of Emotions in Man and Animals.* (London: Fontana Press).

Deigh, J. (1994), 'Cognitivism in the Theory of Emotions', *Ethics* 104, 824–854.

——. (2004) 'Primitive Emotions', in Solomon, R.C. (ed.), *Thinking About Feeling: Contemporary Philosophers on Emotions* (Oxford: Oxford University Press), pp. 9–27.

Downing, G. (2001), 'Emotion Theory Revisited', in Wrathall, M. and Malpas, J. (eds), *Heidegger, Coping and Cognitive Science: Essays in Honour of Hubert L. Dreyfus* (Cambridge MA: MIT Press), pp. 245–270.

Dretske, Fred (1981), *Knowledge and the Flow of Information* (Cambridge MA: MIT Press).

Dretske, Fred (1988), *Explaining Behaviour: Reasons in a World of Causes.* (Cambridge MA: MIT Press).

Dupré, J. (1981), 'Natural Kinds and Biological Taxa', *The Philosophical Review*, 90 (1), 66–90.

Ekman, P. (1972), *Emotions in the Human Face* (New York: Pergamon Press).

Fodor, Jerry (1990), *A Theory of Content and Other Essays.* Cambridge MA: MIT Press.

Frank, R.H. (1988), *Passions Within Reason: The Strategic Role of the Emotions* (New York: Norton).

Goldie, P. (2000), *The Emotions: A Philosophical Exploration* (Oxford: Oxford University Press).

——. (2004), 'Emotion, Feeling and Knowledge of the World', in Solomon, R.C. (ed.), *Thinking About Feeling: Contemporary Philosophers on Emotions* (Oxford: Oxford University Press), pp. 91–106.

Greenspan, P.S. (1988), *Emotions and Reasons* (London: Routledge).

——. (1995), *Practical Guilt: Moral Dilemmas, Emotions and Social Norms* (Oxford: Oxford University Press).

——. (2004), 'Emotions, Rationality and Mind/Body', in Solomon, R.C. (ed.), *Thinking About Feeling: Contemporary Philosophers on Emotions* (Oxford: Oxford University Press), pp. 125–134.

Griffiths, P.E. (1989), 'The Degeneration of the Cognitive Theory of Emotion', *Philosophical Psychology*, 2 (3), 297–313.

——. (1997), *What Emotions Really Are* (Chicago: Chicago University Press).

——. (2003), 'Basic Emotions, Complex Emotions, Machiavellian Emotions', in Hatzimoysis, A. (ed.), *Philosophy and the Emotions: Royal Institute of Philosophy Supplement:* 52 (Cambridge: Cambridge University Press), pp. 39–68.

——. (2004), 'Is Emotion a Natural Kind?', in Solomon, R.C. (ed.), *Thinking About Feeling: Contemporary Philosophers on Emotions* (Oxford: Oxford University Press), pp. 233–249.

Gustafsson, M. (2002), 'Meaning, Saying, Truth', in Gustafsson, M. and Hertzberg, L. (eds), *The Practice of Language* (Dordrecht: Kluwer), pp. 177–197.

——. and Hertzberg, L. (eds) (2002), *The Practice of Language* (Dordrecht: Kluwer).

Hatzimoysis, A. (ed.) (2003), *Philosophy and the Emotions: Royal Institute of Philosophy Supplement*: 52 (Cambridge: Cambridge University Press).

Hutchinson, P. (2008), *Shame and Philosophy: An Investigation in the Philosophy of Emotions and Ethics* (Basingstoke: Palgrave Macmillan).

Hutto, D.D. (2008), *Folk Psychological Narratives* (Cambridge MA: MIT Press).

James, W. (1884), 'What is an Emotion?', *Mind*, 9, 188–205.

Kenny, A. (1963), *Action, Emotion and Will* (London: Routledge).

Lange, C.G. (1885), *Om Sindsbevaegelser: et Psyko-Fysiologisk Studie.* (Kjøbenhavn: Jacub Lunds).

Lazarus, R. (1991), *Emotion and Adaptation* (Oxford: Oxford University Press).

McDowell, J. (1994), *Mind and World* (Cambridge: Cambridge University Press).

——. (1998a), *Mind, Value and Reality* (Cambridge MA: Harvard University Press).

——. (1998b), *Meaning, Knowledge, & Reality* (Cambridge MA: Harvard University Press).

——. (2000a), 'Experiencing the World', in Willaschek, M. (ed.), *John McDowell: Reason and Nature* (London: Lit Verlag), pp. 3–18.

——. (2000b), 'Responses', in Willaschek, M. (ed.), *John McDowell: Reason and Nature* (London: Lit Verlag), pp. 91–114.

Moyal-Sharrock, D. (ed.) (2007), *Perspicuous Presentations: Essays on Wittgenstein's Philosophy of Psychology* (Basingstoke: Palgrave).

Nash, R.A. (1989), 'Cognitive Theories of Emotion', *Nous* 23, 481–504.

Nussbaum, Martha (2004) 'Emotions as Judgments of Value and Importance', in Solomon, R.C. (ed.), *Thinking About Feeling: Contemporary Philosophers on Emotions* (Oxford: Oxford University Press), pp. 183–199.

Prinz, J. (2003a), 'Emotions, Psychosemantics, and Embodied Appraisals' in Hatzimoysis, A. (ed.), *Philosophy and the Emotions: Royal Institute of Philosophy Supplement*: 52 (Cambridge: Cambridge University Press), pp. 69–86.

——. (2003b), *Gut Reactions: A Perceptual Theory of Emotion* (Oxford: Oxford University Press).

——. (2004), 'Embodied Emotions', in Solomon, R.C. (ed.), *Thinking About Feeling: Contemporary Philosophers on Emotions* (Oxford: Oxford University Press), pp. 44–60.

Putnam, H. (1994), *Words and Life* (Cambridge MA: Harvard University Press).

——. (1999), *Threefold Cord: Mind, Body, World* (Columbia: Columbia University Press).

Roberts, R.C. (1988), 'What an Emotion Is: A Sketch', *Philosophical Review*, 97, 183–209.

——. (2003), *Emotions: An Essay in Aid of Moral Psychology* (Cambridge: Cambridge University Press).

Robinson, J. (1995), 'Startle', *Journal of Philosophy*, 92 (2), 53–74.

——. (2004), 'Emotion: Biological Fact or Social Construction?', in Solomon, R.C. (ed.), *Thinking About Feeling: Contemporary Philosophers on Emotions* (Oxford: Oxford University Press), pp. 28–43.

Rorty, A.O. (2004), 'Enough Already With "Theories of the Emotions"', in Solomon, R.C. (ed.), *Thinking About Feeling: Contemporary Philosophers on Emotions* (Oxford: Oxford University Press), pp. 269–278.

Sharrock, W. and Coulter, J. (2007a), *Brain, Mind and Human Behaviour in Contemporary Cognitive Science: Critical Assessments of the Philosophy of Psychology* (New York: Edwin Mellen Press).

——. (2007b), 'Revisiting "The Unconscious"', in Moyal-Sharrock (ed.), *Perspicuous Presentations: Essays on Wittgenstein's Philosophy of Psychology* (Basingstoke: Palgrave), 95–113.

Solomon, R.C. (1976), *The Passions* (Garden City, New York: Anchor/Doubleday).

—— (2003a), 'What is a "Cognitive Theory" of the Emotions?' in Hatzimoysis, A. (ed.), *Philosophy and the Emotions: Royal Institute of Philosophy Supplement: 52* (Cambridge: Cambridge University Press), pp. 1–18.

——. (ed.) (2003b), *What is an Emotion: Classic and Contemporary Readings* (New York: Oxford University Press). (This is the – significantly changed – 2nd edn of Calhoun and Solomon (eds) (1984)).

——. (2003c), *Not Passion's Slave* (Oxford: Oxford University Press).

——. (2004a), 'Emotions, Thoughts and Feelings: Emotions as Engagements in the World', in Solomon, R.C. (ed.), *Thinking About Feeling: Contemporary Philosophers on Emotions* (Oxford: Oxford University Press), pp. 76–89.

——. (ed.) (2004b), *Thinking About Feeling: Contemporary Philosophers on Emotions* (Oxford: Oxford University Press).

de Sousa, R. (1987), *The Rationality of Emotion* (Cambridge MA: MIT Press).

Stocker, M. (1987), 'Emotional Thoughts', *American Philosophical Quarterly*, 24 (1), 59–69.

——. with Hegeman, E. (1999), *Valuing Emotions* (Cambridge: Cambridge University Press).

Taylor, G. (1985), *Pride, Shame, and Guilt: Emotions of Self-Assessment* (Oxford: Oxford University Press).

Travis, C. (2000), *Unshadowed Thought* (Cambridge MA: Harvard University Press).

——. (2005), 'The Twilight of Empiricism', *Proceedings of the Aristotelian Society* XII, 245–270.

Willaschek, M. (ed.) (2000), *John McDowell: Reason and Nature* (London: Lit Verlag).

Williams, M. (1999), *Wittgenstein, Mind and Meaning* (London: Routledge).

Wrathall, M. and Malpas, J. (eds) (2001), *Heidegger, Coping and Cognitive Science: Essays in Honour of Hubert L. Dreyfus* (vol. 2) (Cambridge MA: MIT Press).

5

Capturing Emotional Thoughts: The Philosophy of Cognitive-Behavioral Therapy*

Michael McEachrane

Ever since Albert Ellis introduced his ABC-theory of emotional dysfunction in the 1950s one premise of *cognitive-behavioral therapy* (CBT) has been the idea that emotional disturbances are caused by beliefs. Following Stoic philosophy Ellis argued that emotional disturbances are a *consequence* (C) of *beliefs* (B) rather than of *activating events* themselves (A) (e.g., Ellis 1962). Since then, beliefs have been the focal point of CBT – be it Ellis' *rational emotive behavior therapy* (REBT), Aaron T. Beck's *cognitive therapy* (CT) or the so-called 'new wave' of cognitive-behavioral therapies such as *acceptance and commitment therapy* (ACT) (e.g., Beck 1979; Beck et al. 1979; Ellis and Blau 1998; Hayes, Follette and Linehan 2004).

A second premise of CBT is that emotion causing beliefs are mentally represented; primarily as 'internal dialogues' – what Ellis refers to as 'self-talk' and Beck as 'automatic thoughts' – but also as mental images (e.g., Beck 1979; Ellis 1994; Segal, Williams and Teasdale 2001). On the basis of this second premise, a central idea to the practice of CBT is that we can become aware of the beliefs that elicit our emotional reactions by becoming aware of the words or images that elicit them.

This chapter examines these two premises – that emotions are caused by beliefs and that those beliefs are represented in the mind as words or images. Being a philosophical examination, the chapter also seeks to demonstrate that these two premises essentially are *philosophical* premises. Although the space of a single article does not allow for more than a cursory sketch, its upshot, that CBT in part is based on misleading philosophical assumptions, should come as a great surprise to those who think that CBT is firmly based on science.

The chapter will begin with a brief methodological suggestion of how to properly evaluate the theory of CBT. From there it will work its way from examining the therapeutic practice of capturing the mental representations that supposedly elicit emotional reactions to examining the assumption that emotions are caused by beliefs. The chapter will end by briefly pointing to some consequences of what has been said to the practice of CBT.

1. The theory of CBT: science or philosophy?

How should one examine the two central assumptions of CBT, that emotional disturbances are caused by beliefs and that those beliefs are internally represented? In a relatively recent debate between the Beck-camp of CT and the Ellis-camp of REBT, Christine A. Padesky and Aaron T. Beck criticize REBT for being *philosophical* rather than *scientific* (Padesky and Beck 2003, 2005; Ellis 2005; Still and Dryden 2003).

It is widely known that REBT largely grew out of Ellis' interest in philosophy, particularly Stoicism (e.g., Ellis 1994, p. xv, 1989, p. 215). His development of REBT in the 1950s was not based on empirical research, but on applying Stoic ideas in his clinical practice. As Padesky and Beck point out, CT on the other hand was developed on the basis of Beck's empirical research on depression in the 1950s (and early 60s) (Padesky and Beck 2003, p. 212). On the whole, Padesky and Beck argue, a 'fundamental difference between the two is that REBT is a philosophically based psychotherapy and CT is an empirically based psychotherapy' (Padesky and Beck 2003, p. 211). There is no doubt that CT is deeper rooted in experimental psychology than REBT, and perhaps Padesky and Beck are right that, 'The empirical foundation of CT is undoubtedly one of the reasons it is such a highly regarded therapy approach' (Padesky and Beck 2003, p. 213).

But although it seems fair to say that empirical studies are relevant to, say, pinpointing how people suffering from (or who are particularly susceptible to) certain mental disorders tend to view themselves, other people, certain situations, and so forth, and also to evaluating the efficacy of treatment methods, it does not seem fair to say that empirical studies are sufficient to evaluate what Padesky and Beck refer to as the key assumptions of CT:

> All CT conceptualizations include two key assumptions. The first is that people actively construct meaning and derive rules that guide their behavior. This construction process involves information processing which frequently includes selective filtering and even distortion of what is perceived .... The second is an assumption that cognitions, emotions, behaviors, physical responses and life events are interactively linked to one another .... Although cognitions are not always causally linked to emotional or behavioral disorders, cognitive theory proposes that cognitions mediate all change efforts. For example, regardless of the original causes, someone with a substance abuse disorder may need to change beliefs about the problem before developing a motivation to participate in treatment. There is empirical support for each of these assumptions .... (Padesky and Beck 2003, p. 218)

Here I take the first assumption to mean that people have beliefs and 'automatic thoughts' (that guide their behavior) and the second assumption to mean that emotional disorders are caused by such 'cognitions'. This is in line with what Beck elsewhere has described as the core of the cognitive model of emotions and emotional disorders:

> The thesis that the special meaning of an event determines the emotional response forms the core of the cognitive model of emotions and emotional disorders: The meaning is encased in a cognition – a thought or an image. (Beck 1979, p. 52)

What I am going to try to demonstrate in the remainder of this article is that this cognitive model, what I take to be the two key assumptions of CBT – again, that emotions are caused by beliefs and that these beliefs are mentally represented as words or images – depend on certain understandings (or misunderstandings rather) of the meanings of emotion-reports. What I will try to show is how the theoretical foundation of cognitive therapy hinges on an understanding of the meanings and uses of emotion terms, and such terms as 'thought' and 'belief'. This is also to show precisely how philosophy is relevant to CBT: clarifying the meanings of words by reflecting on their use – what, in philosophy, sometimes is referred to as 'conceptual analysis' – is needed in order to inquire into its underlying theory (cf. McEachrane 2006, and in press).[1] As we proceed, I hope that the practice and relevance of such an approach will become sufficiently clear.

2. Capturing emotional thoughts

The typical course of treatment in CBT is to go from *automatic thought* (CT) or *self-talk* (REBT) to *core belief* (CT) or *core philosophy* (REBT) (cf. e.g., Beck, J.S. 1995, p. 16). The initial focus, in other words, is to seek to capture the thoughts that supposedly elicit emotions in the moment, and then from there explore the deeper lying, general beliefs that these thoughts often are expressive of. Typically, these 'thoughts' are assumed to be in the form of 'inner speech'.

Early on in his career Ellis put an emphasis on such 'inner speech' – which he called *self-talk* – and theorized that what makes humans particularly prone to be emotionally disturbed, and remain so, is their linguistic facility 'to translate their psychological *desires* – such as the desires for love, approval, success, and leisure – into *definitional needs*' and to thereby 'abuse this facility by talking nonsense to themselves: to *define* things as *terrible* and *impermissible* when, at worst, these things are very inconvenient and annoying' (Ellis 1994, pp. 29–30). Over the years, though, Ellis went from putting an emphasis on emotion-eliciting beliefs as *self-talk* to putting a greater emphasis on emotion-eliciting beliefs as a matter of the general *philosophy* of the client.

> When I first started to do REBT, I wrongly thought that disturbed people almost always talk to themselves to create their emotional problems. I now see that they often do this and literally tell themselves, 'I failed again. That means I'll *always* fail and am no damned good as a person!' Now I see that they *sometimes* but not always explicitly say these sentences to themselves. But whether they do or don't tell themselves these negative statements, they have a *core philosophy* (sometimes called, by Aaron Beck and others, a schema) that they implicitly, and usually strongly, believe that underlies their self-statements. (Ellis 1994, p. 28)

REBT's current view on the relation between emotional disturbance, core philosophy, and self-talk seems to be something like the following.[2] Emotional disturbances depend on core philosophies[3] that create tendencies to view events and circumstances in a disturbing manner. Such disturbing perceptions may be 'non-verbal' as initial or momentary reactions, but are typically followed by self-talk resulting from a core philosophy. Nevertheless, these core philosophies are themselves quite literally understood as *statements* – be they *tacit*, as in the case of core philosophies, or *explicit*, as in the case of self-talk (cf. e.g., Ellis 1994, pp. 26–27). And so, a central task of REBT is to track these emotion-eliciting statements down.[4]

CT's analogue to REBT's 'self-talk' is so-called *automatic thoughts* – 'self-talk' which occur 'in a kind of shorthand; ... as in telegraphic style' and not 'as a result of deliberation, reasoning, or reflection' but 'as if by reflex' (Beck 1979, p. 26). According to Beck emotional reactions to external events are made understandable by such intervening automatic thoughts, which people can learn to capture:[5]

> When a person is able to fill in the gap between an activating event and the emotional consequences, the puzzling reaction becomes understandable. With training, people are able to catch the rapid thoughts or images that occur between an event and the emotional response. (Beck 1979, p. 26)

Although emotions are typically mediated by 'automatic thoughts', they may also, as maintained by Beck, be mediated by *mental imagery* (e.g., Beck 1979, p. 26 and pp. 37–38; Beck et al. 1979, pp. 150–157; cf. also Beck, J.S. 1995, p. 88).

However, what is key here, both in Ellis' and Beck's rendition of how thought elicits emotion, is the notion that *thought must consist of some kind of mental representation, be it words or images*. This – I dare say – unexamined presupposition is a central and recurrent theme in REBT, CT, and what sometimes is referred to as 'new wave cognitive therapy' or 'third wave behavior therapy' (cf. Hayes 2004).[6]

3. What are emotional 'thoughts' anyway?

Here is a clinical example by Judith S. Beck of how this cognitive model of emotion might be introduced in a therapy session:

> *THERAPIST*: Now I'd like to spend a few minutes talking about the connection between thoughts and feelings. Can you think of some times this week when you felt upset?
>
> *PATIENT*: Yeah. Walking to class this morning.
>
> *T*: What emotion were you feeling: sad? anxious? angry?
>
> *P*: Sad.
>
> *T*: What was going through your mind?
>
> *P*: I was looking at these other students, talking or playing Frisbee, hanging out on the lawn.
>
> *T*: What was going through your mind when you saw them?
>
> *P*: I'll never be like them.
>
> *T*: Okay. You just identified what we call an *automatic thought*. Everyone has them. They're thoughts that just seem to pop in our heads. We're not deliberately trying to think about them; that's why we call them automatic. Most of the time, they're real quick and we're much more aware of the emotion – in this case, sadness – than we are of the thoughts. Lots of times the thoughts are distorted in some way. But we react *as if* they're true.
>
> *P*: Hmmm.
>
> *T*: What we'll do is to teach you to identify your automatic thoughts and then to evaluate them to see just how accurate they are. For example, in a minute we'll evaluate the thought, 'I'll never be like those students'. What do you think would happen to your emotions if you discovered that your thought wasn't true – that when your depression lifts you'll realize that you *are* like the other students?
>
> *P*: I'd feel better. (Beck, J.S. 1995, p. 78)

As should be clear by now, in CBT a question such as 'What was going through your mind when you saw them?' is asked literally, and the answer 'I'll never be like them' is understood as the actual words (or perhaps image) that went through the client's mind and elicited the sadness. Whether or not this practice reflects an accurate understanding of what it means 'to think' something may seem like hair-splitting, but, as we will see, how the question is answered may significantly change the therapeutic approach.

The assumption underlying the practice of cognitive therapy to ask what is going through a client's mind, what they are telling themselves when they feel a certain way (cf. Ellis 1994), or that they should learn to capture their emotional thoughts, is that the word 'thinking' refers to something particular going on in their mind (e.g., a stream of words) that *is* the thinking. But this wrongly conflates thinking with whatever is going on in a person's mind when they think something.

In the clinical example above, it is possible that the client thought 'I'll never be like them' without formulating those words to herself (i.e., without these words popping in her head) for at least two reasons.

1. What it means 'to think' something is not equivalent to what it means 'to have thoughts' about something.
2. 'To think' something may mean to perceive something a certain way (rather than to have certain words or images before one's mind, as it were).

(1) When speaking of thinking there is a crucial difference between 'to think' and 'to have thoughts' (cf. Malcolm 1977). When speaking of 'to think' or 'thinking' (as in 'to think' that one is living a good life or 'thinking' that one is an intelligent individual) we do not necessarily mean that certain words, or even images, are before our own or someone else's mind. For instance, one need not be entertaining the thought 'I'm an intelligent individual' or have the image of oneself as an 'intelligent individual' (whatever that would mean) present to one's mind so long as one thinks that one is an intelligent individual (which might be practically all the time). A student might be overconfident about her own intelligence and categorically react to something a professor is saying as nonsense since she does not understand it. Here, though, *thinking that she is intelligent* does not imply *having the thought (present to her mind as it were) that she is intelligent.*

In general, to say of someone that they 'thought that *p*' does not imply that they 'thought of *p*' or 'thought about *p*' or formulated *p* or that *p* occurred to them or were in their thoughts. So, for instance, if a client says that in a particular situation they thought that, say, 'I'll never be like them' or 'I'm worthless at interacting with people' or 'I'm not a likeable person', then this does not necessarily mean that the client in that situation thought *of* these things, formulated these things to herself, that these things occurred to her or were in her thoughts. That fact, that the formula 'she thought that *p*' does not imply the formula 'the thought that *p* occurred to her', may perhaps be easier to digest if we keep in mind that,

> The same holds for a host of propositional verbs. You and I notice, for example, that Robinson is walking in a gingerly way, and you ask why. I reply, 'Because he realizes that the path is slippery'. I do not imply that the proposition 'This path is slippery' crossed his mind. Another example: I wave at a

man across the quad. Later on I may say to someone, 'I saw Kasper today'. It may be true that I recognized Kaspar, or recognized that the man across the quad was Kaspar, but not true that I thought to myself, 'That is Kaspar'. (Malcolm 1977, p. 52, cf. also p. 57)

Consider, again, the thought 'I'll never be like them' in Judith Beck's clinical example above. What went on when the client thought that she would 'never be like them' might have been something like this. She saw these other students, talking or playing Frisbee, hanging out on the lawn. It was a sunny day to which she already felt a sense of alienation: merely registering that it was a sunny day but not being able to enjoy it, experiencing it as a sharp contrast to how she felt. Then she saw these contemporaries of hers, students like herself, that seemed to be hanging out and enjoying themselves with ease. The contrast between herself and these students seemed stark and interminable and this saddened her.

Later, during counseling, when asked what went through her mind that made her sad, she said: 'I'll never be like them'. That was what she was thinking. And this thought had saddened her. If she had thought, say, that her generally gloomy frame of mind was merely temporary – like a Sunday evening blues or something of the sort – and that she was likely to feel o.k. tomorrow, perhaps she would not have reacted the way she did. Now note that although it makes perfect sense for her to say that she in fact thought 'I'll never be like them', such words (or equivalent images) need not have flitted through her mind while she thought this. To insist otherwise, to insist that such words *must* have flitted through her mind if this is what she thought, is like insisting that after having sat down on a chair that broke under our weight and saying 'I certainly thought it would hold', then such words *must* have flitted through our mind – as if each time we sit down on a chair we tell ourselves something like, 'This chair will certainly hold'. In fact, when we utter the words 'I'll never be like them' or 'I certainly thought it would hold' to express what we thought at a particular moment it might very well be the first time these words occur to us.

Of course, this is not to deny that we in fact do tell ourselves things – far from it! – and that what we tell ourselves is often what we think. However, if we, for instance, think, as the client in the above example did, that 'I'll never be like them', then that might very well be a matter of how we take things to be rather than what we tell ourselves – which brings us to the second reason why a client may think something, which makes them react emotionally, without the thought being words or images in his or her mind.

(2) Generally speaking, 'thinking that *p*' (e.g., thinking that 'I'll never be like them', 'I'm worthless', 'She's angry with me', 'I don't know what to do', and so on) is not a particular internal representation, but experiencing, acting upon, reflecting upon, reacting to, *something (or someone) as being a*

certain way (cf. Travis 2000, pp. 158–159).[7] That is to say, when we say that we or someone else 'think' or are 'thinking' this or that, we are *reporting on a perceived or appraised state of affairs*, if you will – not on the words or images before our minds. For instance, if I thought that I saw a person in the dark that turned out to be a tree, this 'thought' signifies a perceived or appraised state of affairs ('I saw a person...') and not internal words or images – that is words or images may or may not have occurred to me at the moment I saw a person (...that turned out to be a tree), nevertheless they do not define the 'thought'.

A similar story can be told of 'beliefs'. Sometimes 'thought' and 'belief' may be used synonymously – as in, 'When I sat down on this chair, of course I believed/thought it would bear me' (cf. Wittgenstein 2001, § 575). And just as 'to think' does not imply 'having a thought' (or, on the whole, having an internal representation) neither does 'to believe'. However, there are also obvious differences between 'belief' and 'thought'. Whereas we can 'think of' something, 'think about' something, and the like, we cannot likewise 'believe of' or 'believe about' something. A 'belief', one could say, is more like an attitude than an activity of the mind and in this sense more related to expecting and hoping than it is to thinking (i.e., 'thinking of', 'thinking about', 'thinking over', 'thinking through', etc.) (cf. Wittgenstein 2001, § 574). Therefore, one could also say, we have even less reason to assume that 'belief' is some kind of internal representation like an image or self-talk. Hence, I will not directly address the issue whether or not 'beliefs' are constituted by what we tell ourselves. Besides, I take it that the assumption in CBT is that it is thought that consists of what we tell ourselves and the like, and that a belief can only be what we tell ourselves so long as it is a thought (e.g., there is never any talk of 'automatic beliefs' in cognitive therapy).

4. On declaring one's feelings

However, there is another assumption concerning beliefs that makes CBT put an undue emphasis on automatic thoughts, self-talk and the like. CBT tends to treat any declarative expression of an emotion – such as 'I'm worthless', 'My life's a disaster', or 'I'll never be like them' – as an emotionally constitutive belief. Beck, for instance, asks therapists to be wary of allowing clients to 'preface a wide assortment of opinions, beliefs, speculations, and other attributions with words such as "I feel"' (Beck et al. 1979, p. 37). When a client 'makes a statement such as "I feel I am worthless" or "I feel I have to be successful in order to be happy"', Beck goes on, 'he is verbalizing an *idea* that may be associated with a feeling' (Beck et al. 1979, p. 37). Therefore 'it is desirable for the cognitive therapist to get an early start in making appropriate translations of "I feel..." into "You believe..."' (Beck et al. 1979, p. 37).

In this piece of advice, and in CBT in general, there seems to be at least two related and misleading assumptions about declarative sentences:[8]

1. Declarative sentences are generally treated as constitutive rather than merely expressive of emotional experiences – whereas it would seem that they can be both.
2. Declarative sentences such as 'I feel I am worthless' or 'I feel I have to be successful in order to be happy' are generally treated as *beliefs* without distinction.

(1) What seems misleading about the first assumption is that an internal dialogue, or a statement in therapy, may very well be words that *express* or *describe* an emotional experience rather than words that *constitute* or *cause/determine* it. So, for instance, an internal dialogue, or a statement in therapy, such as 'I'm worse than my mother ever was. I'm not fit to care for my children. They'd be better off if I were dead' (cf. Beck et al. 1979, pp. 150–151) may be words that *express* or *describe* her emotional experience rather than words that *constitute* or *cause/determine* it – much the same way one may, for instance, think or say of a rotten fish that it is disgusting although it is not the thought that makes it disgusting but the way it smells, looks, and tastes. Furthermore, the declaration 'I'm worse than my mother ever was. I'm not fit to care for my children. They'd be better off if I were dead' may not be a literal statement about her motherhood – and, thereby, understood as a statement that may stand in a causal relation to her depression, as CBT would have it – but merely be an *expression* of, say, just how bad a mother the client thinks that she is. In that case it would be off the mark to take the literal meaning as being constitutive of the client's emotional state or to dispute the literal meaning of the expression (unless this indirectly changes the perception of herself as a poor mother).

(2) The mistreatment of declarative sentences in CBT essentially boils down to this: more than merely being beliefs, opinions, or ideas, declarative sentences may have several kinds of meanings. For example, a client may declare that they are worthless or will never be happy without actually believing it. 'I'm worthless', for instance, may be a way of emphatically saying that they are unsatisfied with their life and the way they are living it, or as a way of expressing an experience they have of themselves rather than a literal belief. Saying that 'I feel worthless' may, for instance, be a way of expressing 'a sense of worthlessness' rather than a belief that one lacks worth or value. 'I feel worthless' may be a way of for example saying just how low their confidence in themselves, their likeability, capabilities, and opportunities in life is, and just how bad they feel about this. In such a case, to assume that the client actually *believes* that they are worthless – or even to ask whether or not they believe that they are worthless – would be to misunderstand the meaning of what they are saying. And rather than

translating 'I feel worthless' into 'I *believe* that I am worthless', 'I *feel* worthless' would, in fact, be the more appropriate expression.

An obvious reason why there is a tendency in CBT to interpret any declarative sentence as a belief seems to be the ABC-theory of emotional dysfunction with its emphasis on beliefs as what determines emotional disorders. In the spirit of this theory Ellis writes that in REBT when clients'

> feelings are negative and self-defeating, they are shown how to look for their underlying cognitive and ideational correlates. They are shown how they *create* most of their self-destructive emotions by consciously or (more usually) unconsciously believing and retaining their dysfunctional philosophies. Thus, when they feel hurt about being rejected, they are shown that their feeling probably accompanied (a) the sane Belief 'I don't like being rejected', and (b) the irrational Belief (iB) 'It is *terrible* being rejected. Because I don't like it, I can't *stand* to be rejected in this fashion. I must *always* be accepted!' (Ellis 1994, p. 266)

But how is 'I don't like being rejected' a belief? Would it, for instance, be fitting to ask a person, after they have expressed their hurt about being rejected, whether they are sure that they did not like being rejected, what their reason or evidence for claiming this is, and so forth? That would generally be nonsense. Now, if a person upon having being rejected and hurt says how *terrible* it is and that they can't *stand* it, are they stating a belief? What is obvious is that they are saying something about how they feel about the rejection. But what, if anything, makes it a belief-statement? Ellis would presumably say that it is a belief because it is a self-defining statement about a rejection as 'terrible' and 'unbearable', whereas there is nothing inherently terrible or unbearable about being rejected (cf. e.g., Ellis 1994, p. 117). But how does this make saying that a rejection is 'terrible' a belief? This seems to depend on what the client means by saying that the rejection is 'terrible'. If the client merely is saying, for instance, that the person that did the rejecting meant a lot to the client and that the client is very disappointed, that alone will not make it a belief. How could it? On the other hand, if the client by 'terrible', and especially 'I can't stand it', is thinking for example that they will never meet another person to love, that the person that did the rejecting is a bad person because of it, or that there is no life worth living without this person, then there does seem to be some 'belief' involved. Again, this is just to say that whether or not a declarative expression of an emotion is a belief, or involves a belief, depends on its meaning.

5. The 'B' in the ABC-theory

This naturally brings us to the central idea of CBT, that emotional disturbances are caused by ('irrational' or 'dysfunctional')[9] beliefs (e.g., Beck 1979;

Ellis 1994).[10] As I am about to argue, this ABC-model carries with it at least three misconceptions:

1. Emotional reactions are caused by beliefs which are mentally represented as words or images.
2. To believe something (that disturbs us) is to entertain a proposition.
3. Emotional dysfunction is caused by belief.

Contrary to (3), both (1) and (2) are presuppositions rather than explicit theories, and do not follow from the ABC-model itself. Fair to say, though, especially (1), but also (2), are widespread presuppositions in CBT. And, as we will see, their correctives – as, obviously, the corrective of (3) – should lead to a significant change in therapeutic practice.

(1) To repeat, there is a tendency in CBT to treat beliefs as words or images in our minds waiting to be tracked down and observed. Although I have already addressed this issue above in showing that thinking or believing that p does not imply having the thought that p, and that speaking of beliefs generally is a way of indicating how we take something to be, not a way of naming an internal representation, let me still add a few words regarding mental imagery.

It may be tempting to assume that if a belief is not something that we tell ourselves, then it must be represented in our minds in some other way and that that other way is as an image. In that view, a belief is an image in our minds representing a certain state of affairs. But – to reiterate the point that to believe something generally is a way of indicating how we take something to be, not a way of naming an internal representation – insisting on mental imagery is to misunderstand what it may mean to take something to be a certain way. For instance, if I believe that a tree seen at night is a person, then, surely, it is not a picture in my mind of a person that I see, but simply a person (although it is a misperception; an optical illusion if you will).

Similarly, it would be wrongheaded to presume that if a client believes, say, that he or she is not a likeable person, then that belief is a mental image that the client has of him- or herself as not being likeable. Although it seems fair to describe the belief that one is not likeable as a self-perception, it seems unfair to presume that this belief/self-perception is a mental image. Because a client believes that he or she is not likeable a client might expect that people are going to respond to him or her accordingly. But that does not mean that so long as the client has such expectations because of such a belief, then there must be a mental image present to the client of him- or herself as not being likeable. If anything, rather than describing the belief/self-perception as a *mental image*, it would be more appropriate to describe it as a *propensity* of the client to have thoughts (including mental images) about him- or herself as not being likeable and to make assumptions about how other people relate to, think of, respond to, and so forth, him or her as not being likeable. For instance, because the client believes that he or she is not likeable he or she might incorrectly think that a facial expression is contemptuous and feel dismayed. However, despite the thinking, believing, and the emotional reaction, no mental image needs be present – merely a perception, even if false, of a contemptuous face of flesh and bone.

(2) A related assumption of CBT is that to believe something that disturbs us – whether the belief is conscious, semiconscious or unconscious – is to entertain a proposition (e.g., the proposition, 'I'm unlovable'). This assumption generally seems to go with the assumption that beliefs are internally represented as words or images. But there is another way in which the assumption that to believe something is to entertain a proposition may mislead. One might identify – or rather *mis*identify, as I will argue – a 'belief' with a proposition (or, perhaps more accurately, with an attitude toward a proposition) and assume that a belief simply *is* to entertain a proposition, and, thus, that without the proposition, no belief. However, at least typically, this would be to confuse the linguistic expression of a belief – which is done in propositional form – with the belief itself.

Again, speaking of beliefs may simply be a way of expressing how we take something to be – that is to say, how we perceive, or, more generally, experience something. This is an important point to keep in mind in doing therapy since it points to what the therapeutic focus ought to be and what needs to change in order to change an emotionally held belief. Consider, for instance, the following clinical example by Ellis about a patient who is having problems in seeing that feelings depend on beliefs:

'(...) I know I'm doing better of course, and I'm sure it's because of what's gone on here in these sessions. And I'm pleased and grateful to you. But I still feel basically the same way – that there's something really rotten about me, something I can't do anything about, and that the others are able to see. And I don't know what to do about this feeling.'

'But this "feeling", as you call it, is largely your *belief* – do you see that?'

'How can my feeling be a belief? I really – uh – *feel* it. That's all I can describe it as, a feeling?'

'Yes, but you feel it *because* you believe it. If you believed, for example, really believed you were a fine person, in spite of all the mistakes you have made and may still make in life, and in spite of anyone else, such as your parents, thinking that you were not so fine; if you really *believed* this, would you then feel fundamentally rotten?'

'Oh. Hmm. No, I guess you're right; I guess I then wouldn't feel that way.' (Ellis 1994, pp. 32–33)

Here, again – as I pointed out in the previous section – 'I feel rotten', may in fact be the more accurate expression, rather than 'I believe that I'm rotten' or the like. However, let us, for the sake of argument, go along with Ellis and assume that, in this case, 'I believe that I'm rotten' would be an accurate depiction. In this case, Ellis may indeed be right that the patient would not feel rotten if he believed that he was a fine person. Nevertheless, here one need to keep in mind that what constitutes the belief is not the proposition 'I'm rotten', but the client's self-perception. In fact, the therapy session may be the first time he has formulated his belief as a proposition. For example, the client might be putting himself down a lot (e.g., he thinks that he is too fat, that he will never find someone to love, that he is incapable of bonding with people, and that he is professionally incompetent); he might have a tendency to interpret gestures, facial expressions, comments, and so on, as personal rejections, and might not be able to see how his future could possibly be bright. Of such a self-conception it might be accurate to say that, 'I believe that I'm rotten' or 'He believes that he is rotten'. But note that speaking of *belief* here is a depiction of how he sees himself in the world, as it were. What is primary to the clients' belief is the perception of himself as 'rotten', whereas the proposition 'I'm rotten' is a linguistic expression of his self-perception.

One might want to object to this order and claim that the clients' perception of himself as rotten has to flow from his (propositional) belief 'I'm rotten', and not the other way around. A likely rationale for this assumption is that one cannot perceive that *p* (e.g., 'I'm rotten') unless one has a concept of what the perception is a perception of (e.g., 'being a rotten person'), and that the perception 'I'm rotten' is not possible without applying the concept 'rotten' to oneself. On this account, the client would not have any perception of himself as *rotten* if he did not entertain the proposition that he is 'rotten'. But this exaggerates the power of words. 'I'm rotten' may very well be exchanged by, say, 'I'm nothing', 'I'm worthless', 'I'm a failure' or 'I don't amount to much' – although, perhaps, the word 'rotten' may better capture this clients' particular sense of self – which is to say that 'rotten' is a way of articulating an experience rather than a prerequisite of it. In a similar fashion we should not confuse how something smells with the expression 'What an odor!', or how we take someone's behavior with the expression 'He's being hostile', or our impression of a book with the expression 'It sucks!'[11]

(3) Let us now turn to the general claim that emotions are caused by beliefs. Besides the reservations that CBT misunderstands beliefs as mental representations in the form of words or images, CBT also, I will argue, exaggerates the role of beliefs in our emotional lives. Not only are emotion-eliciting beliefs, as I have mentioned, best understood in terms of how we take things to be. I would like to go further and suggest that how we take things to be is fundamental to our emotions and not always a matter of belief.

Without much ado it seems fair to assume that emotions typically are about something, that they have what philosopher's call *intentionality* (cf. e.g., Kenny 1963; Nussbaum 2001). Anger, sadness, jealousy, anxiety, and so on, are typically about something – say, an offense, the loss of a loved one, someone else's success, or an uncertain outcome. The ABC-theory, as I will argue, mistakenly reduces this aboutness or intentionality of emotions to beliefs.

Consider the following example. A client, Jill, is depressed. When asked what makes her depressed she describes that she is one year away from turning forty and that what pains her more than anything else is that she is childless, without a partner and that her chances of ever having a family seems slimmer by the day. Granted that Jill's depression actually is about these circumstances, then, according to the ABC-theory, it is not the circumstances per se that depresses her, but the beliefs that she has about them (or, more generally, the beliefs that are activated by them). But is this assumption correct?

Let us examine the supposition that Jill's depression is caused by belief. Could it be that her depression simply is caused by the belief that her chances of ever having a family are becoming slimmer by the day? Well it might certainly be true that her depression depends on this belief in that if she did not have it then neither would she be depressed. On the other hand, the logic of the ABC-theory seems to suggest that this belief alone is not sufficient to make someone depressed. On the logic of the ABC-theory, Jill's belief, that her chances of ever having a family are becoming slimmer by the day, is arguably the activating event (A), while the cause of her depression needs to be a belief (or several beliefs) of a more evaluative kind (cf. Daniel 2003). For instance, it may, at least in principle, be possible for Jill to believe that her chances of ever having a family are becoming slimmer by the day and yet not be depressed. In fact, this seems to be a condition for the therapy to be relevant, not to mention successful – for it might very well be a true belief.

So it would seem that a therapist need dig deeper as to what this belief means to Jill in order to understand what causes her to feel depressed.[12] However, although it seems right to assume that the diminishing prospect of ever having a family is depressing to Jill because of what this means to her, it seems wrong to assume that the meaning is a matter of belief. Suppose that Jill has dreamt of having a family her whole life and made that prospect a central part of how she envisions a happy life for herself – so much so that the prospect of not attaining that dream depresses her. How is this necessarily a matter of belief? Here a traditional cognitive-behavioral therapist might suggest (especially if the therapist practices REBT) that Jill believes that she *cannot be happy without a family* (i.e., that she *must* have a family in order to be happy) or that *her life will be awful without a family*. It may also be that she simply believes that she *must* have a family, period (without any specific conditional). In either case, a traditional cognitive-behavioral therapist might argue, her depression may be caused by such beliefs.

However, this is likely to be a mischaracterization of Jill's depression. What is likely to cause Jill's depression is not literal beliefs such as, 'I cannot be happy without a family' or 'My life will be awful without a family', but more fundamentally how she sees her life, as it were, with and without a family. 'My life would be empty without a family' or 'My life would be pointless without a family' may be further ways, alongside the other two beliefs, of expressing how she sees her life with and without a family – where what is critical is not any of these literal expressions, but the outlook that they are expressive of.

Understanding the significance to Jill's depression of how she takes her life to be with and without a family is critical to understanding the role beliefs, and the changing of beliefs, actually may play. For instance, once we realize that, say, how Jill envisions a happy life for herself as one with a family, perhaps a certain kind of family, and how much she desires this, is more fundamental to her depression than any belief, then it should come as no surprise if she remained depressed although she believed that she, at least in principle, in fact could lead a happy and fulfilling life without a family. Changing Jill's beliefs – say, 'I cannot be happy without a family' or 'I'm worthless without a family' – may very well be critical to alleviating her depression. But a change of belief without a corresponding change of perception – say, helping her envision the possibility of a happy and fulfilling life for herself without a family – will be of little help.

In addition to implying what the therapeutic focus ought to be, getting this point says something about the kind of role beliefs play in emotions – where what is essential to the beliefs (and the emotions) are perceptions, not propositions. It also says something about the role speaking of emotions in terms of beliefs may have as a shorthand for a way of seeing something, for how one takes something to be. And, it shows how one can feel something against one's best judgment, as it were (e.g., feeling rotten although one does not believe that one is rotten, or being terrified of the sight of a spider in a book although one knows it is not an occasion for danger).[13]

6. A more philosophically accurate CBT?

Then what are the consequences, if any, of all this to cognitive-behavioral therapy? Here are some brief suggestions.

First, there is the notion of 'automatic thoughts'/'self-talk' as emotion-eliciting words (or images) in our minds. In the practice of CBT, this notion may become falsely asserted and reaffirmed in the relationship between therapist and client as well as in the clients' own therapeutic work outside the therapists' office. For instance, to borrow an example from Albert Ellis, cognitive-behavioral therapists may be in the habit of asking leading questions such as, 'What are you telling yourself anxious and depressed about failing some important project?' And in response a client might rummage for self-statements and reply, 'If I fail at this project, everyone will despise me' or 'If I fail at this project, I'll never succeed at anything important' even if such statements never actually ran through their mind (cf. Ellis 1994, p. xx). Both therapist and client may also falsely assume that if the client cannot find such words or images in their minds, then it is because they are not being conscious enough.

An alternative, and more accurate practice, would be to *not* assume the existence of such emotion-eliciting words and images in the minds of clients. To ask clients, or to make clients ask themselves, what they were thinking when they reacted a certain way may be fine. However, as I have argued, rather than understanding such talk of emotion-eliciting 'thoughts' as representing words or images in our minds, it would be more accurate to understand them as representing how we, as I have put it, *take something to be* or broadly speaking *perceive* something. This means that it should never be assumed that when a client 'thought' something then this 'thought' was words or images in the client's mind, or that the verbal expressions of what he/she was thinking when he/she, say, felt a pang of guilt must reflect a mental process that took place at the time. So, for instance, in finding out what a client was thinking that made them react in a certain way to a situation, we had better focus on the particulars of the situation and what it meant to the client than on what was running through the client's mind at that moment.

Still, encouraging clients to become more aware of what is going on in their minds may be fine so long as this is accurately understood in the broader context of trying to get a handle on how they take things to be. In addition to that it should not be assumed that it is a client's 'self-talk' (or mental images) that causes him or her to react the way he or she does, neither should it be assumed that when such 'self-talk' (or mental images) *does* cause a client to react the way he or she does then it must be in the form of a 'belief'. Moreover, if, as I have argued, a declarative expression of an emotion can be both expressive *and* constitutive of an emotion, and it would be wrongheaded to treat all declarative sentences as beliefs, then this is true of self-talk too.

Secondly, there is the general notion that emotional disturbances are caused by beliefs – be they 'automatic thoughts'/'self-talk' or 'core beliefs'/'core philosophies'. As I have argued, a client's 'beliefs' should not be understood as words or images in the client's mind either. CBT seems generally to have fallen for the misleading temptation of understanding 'beliefs' literally as propositions. Instead beliefs are, again, more properly understood as *how we take something to be* or more broadly *perceive* something. This means that, in the practice of CBT (as elsewhere), the expression of 'beliefs' in propositional form should be understood as *descriptions* (of which there may very well be several alternative ones) rather than expressions of propositions (or equivalent images) in our minds. This also means that the challenge of formulating clients' beliefs is typically not to unearth propositions in their mind, but to find the words that accurately describe how they understand or see something (where how the client understands or sees something cannot be reduced to propositions in the client's mind).

Moreover, as I have argued, although emotions may be said to be caused by how we take things to be, how we take things to be is not always a matter of 'belief'. What this means to the practice of CBT is that rather than exclusively focusing on 'beliefs' it would be more accurate to focus on the outlook of the client more generally. Then, the primary goal of CBT would not be to change the beliefs of the client – especially if these are understood as propositions – but to change how the client, more broadly, sees things. From this perspective focusing on beliefs may be a pragmatic way of challenging, and changing, how a client sees things – but only to the extent that such a focus actually leads the client to develop emotion-altering outlooks.

Notes

*I would like to thank Ylva Gustafsson, Lars Hertzberg, Camilla Kronqvist, and Thomas Teufel for helpful comments on earlier drafts of this paper.

1. Given this approach it is secondary how the cognitive model initially was reached at (cf. Beck 1979, pp. 52 and 83).
2. Exchange 'core philosophy' with 'core belief', and 'self-talk' with 'automatic thoughts', and you will find the same general idea in CT.
3. Characteristically so-called 'masturbatory philosophies'.
4. Some followers of REBT might disagree with this characterization as did Ellis himself who, in the 1990s, claimed that he nowadays emphasized clients' 'self-*meanings* and self-*philosophies*, which may be held in the form of self-sentences or self-talk but also in more complex or more tacit kinds of self-communication' (Ellis 1994, p. 39). But, as I will try to show, there is nonetheless some unclarity concerning the nature of beliefs and thoughts in REBT (and cognitive-behavioral therapy in general) that once resolved should suggest an entirely different approach than the current one. Besides, anyone in disagreement with my characterization should, for instance, consider this relatively recent statement by Ellis (2004):

    People have a basic belief system, or system of values, which they consciously or unconsciously strongly and emotionally believe. And this belief system instantaneously flashes, if you want to use that term, into their heads every time they contemplate a certain feared activity.

    Thus, in the illustration just given, the man who fears subway rides may have the basic philosophy, or set of beliefs, that it is terrible if people stare at him in a pitying manner. And this philosophy, this series of fundamental *assumptions* that he holds at point 'B', induces him, in any given case where he contemplates taking a subway ride, to 'flash' to himself, 'Oh, no! I couldn't do that!' – which is a logical deduction from his illogical or irrational premise – namely, that it is terrible if people stare at him in a pitying manner.

    It is this irrational premise we would clearly bring to awareness and persistently and strongly (emotionally) challenge. (Ellis 2004, pp. 35–36)
5. A first step in the therapeutic process of CBT is to teach a client 'to monitor his negative, automatic thoughts (cognitions)' (Beck 1979, p. 4). How this is done may vary depending on the emotional problem and the clients' capabilities. In the

treatment of depression, however, the client is typically 'instructed to "catch" as many cognitions as he can and to record them' (Beck et al. 1979, p. 150). This is preferably done right after they occur. But if, for whatever reason, a client may not be able to record his cognitions immediately, 'a second method', Beck goes on,

> is to direct the patient to set aside a specific brief period of time, for example, 15 minutes each evening, to replay the events that led to his cognitions as well as the actual cognitions. The therapist instructs the patient to record any upsetting thoughts as precisely as possible. That is, rather than noting, 'I had the feeling I was incompetent in my job', as he would be likely to report the thought in a conversation, the patient would write, 'I'm incompetent in my job', a more precise reproduction of the thought. (Beck et al. 1979)

Beck also suggests further methods in assisting clients to capture their emotional thoughts (cf. Beck et al. 1979).

6. Rather than seeking to 'correct' the thoughts involved in emotional disturbances *new wave cognitive therapies* (such as *acceptance and commitment therapy, mindfulness-based cognitive-behavior therapy* or *dialectical behavior therapy*) seeks to help patients loosen their identification with such thoughts (so-called 'decentering'), to become less caught up and more accepting and mindful or witnessing of them, to be able to see them as 'just thoughts', and thereby change their context and function (rather than content) (cf. Hayes 2004; Marra 2005; Segal et al. 2001).

7. What may easily mislead us into to assuming that thinking consists of an internal representation is a picture of thinking as having an *essence* so that each time we speak of 'thinking' we mean the same thing – a particular kind of activity, process, or phenomena in our minds (cf. Canfield 1994; Hanfling 2002, pp. 135–140; Malcolm 1977, p. 55). If we actually study the circumstances of which we speak of 'thinking' we should notice, however, that it is a term with diverse uses and meanings that need not refer to any particular kind of mental activity. One need only remind oneself of such uses as 'He thought a tree he saw in the dark was a person', 'It was a difficult equation that he thought about for over an hour before he solved it', 'I was thinking to myself what would have happened if I hadn't surprised her', 'It took a lot of thinking to figure out how to carry that sofa up those stairs and into her apartment', 'And all those years I thought she loved me'. It would no doubt be in vain to insist that everyone of these examples have a particular mental activity in common (such as self-talk or mental imagery) that constitutes or defines the thinking.

8. Not surprisingly, from the very beginning cognitive-behavioral therapy has based many of its theoretical assumptions on clients' verbal reports during therapy sessions (cf. e.g., Beck 2005, p. 955).

9. Although both Ellis and Beck emphasize the significance of beliefs in emotional disorders, there are some crucial differences in the kind of beliefs they think are involved. Whereas Ellis typically labels some beliefs as categorically *irrational* – by which he essentially means 'self-defeating' (e.g., Ellis 1994, pp. 25 and 70) – Beck puts an emphasis on the *functionality* vis-à-vis *dysfunctionality* of beliefs. And whereas Ellis thinks that emotional disorders typically involve faulty *global philosophies* (e.g., so-called 'musturbatory philosophies'), Beck thinks that emotional disorders involve *local beliefs* specific to the emotional disorder and life-circumstances of the person suffering from the disorder (cf. Backx 2003, p. 56; Beck 1967,1979, 1999; Beck et al. 1979, pp. 11, 12–13; Beck, J.S. 1995; Dryden 2003b; Ellis 1994, pp. 34–35 and 29–30, 2005, p. 182; Ellis and Blau 1998; Ellis and Dryden 1997, p. 14; Ellis and Harper 1975, pp. 138–139; Padesky and Beck 2003, p. 217).

10. Although both Ellis and Beck emphasize the significance of beliefs, Beck sometimes expresses himself more ambiguously as to exactly what sorts of 'cognitions' determine emotional disorders. For example, in a book coauthored with David A. Clark and Brad A. Alford he writes that,

> The cognitive content or meaning of an event determines the type of emotional experience or psychological disturbance an individual experiences.... Thus (a) sadness involves appraisals of personal and significant loss or failure leading to a sense of deprivation, (b) happiness is associated with thoughts of personal gain or enhancement, (c) anxiety or fear results from evaluations of threat or danger to one's personal realm, and (d) anger the perception of an assault or transgression to one's personal domain .... (Clark et al. 1999, pp. 62–63)

Here Beck and his coauthors describe what determines emotions in terms of 'cognitive content', 'meanings', 'appraisals', 'thoughts', 'evaluations', and 'perceptions'. Are these 'cognitions' identical? But, then, how? However, if one studies the examples Beck gives of the sort of 'cognitions' involved in emotional disorders and how he tends to describe the practice of cognitive therapy, it seems fair to say that he thinks that beliefs are what essentially determines emotional dysfunction. For example, in a book aimed at fleshing out the methodology of cognitive therapy of depression he explicitly writes that its final goal is to help the patient 'learn to identify and alter the dysfunctional beliefs which predispose him to distort his experiences' (Beck et al. 1979, p. 4).

11. Not identifying beliefs with propositions (or attitudes toward propositions) is essential to understanding how we appropriately can ascribe beliefs to infants and animals without linguistic competence (cf. Hutchinson's contribution to this anthology). This is not to deny, though, that some beliefs cannot be had without linguistic competence or that some beliefs (say, in doing philosophy) cannot be divorced from their linguistic expression.

12. For instance, by using the so-called 'downward arrow technique' – a staple technique of cognitive therapy – a therapist could ask, say, 'What is it about the thought of not having a family that you find so depressing?' or 'What would it mean to you if it were true that you would never have a family?' (cf. DeRubeis et al. 2001, pp. 361–362).

13. A paradigmatic example of how emotions may be caused by how we perceive something or take something to be, rather than by beliefs, may be phobic fears of, for instance, spiders – where a person may believe that a spider is harmless and still be terrified by it. Compare this to what David Hamlyn has to say about an irrational fear of mice (Hamlyn 1983, 271–272).

Bibliography

Backx, W. (2003), 'REBT as an Intentional Therapy', in Dryden, W. (ed.), *Rational Emotive Behavior Therapy* (East-Sussex, England, New York: Brunner-Routledge), pp. 55–76.

Beck, A.T. (1967), *Depression: Clinical, Experimental and Theoretical Aspects* (New York: Harper & Row).

——. (1979), *Cognitive Therapy and the Emotional Disorders* (New York, London, Victoria, Australia, Auckland, New Zealand: A Meridian Book).

——. (1999), 'Cognitive Aspects of Personality Disorders and Their Relation to Syndromal Disorders: A Psychoevolutionary Approach', in Cloninger, C.R. (ed.), *Personality and Psychopathology* (Washington, D.C.: American Psychiatric Publishing).

Beck, A.T. (2005), 'The Current State of Cognitive Therapy: A 40-Year Retrospective', *Archives of General Psychiatry*, 62, 953–959.

——., Rush, A.J., Shaw, B.F. and Emery, G. (1979), *Cognitive Therapy of Depression* (New York: Guilford Press).

Beck, J.S. (1995), *Cognitive Therapy: Basics and Beyond* (New York and London: The Guilford Press).

Bernard, M.E. and DiGiuseppe, R.D. (eds) (1989), *Inside Rational-Emotive Therapy: A Critical Appraisal of the Theory and Therapy of Albert Ellis* (San Diego, New York, Berkeley, Boston, London, Sydney, Tokyo, Toronto: Academic Press).

Canfield, J.V. (1994), 'The Phenomena of Thinking', in Teghrarian, S. (ed.), *Wittgenstein and Contemporary Philosophy* (London: Continuum International Publishing Group).

Clark, C.A., Beck, A.T. and Alford, B.A. (1999), *Scientific Foundations of Cognitive Theory and Therapy of Depression* (New York, Chichester, Weinheim, Brisbane, Singapore, Toronto: John Wiley & Sons, Inc.).

Cloninger, C.R. (1999), *Personality and Psychopathology* (Washington, D.C.: American Psychiatric Publishing).

Daniel, D. (2003), 'Rational Emotive Behavior Therapy (REBT): The View of a Cognitive Psychologist', in Dryden, W. (ed.), *Rational Emotive Behavior Therapy. Theoretical Developments* (East-Sussex, England, New York: Brunner-Routledge), 130–159.

DeRubeis, R.J., Tang, T.Z. and Beck, A.T. (2001), 'Cognitive Therapy', in Dobson, K.S. (ed.), *Handbook of Cognitive-Behavioral Therapies* (New York and London: The Guilford Press), pp. 349–389.

Dobson, K.S. (ed.) (2001), *Handbook of Cognitive-Behavioral Therapies* (New York and London: The Guilford Press).

Dryden, W. (ed.) (2003a), *Rational Emotive Behavior Therapy. Theoretical Developments* (East-Sussex, England, New York: Brunner-Routledge).

——. (2003b), ' "The Cream Cake Made Me Eat It": An Introduction to the ABC Theory of REBT', in Dryden, W. (ed.), *Rational Emotive Behavior Therapy* (East-Sussex, England, New York: Brunner-Routledge), pp. 1–20.

Ellis, A. (1989), 'Comments on Mahoney, Lyddon, and Alford's Chapter', in Bernard and DiGiuseppe (eds.), *Inside Rational-Emotive Therapy: A Critical Appraisal of the Theory and Therapy of Albert Ellis* (San Diego, New York, Berkeley, Boston, London, Sydney, Tokyo, Toronto: Academic Press).

——. (1994), *Reason and Emotion in Psychotherapy* (Secaucus, NJ: Lyle Stuart).

——. (1994), *Reason and Emotion in Psychotherapy. Revised and Updated* (New York; Toronto: Carol Publishing Group).

——. (2004), *The Road to Tolerance: The Philosophy of Rational Emotive Behavior Therapy* (Amherst, New York: Prometheus Books).

——. (2005), 'Discussion of Christine A. Padesky and Aaron T. Beck, "Science and Philosophy: Comparison of Cognitive Therapy and Rational Emotive Behavior Therapy"', *Journal of Cognitive Psychotherapy: An International Quarterly*, 19 (2), 181–185.

——. and Blau, S. (eds) (1998), *The Albert Ellis Reader. A Guide to Well-Being Using Rational Emotive Behavior Therapy* (Secaucus, NJ, Toronto: A Citadel Press Book Published by Carol Publishing Group).

——. and Dryden, W. (1987), *The Practice of Rational-Emotive Therapy (RET)* (New York: Springer Publishing Company).

——. and Harper, R.A. (1975), *A New Guide to Rational Living* (Eaglewood Cliffs, New Jersey: Prentice-Hall, Inc.).

Hamlyn, D.W. (1983), *Perception, Learning and the Self: Essays in the Philosophy of Psychology* (London, Boston, Melbourne, Henley: Routledge & Kegan Paul).

Hanfling, O. (2002), *Wittgenstein and the Human Form of Life* (London and New York: Routledge).

Hayes, S.C. (2004), 'Acceptance and Commitment Therapy and the New Behavior Therapies: Mindfulness, Acceptance and Relationship', in Hayes, S.C., Follette, V.H. and Linehan, M.M. (eds), *Mindfulness and Acceptance: Expanding the Cognitive-Behavioral Tradition* (New York and London: The Guilford Press), pp. 1–29.

——., Follette, V.H. and Linehan, M.M. (eds.) (2004), *Mindfulness and Acceptance: Expanding the Cognitive-Behavioral Tradition* (New York and London: The Guilford Press).

Kenny, A. (1963), *Action, Emotion and Will* (London, New York: Routledge and Kegan Paul).

Malcolm, N. (1977), *Thought and Knowledge* (Ithaca and London: Cornell University Press).

Marra, T. (2005), *Dialectical Behavior Therapy* (Oakland, CA: New Harbinger Publications).

McEachrane, M. (2006), 'Investigating Emotions Philosophically', *Philosophical Investigations*, 29 (4), 342–357.

——. (in press), 'Emotion, Meaning and Appraisal Theory', *Theory & Psychology*.

Nussbaum, M.C. (2001), *Upheavals of Thought. The Intelligence of Emotions* (Cambridge, New York: Cambridge University Press).

Padesky, C.A. and Beck, A.T. (2003), 'Science and Philosophy: Comparison of Cognitive Therapy and Rational Emotive Behavior Therapy', *Journal of Cognitive Psychotherapy*, 17 (3), 211–224.

——. and Beck, A.T. (2005), 'Response to Ellis' Discussion of "Science and Philosophy: Comparison of Cognitive Therapy and Rational Emotive Behavior Therapy"', *Journal of Cognitive Psychotherapy: An International Quarterly*, 19(2), 187–189.

Segal, Z.V. Williams, J.M.G. and Teasdale, J.D. (2001), *Mindfulness-based Cognitive Therapy for Depression: A New Approach to Preventing Relapse* (New York: The Guilford Press).

Still, A. and Dryden, W. (2003), 'Ellis and Epictetus: Dialogue vs. Method in Psychotherapy', *Journal of Rational-Emotive & Cognitive-Behavior Therapy*, 21 (1), 37–55.

Travis, C. (2000), *Unshadowed Thought: Representation in Thought and Language* (Cambridge MA, London: Harvard University Press).

Wittgenstein, L. (2001), *Philosophical Investigations: The German Text, with a revised English translation*. 3rd edn (Malden, Oxford, Victoria, Berlin: Blackwell Publishers Ltd).

6

The Self and the Emotions

John V. Canfield

There is no unowned fear, happiness, or grief – these and their brethren always belong to someone. Apparently, then, to get clear on the meaning of first-person emotion utterances like 'I am afraid' or 'I am angry,' we must consider both components; on one hand the fear, anger, and so on, and on the other the I that is afraid, or angry, or the like. In addition it seems plausible that light cast on either of the two – self or emotion – will provide a better understanding of the other. Thus the question, 'So what do we learn about the emotions when we settle on a viable account of the I that has them?' And conversely, what do we learn about the self given a correct interpretation of the emotions. This chapter is an attempt to answer those questions. Insight into what the I is allows us to see aspects of the emotions we might otherwise miss. What surprised me was the reverse: clarity about the emotions leads to a better grasp of the I.

Of course it's not as if everyone agrees on what the self is, and what an emotion is, so that all we would need do is bring the two commonly understood items together and observe their effects on one another. Rather, we can examine those interrelations only under some assumed interpretation of each. According to the account I shall draw on here our common idea of the self is a false or delusory one. This portrayal of the self derives in part from the later Wittgenstein's remarks on 'I'. (See, for example, *BB*, p. 67ff.) As for the emotions side, no general account is possible; the emotional concepts differ significantly. Even in dealing with one idea, such as *fear*, it turns out that there is not one concept to be acknowledged but a range of them. The multi-concept view of fear I work with here is drawn wholly from Wittgenstein. (See Canfield 2007b, pp. 12–27.) My task in this chapter, then, is to see what we can learn about the emotions, and in particular the emotion *fear*, when we assume the interpretation of the self I have been speaking of. And the reverse: what does a multi-concept account of fear tell us about the false self? Otherwise put, given a certain analysis of 'I' and of 'fear' what follows for the analysis of 'I am afraid'? I begin in Section 1 with an account of the false self, and go on in Section 2 to sketch out a multi-concept treatment of the emotion *fear*. I then turn in Sections 3 and 4 to examine 'I am afraid'.

1. The false self

What is the self – the I of 'I think', 'I am afraid', and like pronouncements with 'I' in the subject place? There is a strong tradition that denies the existence of such a thing, but such a rejection is puzzling. It is one thing to present a theoretical account of the I and then deny its existence, but some of the traditions that reject the self are after bigger game. Religions such as Buddhism want to disavow not merely some erudite or technical vision of selfhood but the gut level unsophisticated and simple one we all operate with day in day out. That self, it seems, cannot sensibly be forgone. A philosopher once told me that if someone were to say there is no self, she would ask him who is saying that, and to whom is he saying it. Indeed it seems patently absurd to disavow what seems the core of our being, the very center of the universe, the I that is writing these words or the I that reads them. Hence the puzzle Buddhism sets: what is that common-garden self, that it might not exist?

At one level it seems perfectly obvious what the I is. For us English speakers it is the referent of the words 'I' or 'me' as we use them in daily life; when we say for example, 'I'll get the phone', or 'I'm hungry', or, with Steve Martin, 'Well, enough about me, now what do *you* think of me?' And on and on. In whatever other ways one might wish to categorize the I this much seems certain: it is the thing I am talking about when, as we say, I speak about myself.

So the first step in examining the self is to recognize that it is the assumed referent of 'I', 'me' or 'myself' – or their equivalents in other languages. (For simplicity I ignore those other-language words and focus on the pronoun 'I'.)[1] The I, of course, is taken to be one and the same entity across the spectrum of a given person's many uses of the word. The child's 'I am happy', and the now grown-up person's 'I am tired', talk about the same thing, as do my 'I am angry' and my later 'I feel good'. In all my uses of the word I take it for granted that I'm talking about the same thing, the subject.

The second step in searching out the self is to recognize that this assumption of a common referent for each person is mistaken. An examination of how we use the word 'I' reveals three distinct uses, not one. This plurality of uses results in there being two distinct referents of 'I' for each person and in addition one, as it were, nonreferent. (On this latter point see just below.) I call the corresponding entities the I as person, as narrative self, and as grammatical fiction. To take up the first of these, sometimes when we use the word we are talking about a certain space-time biological and social animal. I will also speak in this case of the empirical self. Examples are: 'I bought a book', 'I live in that house', 'I was born in Switzerland'. The hallmark of these uses is that they refer to actual entities in the world. Claims about them are to be decided on roughly empirical grounds, such as observation or by perusing birth records, and the like.

This type of use is best understood as standing in contrast to the third type I mentioned, self as grammatical fiction. Wittgenstein distinguishes the two uses in the *Blue Book*, calling the one just canvassed the use as object and the other the use as subject. He gives examples of each type. For the first: 'My arm is broken', 'I have grown six inches', 'I have a bump on my forehead' (*BB*, p. 66). For the second: 'I see so-and-so', 'I hear so-and-so', 'I try to lift my arm', 'I think it will rain' (*BB*, p. 67). He distinguishes the two as follows:

> The cases of the first category involve the recognition of a particular person, and there is in these cases the possibility of an error. ... On the other hand there is no question of recognizing a person when I say I have toothache. ... To say 'I have pain' is no more a statement *about* a particular person than moaning is. (*BB*, p. 67)

We can put the distinction in terms of reference: 'I' on its object use refers, 'I' in its subject use does not. One use picks something out from an array of entities, the other does not. When the use of 'I' belongs to the non-referring class of cases I shall speak of the I, there, as a 'grammatical fiction'. It is a *grammatical* fiction because its place as subject term in a statement makes us expect that something corresponds to it. But grammar here misleads us. The I in question is a *fiction* because in fact – as a survey of depth grammar would show – 'I' here has no referent. The point I am defending was made, in essence, long ago in Lichtenberg's well-known remarks on Descartes' cogito argument. Instead of saying 'I think' Descartes ought to have said 'It thinks' as in 'It thunders'. The 'I' of 'I think' has the same status as the 'It' of 'It thunders': on a proper understanding of how in fact those words are used neither functions to pick out a referent. 'The philosophical question, What is the nature of the "I" of "I think"?' is like the question, 'What is the nature of the "It" of "It thunders" or "It is snowing"?' But the mistake of thinking of some uses of 'I' as referring when they do not is not merely a philosophical error; it is rather an unspoken assumption we all make. We all unthinkingly believe that the I that thinks or that is afraid is one and the same as the I that needs a haircut or weighs 160 pounds, and so on.

The other component of our everyday picture of the I is the narrative or fictional self. One of the things that distinguishes a type of use is the nature of the criteria governing the truth of claims made within it. Thus the name 'Robspierre' has a different kind of use than the name 'Julien Sorel' (the hero of *The Red and the Black*), in the main because truths about the former are decided on different grounds from those about the latter. 'Robspierre was executed' and 'Julien Sorel was executed' are each true, but the first is decided on empirical grounds, the second on what Stendhal says in his book.

Some uses of 'I' are fiction-like in significant ways. They are not purely fictional in that no one has authorial control, making it the case that what the writer says about his characters is true. (True of course in the way that fictional statements are true.) But they are fiction-like in that the person who makes them does not do so on empirical grounds. Rather there is in some cases a disconnect from the empirical. These protected instances always concern, directly or indirectly, someone's self-image, his idea of who he or she is.

The contrast between what I called the use as person and the use as narrative self is reflected in the following remark by Bernard Shaw:

> Men and women play at being heroes and heroines, saints and sinners; but they are dragged down from their fool's paradise by their bodies: hunger and cold and thirst, age and decay and disease, death above all make them slaves of reality. (Shaw 1977, pp. 261–262)

Thus while many claims about oneself – about having a certain disease, for example – are subject to empirical criteria, many are not. Those of the latter type may involve what might be called axioms of the self system. We may not think of ourselves overtly as heroes or saints, but merely as, say, fair-minded, diligent and honest, in that we could not be the sort of person who, say, as prosecutor convicts a patently innocent man. Thus even in the face of overwhelming evidence of the convicted person's innocence, a prosecutor might cling to his idea of himself by refusing to admit the truth of 'I brought about the death of an innocent man'. Empirical criteria are here withheld, in the service of one's self-image. Other types of blocking out the empirical are found in society-sanctioned beliefs and ways of action such as those involving ethnic or racial characterizations, whether for good or bad. Thus such and such a group is subhuman and to be exploited or killed without compunction.

There are then three distinct uses of 'I', and these give rise to three different things which we unknowingly treat as identical. All of my uses of 'I' are taken by me to stand for one and the same thing; they stand for *me*. Thus the self qua referent of 'I' is implicitly taken to be the amalgam of empirical self or *person*, 'I' qua *grammatical fiction*, and the *narrative I* just touched upon. We might call this implicitly pictured threefold being the *persona*. However, the cross-category identity we unthinkingly assume to hold across the three distinct entity types is conceptually impossible. There can not be an amalgam of the empirical I and, say, the narrative one. Similarly we cannot say that the numeral 2 on my door and the square root of four are identical. Identities hold only within categories. Thus to the question, 'What makes the false self false?' I would answer that it assumes a cross-category identity that cannot possibly obtain.

2. The multi-concept fear

It is the false self we take to have a given emotion, but what is it we attribute to it? What is an emotion? In sketching out an answer I shall concentrate on the case of *fear*, but not with the idea of finding a general account of it which holds for any of the standard emotions. I will not treat fear as a paradigm case the essential features of which are to be found also among the other feelings. On the contrary, we deploy a great many significantly different language-games with the word 'fear', and the same for all the other emotions. An approach that recognizes that diversity stands in contrast to one which seeks a general account of fear. Why are we inclined to the contrary, general view of fear as the same in all instances? Well, we use the same word in a variety of different occasions, and thus it is tempting to assume that we refer to the same one thing in each case. The problem then becomes to say what that one thing is.

In saying that the question 'What is the emotion *fear*?' has no general answer – that there is not one concept of fear, but many – I follow Wittgenstein, who writes, for example:

> We ask 'What does "I am frightened" really mean, what am I referring to when I say it?' And of course we find no answer, or one that is inadequate. The question is: 'In what sort of context does it occur?' (*PI*, p. 188c)

One reason we find no answer or only an inadequate one is because we are, as suggested, looking for one thing not many, and there is no such one thing. Instead of asking 'What is fear?' we should inquire into the various language-games in which we use the word 'fear' or 'afraid' and so on. These various language- games will be differentiated in part in terms of the contexts in which utterances like 'I am frightened' occur, and it is for that reason that Wittgenstein wishes to address the question of context. The issue now is to identify various of these language-games, and to show how they differ.

There are several ways in which Wittgenstein seeks to highlight the differences between fear language-games. One is to suggest that we develop a genealogy of concepts: 'I should like to speak of a genealogical tree of psychological concepts' (*RPP I*, § 722).

Let us follow for a while the strategy suggested by that remark. Such a genealogical tree might begin with a description of the situation out of which talk of fear might have arisen. In particular, what context might have supplied the foundation for the development of talk of fear? The answer is twofold. What is needed is, first, a world containing danger – predatory animals, harmful events like sudden floods, angry fellow humans, and so on. Second, we need awareness of and spontaneous reactions to such potentially harmful things. Given those responses we can imagine the development of a word-signal indicating someone's fear. There could be a prelinguistic form of such a signal. In a certain context, such as a hunting party stalking a wounded animal that has taken refuge in the bush, one Pearson, J., sees another's (S's) fear-reaction – for example S's sudden adoption of a wary, skittish way of moving – and, catching the attention of others, points to S and mimics his reaction. Given a background of similar events the custom might evolve of saying 'Afraid!' of someone in such a context. Instead of mimicking, a word is used. Both the prelinguistic signal and the verbal one might have the same point, serve the same purpose. Knowledge that someone is afraid might serve to warn us of the danger that person senses, or might, in a more complex, genealogically later case, serve to justify or explain someone's actions. So a primitive language-game for 'fear' or 'afraid' might be one based on observation of another's fear-behavior. We see the person's changed mode of moving in the world, and say of him, 'Afraid!'

We can also imagine a people's development of a first-person version of the use of 'fear' or 'afraid'. In this case 'I am afraid!' or the simpler 'Afraid!' or 'Fear!' would be what Wittgenstein calls an 'Äusserung' – a spontaneous replacement of a behavioral fear-reaction by a verbal or word-borne one. We have then several items to list in our attempts at a genealogical tree: the background context – (danger and a spontaneous fearful physical reaction to it); first- and third-person single word versions of 'fear!'; and their embellishments: 'I am afraid', 'He or she is afraid'. With regard to the latter two we can imagine either that the first-person version preceded the third-person one, or vice versa.

I have indicated something of what Wittgenstein means by a genealogy of concepts; now I want to turn directly to some related remarks of his concerning what I have called a multi-concept reading of 'fear'. Let us look at some of his lists of what he takes to be different language-games with 'fear'. He writes:

> I say 'I am afraid'; someone else asks me: 'What was that? A cry of fear; or do you want to tell how you feel; or is it a reflection on your present state?' (*PI*, p. 187g)

He goes on to say:

> We can imagine all sorts of things here, for example:
> 'No, no! I am afraid!'
> 'I am afraid. I am sorry to have to confess it.'
> 'I am still a bit afraid, but no longer as much as before.'
> 'At bottom I am still afraid, though I won't confess it to myself.'
> 'I torment myself with all sorts of fears.'
> 'Now, just when I should be fearless, I am afraid!' (*PI*, p. 188a)

Wittgenstein then makes the crucial remark that for each of these utterances 'a special tone of voice is appropriate and a different context'. Is it plausible to differentiate concepts in terms of use, and in particular in terms of context and tone of voice? It may appear that if I say 'I am afraid' on several occasions, then no matter what the context and no matter what the tone of voice – whether whisper or shout, say – still I am saying the same thing. Are the instances Wittgenstein alludes to really significantly different? Let us consider some of them, as given in *PI*, p. 187g.

There a cry of fear is set in contrast to a reflection on one's present state. We need a better understanding of each and that is to be gained by the consideration of examples. Walking with others along a narrow path on the edge of a precipitous canyon, a person sees a sudden landslide knock out a portion of the trail in front of them, and cries out: 'I'm afraid!' This is Wittgenstein's 'cry of fear' – our familiar *Äusserung*. In the other case, sitting quietly in the evening I reflect on the day's events. I recall my shock at my friend's news of awaiting the results of a biopsy; I remember thinking that I was overdue for a check up; I think about how nervous and irritable I have been. It dawns on me: 'I am afraid!' What about the third case mentioned in *PI*, p. 187g? I say 'I am afraid' in order to tell you how I feel? We can suppose that what I say is neither a cry of fear evoked by the sight of some immanent danger, nor a report based on a memory-search through the past day's events. Also the tone of voice could differ. I say, in the second case, 'I am afraid' as announcing a revelation: I speak as it were with wonder at what I have discovered. In the third case the context might be that I have been told some while ago that I must undertake a perilous journey. Someone seeing my indrawn demeanor asks me what is wrong and I say 'I am afraid'. Anyone in that context might be. The tone of voice is neither that of a cry nor of an announced revelation; it rather relates what is obvious to me, and what explains my demeanor, namely that I am afraid. Other differences between fear language-games would be revealed by an example-driven examination of the items on the longer list at *PI*, p. 188a.

In *PI*, p. 188a, Wittgenstein then makes this observation: 'It would be possible to imagine people who as it were thought much more definitely than we, and used different words where we use only one'.

We can easily imagine a people who use three different words in the above discussed three instances. Indeed let us suppose they use the terms 'afraid$_1$' 'afraid$_2$' and so on (or 'fear$_1$' etc.). Furthermore a close reading of the list given at *PI*, p. 188a will reveal further marked differences, and justify the employment of distinct words in the disparate cases.

3. 'I am afraid' – part one

On the interpretations I have just sketched there are three versions of the self (that is, three distinct language-games for 'I') and an indeterminate number of versions of (or language-games concerning) 'fear' or 'afraid'. We have already introduced names or labels for different language-games for 'fear' or 'afraid'; let us do the same for 'I'. 'I_1' will stand for 'I' when it is used in cases like 'I am in pain'; I_2 on its use to denote a certain type of animal – a person – and I_3 as standing for the narrative self. What results when we combine that three-part account of 'I' with the previously sketched take on 'fear'? That is, what do we learn when we start with the term 'I' in focus and consider what happens when we attach this or that instance of the multi-concept understanding of 'fear' to produce the various possible utterances of 'I am afraid'? Conversely, what result does our account of 'fear' have for the understanding of self.

I begin with the first question. It would seem that the logical space of language-games for 'I am afraid' could be displayed as follows:

I_1 *or* I_2 *or* I_3 am afraid$_1$ *or* afraid$_2$ *or* afraid$_3$ *or* ... afraid$_n$

Here, as stated, 'I_1' is the use of 'I' as part of an Äusserung, 'I_2' denotes a biological entity and I_3 the self as creature of narrative creature. 'Afraid$_1$' (or 'fear$_1$') is the term used as substitute for a cry of fear, 'afraid$_2$' the word used in the case discussed above, where someone examines his past behavior and feelings and concludes he is afraid, and so on.

It might at first appear that we can combine any of the three language-games for 'I' with any of the different language-games for 'fear' or 'afraid', but this is not so. When 'I' is used as part of an Äusserung – as part of an utterance that substitutes for a cry of fear – it cannot be combined with uses like 'fear$_2$' or 'afraid$_3$' or with any other of the uses we might distinguish, except for 'fear$_1$'. Thus ' I_1 am afraid$_2$' or 'I_1 am afraid$_3$' and so on do not make sense. 'I am afraid' cannot be at the same time a cry of fear and the result of a memory-based investigation into the past day's fearful events.

The case is different with regard to 'I_2' and 'I_3'. When 'afraid' in 'I am afraid' is uttered in its memory-based use, the 'I' in question can be either the biological or the narrative one. From the speaker's point of view, which alternative is the case will be a function of which criterion he, wittingly or unwittingly, employs. The criterion will be either empirical in nature, or fictional, or somewhere in between. Similarly for 'afraid$_3$'.

Without carrying the investigation into the different fear language-games any further, we can see the general purport of looking at that emotion from the perspective of self. The result is simply a further set of distinctions, a finer grained view of the phenomenon. Thus, having characterized, say, the memory-based use of 'fear' we can now see that such a use can be further divided, given the distinction between the narrative and the empirical self. So in general the result of looking at fear from the vantage point of the several uses of 'I' is further to fracture 'I am afraid' into parts. For example, consider the situation described earlier where 'I am afraid' is said by someone after their reflection on the day just spent. The criterion the speaker presupposes might be straightforwardly empirical. Anyone, given the evidence uncovered by his reminiscing – the news of the friend's biopsy, his own nervousness, his irritable reactions and general uneasiness – would rightly conclude that his 'I am afraid' is true. This use is that of 'I_2 am afraid$_2$'. But 'I_3 am afraid$_2$' is also possible. That is, there is a fiction-like use of 'I am afraid$_2$' in addition to one governed by empirical criteria. There are negative as well as positive self-images. 'I am afraid' might conceivably be an axiom of someone's self-narrative. The things that happen to him, the reactions he has to them, and his general demeanor, might all be systematically misread to uphold his belief in himself as a fear-ful person. The narrative self is in charge; the case is one I would depict as 'I_3 am afraid$_2$'. The doubling up we see here will hold across the spectrum of first-person emotion utterances. The fractured I produces twice as many language-games as our original survey of versions of 'I am afraid' might have led us to expect.

4. 'I am afraid' – part two

To take up the converse case, how does it further our understanding of the concept 'I' to consider it from the perspective reached by a study of the emotion *fear*? Well, what was the situation prior to the examination of fear-talk? Uses of 'I' were divided into three types – one giving rise to a grammatical fiction, one concerning a certain biological cum social ani-mal, and one denoting a fiction-like being. Leaving to one side, here and below, the case of *Äusserungen*, I was inclined to picture the field of I-assertions as divided in two: on the one hand those concerning the empirical self and on the other those concerning the narrative one. Thus 'I convicted an innocent man' could be taken as governed by empirical or by quasi-fictional criteria. In general, propositions with 'I' were seen as falling in one or another of those two classes. But a survey of first-person uses of 'fear' shows that this twofold distinction, while viable in itself, is crude; it needs to be augmented by a vast array of further distinctions. Examining the multi-concept view 'fear' shows, as we have seen, that there are not just two forms – empirical and fictional – of 'I fear...' state-ments, but a whole host of them, distinguished in part by context of utterance and tone of voice. 'Empirical', and by extension 'fictional', are family resemblance concepts.

The pay-off of these considerations is a philosophical-anthropological insight into how we proceed through life. Each language-game can be seen as a custom in which such and such sounds have such and such a place in human life. When this particular language-game is in play, things look like *this.* These sounds, with that emphasis, uttered in that context, call forth this reaction. And on and on.

5. Addendum

It might help to bring out the point I am belaboring to consider a position that has been attributed to Heidegger. In an essay in the anthology *What is an emotion?* (Calhoun and Solomon 1984) Charles Guignon writes:

> To be human...is to be contextualized in a world. But that world is not 'private' in any sense. Heidegger...emphasizes the fact that we are contextualized in a culture and in history. In our everyday lives, our routine tasks follow the norms and conventions that are laid out for us in the social world in which we live. (p. 234)

If we add in the norms implicit in the various language-games, the above words could serve to describe Wittgenstein's view of things. Apparently Wittgenstein and Heidegger might agree: Humans must follow the paths set out in the social structures they are acculturated into. The difference between the two thinkers comes out when we ask where each would go from there. Heidegger goes in the direction of the abstract – the highly abstract, or, as the positivists liked to say, of the unintelligible. In contrast Wittgenstein moves in the direction of the specific, the concrete – the individual language-games. Clarity is not sought by means of Heidiggerian neologisms like *Befindlichkeit,* used in an attempt to lay out the essential structures that constrain our 'being-in-the-world'. It is sought rather in a close examination of the mini-customs that constitute our multifarious language-games. The investigation of utterances like 'I am afraid' is one step toward a clear view of human life.

Note

1. See Canfield (2007a), chapters six and seven, for an extended discussion of the false self, including an account of cases where a language lacks an equivalent of our word 'I'.

Abbreviations of works by Wittgenstein

BB   *The Blue and Brown Books* (New York: Harper, 1958).
PI   *Philosophical Investigations* (Oxford: Blackwell, 1967).
RPP I   *Remarks on the Philosophy of Psychology,* Vol. I, Anscombe, G.E.M. and von Wright, G.H. (eds) (Oxford: Blackwell, 1980).
RPP II *Remarks on the Philosophy of Psychology,* Vol. II, Anscombe, G.E.M. and von Wright, G.H. (eds) (Oxford: Blackwell, 1980).

Bibliography

Calhoun, C. and Solomon, R.C. (eds) (1984), *What is an Emotion?* (Oxford: Oxford University Press).

Canfield, J.V. (2007a), *Becoming Human* (Hampshire: Palgrave Macmillan).

——. (2007b), 'Wittgenstein on Fear', in Moyal-Sharrock, D. (ed.), *Perspicuous Presentations* (Hampshire: Palgrave Macmillan).

Shaw, B. (1977), 'Don Juan in Hell', in Weintraub, S. (ed.), *The Portable Bernard Shaw* (New York: Penguin Books).

7
What's in a Smile?

Lars Hertzberg

1. Nature or convention?

Webster's Third International Dictionary defines the word 'smile' as follows:

> smile, *n*.: a change of facial expression involving a brightening of the eyes and an upward curving of the corners of the mouth with no sound and less muscular distortion of the features than a laugh that may express amusement, pleasure, tender affection, approval, restrained mirth, irony, derision, or any of various other emotions.

There are two sides to the definition: certain facial movements on the one hand, and the feelings or attitudes expressed by those movements on the other hand. The definition seems commonsensical enough. However, in reflecting on it we might be led to ask: how is the relation between the movements on the one hand and the feelings and attitudes on the other hand to be understood? There appear, on the face of it, to be two alternatives: either the relation is somehow natural, laid down in the constitution of the human organism, or is it a matter of convention, of rules of expression formed by our culture, and thus, conceivably, varying from one culture to another. Furthermore, it would seem that the way to resolve this issue is through empirical research. Thus, one might try to establish what degree of variation there is between the expressive force of smiles in different societies.

In this chapter, my aim is to show that this view of the issue is misconceived. On the one hand, I want to argue that the question cannot be construed as empirical, but rather is dependent on logical considerations concerning the concept of a smile. On the other hand, I wish to show that, where genuine smiles are concerned, the natural–conventional distinction does not apply. Similar considerations could probably be brought to bear on many other types of facial and bodily expressions; in this chapter, however, I shall in the main limit myself to smiles.

The question whether facial expressions are natural or conventional is pondered by Charles Darwin in *The Expression of Emotions in Man and Animals*. For Darwin, the issue is to be settled by the methods of natural science. He set out 'to ascertain', as he put it,

> independently of common opinion, how far particular movements of the features and gestures are *really* expressive of certain states of the mind. (Darwin 1872, p. 13, emphasis added)

Obviously, what he meant by the features and gestures 'really' being expressive of certain states of mind is that the link was biological. For this reason he considered it

> highly important to ascertain whether the same expressions and gestures prevail ... with all the races of mankind, especially with those who have associated but little with Europeans. Whenever the same movements of the features or body express the same emotions in several distinct races of man, *we may infer with much probability, that such expressions are true ones, –* that is, are innate or instinctive. (Darwin 1872, p. 15, emphasis added)[1]

For Darwin, in other words, studying the meanings of human expressions is a matter of establishing empirical hypotheses concerning the functioning of the organism. Accordingly, the evidence would be the more reliable, the less it was tainted through possible cultural interaction. Apart from alien cultures, Darwin also laid emphasis on observations of infants and the insane. An interpretation is corroborated even further if the corresponding correlations can be found in animals. This would confirm the assumption that they are grounded in some physiological mechanism linking the state of the organism to contractions of the facial muscles. (See Darwin 1872, pp. 81, 204f, 212ff.) On the other hand, any counter-instances – that is, cases of the expression occurring in the absence of the relevant emotion (or, I suppose, the emotion being present without the expression) – would diminish the reliability of the hypothesis.

If Darwin was inclined to regard smiles as natural in the sense defined by him, others have wanted to draw the opposite conclusion, arguing that the meaning of expressions such as smiles is conventional. On this view, our ability to understand the expressions of others as well as our ability to express ourselves depend on our having learnt shared ways of expressing various feelings and attitudes. Putting this point in philosophical jargon, it means that the question of how a smile is to be understood is not, ultimately, an empirical issue, but a normative one. There are rules, or something like rules, for the expression of delight, or amusement, or friendliness, and so on, and our knowledge of these rules enables us not only to make our own feelings known to others, but also to understand how others feel.

What is often advanced as a point in favour of this view is the fact that human expressiveness is subject to cultural variation. This point is emphasized by Nelson Goodman in discussing the concept of expression in *Languages of Art*:

> it seems that a smiling face can hardly express grief, a drooping figure elation... If the connection is not causal, at least it seems constant. But this distinction evaporates too. When the first Japanese films reached us, Western audiences had some difficulty in determining what emotions the actors were expressing. Whether a face was expressing agony or hatred or anxiety or determination or despair or desire was not always instantly evident; for even facial expressions are to some extent molded by custom and culture. What the insular and amateur spectator may take to be instinctive and invariable, the professional actor or director knows to be acquired and variable. (Goodman 1969, pp. 48ff.)

In support of his view, Goodman invokes the following statement by the anthropologist Ray Birdwhistell:

> Insofar as I have been able to determine, just as there are no universal words, sound complexes, which carry the same meaning the world over, there are no body motions, facial expressions or gestures which provoke identical responses the world over. A body can be bowed in grief, in humility, in laughter, or in readiness for aggression. A 'smile' in one society portrays friendliness, in another embarrassment and, in still another, may contain a warning that, unless tension is reduced, hostility and attack will follow. (Goodman 1969, p. 49)[2]

What Goodman and Birdwhistell are claiming then is that the universal of human behaviour sought for by Darwin simply does not exist. How is this disagreement between Darwin on the one hand and Goodman and Birdwhistell on the other hand to be resolved? What is the nature of the disagreement in the first place?

2. Duchenne smiles and non-Duchenne smiles

The question whether smiles are natural or conventional expressions of feeling is actually intertwined with another question: are smiles actions or events? Is smiling something we do, or something that occurs to us? In order to get clear about the first question, I would suggest, we must start by addressing the second.

Now, for a smile to constitute a natural expression in the sense intended by Darwin, it cannot be something *the agent does intentionally*. As we said, for

Darwin the meaning of smiles had to be decided by the methods of natural science. Now, as in any scientific investigation, if the observations are to be trustworthy, no one may interfere with the process. This of course includes the test subjects themselves, that is the persons whose smiles we are observing. If someone, for one reason or another, decides to put on a smiling face, then in that case we would not be dealing with a causal response, untainted by cultural influences. Similarly, the fact that someone might suppress a spontaneous smile brings in an element of uncertainty into the investigation. This fact, it seems, places the study of human expression on a different plane than that, say, of changes in the pulse rate or the dilation of pupils. Darwin, for his part, set this difficulty aside by working on the assumption that facial expressions reveal a person's intentions and thoughts *more* reliably than do words or bodily movements, since they are not as strongly controlled by the will. (On this, see Ekman 2003.)

On the other hand, if smiling is a matter of applying the conventions taught by our culture, as Goodman and Birdwhistell argue, then smiles must, in some sense, be intentional actions on our part. (I shall elaborate on this point in Section 4.) If this is so, then what appeared to be a disagreement about the actual universality or variability of this form of human expression is actually dependent on what I shall argue is a question of logic.

Darwin's problem was picked up in a recent article by Paul Ekman, a leading representative of the psychological study of human expression and follower of Darwin (Ekman 2003).[3] Ekman points out that recent researchers in the field have not shared Darwin's confidence in the reliability of the smile. However, according to Ekman, it all depends on how smiles are defined. He distinguishes between two types of smiles, one of which is reliable while the other is not. To do so, he invokes a classical experiment conducted in the nineteenth century by G.-B. Duchenne (Ekman 2003, pp. 211ff.) (of which there is an illustration in Charles Darwin's *The Expression of the Emotions in Man and Animals*). In the experiment a person's *zygomatic major* muscle is electrically stimulated, causing the corners of his mouth to be strongly pulled backward, producing a powerful wrinkling of his cheeks below the eyes. This contraction is compared to the same man's expression when told a joke. When he was responding to the joke, then in addition to the *zygomatic major*, the *orbicularis oculi* muscle (which orbits the eye) was also active, 'pulling the cheeks up, producing crow's feet, and slightly lowering the brows' (Ekman 2003, pp. 211ff.).[4] In the first case, however, when this muscle was not active, according to Duchenne, 'no joy could be painted on the face truthfully...it is only brought into play by a genuinely agreeable emotion' (Quoted in Ekman 2003, pp. 211ff.)

Ekman introduces the terms 'Duchenne smile' and 'non-Duchenne smile' to distinguish between cheek contractions with and without involvement of the eye-orbiting muscle. According to Ekman, what makes this distinction important is that non-Duchenne smiles can easily be produced at will, while most people are unable to bring about a contraction of the eye-orbiting muscle on demand. Accordingly, his solution to Darwin's problem, in short, is simply to suggest that Duchenne smiles, being independent of our will, are reliable indicators of emotion (in Darwin's sense), while non-Duchenne smiles are not.

3. Actions and expressions

Does this get rid of the problem? I would suggest that it does not. We must ask ourselves: what is the basis for the claim that a certain facial movement is or is not dependent on our will? Ekman suggests a simple test: it is a matter of whether or not the movement can be produced on demand. This seems to presuppose a neat dichotomy between voluntary and non-voluntary movements. In fact, though, I would suggest that matters are more complicated than that. Movements might more adequately be thought of as ranged along a scale. At one end are those that are clearly constitutive of an activity: say, one's hand movements in drawing a picture or putting a needle on a thread; though even here, as we all know, in spite of the high level of attention, the hand will not always do what we mean for it to do. At the opposite end are those that are wholly out of one's control: say, the beating of the heart (even here, one might want to modify this by saying that the heart beats are out of one's *direct* control: one may still be able control it indirectly by various methods). Now breathing or blinking, for instance, fall somewhere between the voluntary and the non-voluntary. I may temporarily take control of them, but normally they occur independently of my conscious intervention. In fact, breathing and blinking are independent of my control in two different senses. On the one hand, they normally go on in their own rhythm without my giving the matter the least bit of thought from one week to the next, and yet I *may* decide to monitor them at any given moment. On the other hand, even if I do try to control them, say, by suppressing them, my ability to do so is limited: sooner or later I am forced to breathe or blink whether I choose to or not. We might say that, while breathing and blinking can be actions, in an important sense they often are not. They can be both *not controlled* in the sense that they normally go on without my attending to them, and *uncontrollable* in the sense that in certain circumstances they will take place even if I try to prevent them.

Now something similar holds for smiles. We may frequently smile without being aware of it, say, in meeting an acquaintance, during friendly conversation or in polite company. On the other hand, on occasion we may find ourselves unable to suppress a smile even though we try (say, on hearing about some misfortune having befallen a rival), or (unlike the case of breathing or blinking) may find ourselves unable to bring off a smile even though we try to (say, in greeting a person we deeply detest). My smiling, when it is not controlled, may be in harmony with my intentions or go against them (I may have decided not to smile when I met this person as a way of showing my displeasure, however, when we met I forgot to check myself). Many other aspects of our bodily demeanour are like this too: laughing, weeping, grimacing, gesturing, bodily posture: they are often not controlled and sometimes uncontrollable.

There is an important difference between smiling and breathing, however. The question what a smile means can be raised in a different sense than the question of what breathing means. Paul Grice has famously distinguished between what he called natural and non-natural meaning (Grice 1957). The fact that someone is breathing heavily may mean that he has a heart condition, or it may mean that he has just been doing some heavy exercise. This would be an instance of what Grice called natural meaning, that is, roughly, a case in which certain causal regularities permit us to infer some condition from the occurrence of a specific phenomenon. On the other hand, when an agent uses words, gestures or other signals in order to convey his intention to get an audience to believe or do certain things, those would be instances of what Grice calls non-natural meaning. In the one case, the person's *heavy breathing* means something, in the other case *he* means something by his words or actions. Now some cases of smiling would fit Grice's definition of non-natural meaning. Thus, if I smile deliberately in order to convince someone of my friendly intentions (and thus perhaps to hide my ill will for him), this would be an instance of non-natural meaning. The problem, however, is that Grice's distinction is too crude to bring out some of the differences that are important in this connection. A deliberate smile would not be called a genuine smile. But on the other hand, there are important differences between genuine smiles and natural signs of the type Grice has in mind.[5]

If you suddenly smile in the course of a conversation and I ask you why you smiled, I expect you to be able to tell me why (although you may not wish to), just as I expect you to be able to tell me why you picked up the phone just now. And there would be nothing hypothetical about your answer, the way there may be if I ask you what made you suddenly breathe so heavily. You may have a heart condition without knowing it, but the suggestion, say, that you might be amused or delighted without being aware of it is incongruous; or better: this is something that would require a special explanation (such as your being ashamed of taking delight in something and hence concealing it from yourself). So even though you did not smile intentionally, and hence *you* did not mean anything by your smile, still your *smile* meant something. In fact, if you honestly have no idea why you made this face, or you come up with an explanation but it has nothing to do with how smiles are normally understood (e.g., you made this face because you suddenly realized you forgot to buy coffee), our response would be to say that you had not really been smiling. In this respect, the kind of meaning smiles have is more similar to the kinds of meaning actions have than to paradigm cases of natural meaning. Analogously, if you have no idea why you picked up the phone, or come up with an incoherent explanation, this would indicate that picking up the phone was not really an action of yours.

Even if I am not controlling my smile, then, it will normally be understood as my response to a situation. And I may be held accountable for smiling or failing to do so. Someone may be insulted by my smile; on the other hand, my failing to smile on a certain occasion may be taken as a mark of grumpiness.[6]

Although (genuine) smiles, then, are not paradigmatic actions, they are part of the way a person becomes intelligible to others. More generally, our intentional actions are embedded in a kind of bodily openness which is to some extent independent of our intentions. Our bodily expressions – facial expressions, postures, gestures, tones of voice – may confirm or belie what we are conveying (as when I fail in faking the warm feelings I do not really have, or fail in concealing the revulsion I feel). Of course, this does not mean that bodily expressions are a fail-safe clue to a person's true feelings. Some people are more at the mercy of their bodily expressions than others. Having control of them is a condition for being adept at poker, and, I imagine, for succeeding as a spy. (Of course, the best way of hiding one's feelings is to give the appearance that one is not controlling one's expressions, rather than simply to blank them out.) One's bodily openness is an aspect of what it means to be an agent. Bodily expressions make it manifest whether someone is acting willingly or reluctantly, confidently or with hesitation, deliberately or absent-mindedly. They mediate her relation to what she is doing, thus making her actions her own (as distinct, say, from the movements of a robot). And it is precisely because in the normal course of affairs people will not or cannot wholly control these expressions that they have this role.

Ekman's suggestion, then, that a certain type of smile (the Duchenne smile) is genuine because it is not under the control of the will is problematic, since it is dependent on a clear-cut dichotomy between voluntary and non-voluntary behaviour which, I have argued, cannot really be upheld. Actually, a central characteristic of expressions such as smiles is that they are on the borderline between intentional actions and involuntary reactions.

4. Smiles and conventions

Smiles then, are not natural expressions in the straightforward sense intended by Darwin (or by Grice). Does this mean that they are to be regarded as conventional expressions?

Consider, once more, the passages from Goodman and Birdwhistell quoted in the introduction. It might appear that they are making an important point there. They seem to be exposing what might be thought to be a naïve view of human expressiveness: the failure to realize that human expressions are not immutable and universally intelligible. However, I would argue that it is actually Birdwhistell who is adopting the naïve view. Thus, in writing, '[a] "smile" in one society portrays friendliness, in another embarrassment and, in still another, may contain a warning that, unless tension is reduced, hostility and attack will follow', he is evidently assuming that smiles in our society always have one and the same meaning[7]: in 'our culture', of course, there are not only friendly smiles, but also smiles from embarrassment, menacing smiles, and so on. The variations to which he is drawing attention are not dependent on differences between cultures, but differences between different kinds of smile in different situations.

A celebrated case of cultural variation is that of the Japanese servant who smiles when telling his master his child has just died. However, the fact that a Japanese may smile in a situation when a European would be expected to express grief does not mean that smiles are expressions of grief in Japanese culture. The story of the smiling servant is usually accompanied by the explanation that it is considered unseemly for the servant to burden his master with his own grief, thus hiding his feelings under an expression of well-being. As a matter of fact, it is only because we see the Japanese servant's smile in the light of some such comment that we are able to see it *as a smile*. If we were to see it as an expression of grief, it would have nothing smile-like about it, no matter how similar a smiling face and a grieving face might be from an anatomical point of view.[8] In fact, the case of the Japanese servant is not, perhaps, altogether different from that of someone in our culture who makes a funny story out of her dread for an impending operation. Her laughter may be a way of covering up her worry or giving vent to it, but for all this laughter is not a conventional expression of worry.[9] The Japanese servant smiles precisely because of what smiles mean both to Japanese and to Westerners.

In fact, Birdwhistell is wrong in suggesting that his examples of what smiles may mean constitute discrete and disparate units of meaning. Rather the various feelings a smile may express are related to one another like a family: if a smile is menacing it is because it is seen as projecting superiority and self-assurance; an embarrassed smile is also disarming, and so on. (Think also about the ambiguity of a sardonic smile.)

Just like the different feelings and attitudes smiles express do not constitute disparate units, smiles form part of a continuum of human expressions. Part of what is involved in smiles being, as I suggested, a form of bodily openness, is that they are a living, organic feature of the human face. In *Remarks of the Philosophy of Psychology* (Vol. II) Wittgenstein writes about the difficulty of imagining

a facial expression not susceptible of gradual and subtle alterations; but which had, say, just five positions; when it changed it would snap straight from one to another. Would this fixed smile really be a smile? And why not? (Wittgenstein 1980, § 614)[10]

A face which switched from neutral to a broad grin and then back again without transitions would not really come across as smiling or indeed as expressive in any way, rather it would strike us as undergoing some strange contortions. The face would not *be alive* with the smile. In the light of this, we can understand why there is an internal connection between smiles and laughter: a genuine laughter is normally preceded and followed by a smile. A smile, we might say, holds the *potential* of laughter.[11] If someone produced a laughter-like sound and face preceded and followed by a straight face, this would simply strike us as bizarre.

Smiling might be compared with the tone of voice in which something is said, not with the particular things said. Words do not form a continuum the way smiles or tones do. In this way, too, smiles are different from conventional signs like shrugging one's shoulders to express ignorance or indifference, shaking one's head in negation, etc. These are signs that we are taught to use, their meaning varying between cultures (thus, the Indians shake their heads in affirmation). Smiles hold a different relation to the feelings they express. The expressiveness of a smile is dependent on the fact that we do not normally smile for some particular purpose. In the case of intentional smiles, we might conceivably use a vocabulary of instruction and criticism, we might speak about someone's 'trying to smile', about 'convincing' or 'unconvincing' smiles, or say things like, 'Is that supposed to be a smile – you have to pull the corners of your mouth much further back', 'Am I smiling broadly enough?', 'What's wrong with this smile?', and so on. These kinds of remarks make sense because of the contrast with genuine smiles: it is genuine smiles we are trying to emulate. A genuine smile is not something put forward for approval. Again, it would be strange if someone explained having smiled in an inappropriate situation by saying he had forgotten what a smile meant, or that he had got the meanings of smiles mixed up (the way a visitor to India might shake her head in denial by mistake).

We should note that this difference is not just psychological. Someone might think that the reason we do not normally use a vocabulary of instruction and criticism in speaking about people's smiles is that we usually follow the procedure 'unthinkingly', just as when riding a bike or driving a car we do not usually have to think about the way to do it. Sometimes such an idea will be put by saying that we have 'internalized' the skill of smiling. In saying this, however, we would be missing the point. If we see someone riding a bike it makes no difference to our description if we find out that he is continually thinking about the way he does it, rather than doing it all automatically. However, if we found out that someone we took to be smiling had all the while been rehearsing the correct ways of curling her lips, had calculated the correct moment at which to let her smile break out, and so on, this would probably make us withdraw the claim that she had been smiling, or at least modify it: we would no longer use terms like 'warm', or 'shy', or 'irrepressible' in characterizing the smile (except ironically), and we would no longer, for instance, regard her expression as a reason for thinking she was pleased or was a friendly person.[12]

In sum, then, to view human expressions as conventional signs is to think of them as involving mastery of expressive conventions. But this presupposes that in expressing ourselves, in smiling, or frowning, or weeping, or in making angry or contemptuous faces, and so forth, we are normally making intentional use of those forms of expression, rather as in speaking we normally use the words we do by intention. In adopting such a view, however, we should be obliterating the distinction between natural and intentional, between genuine and counterfeit expressions. This would mean rendering the significance we attach to the expressiveness of other people unintelligible.[13]

5. Two answers in search of a question

It seems, then, that there is no answer to the question with which we began. The idea that smiles might be connected to feelings such as pleasure, friendliness, and so on, through some natural law is problematic, since smiles are not, normally, beyond our control, and hence it is unclear how those connections could be checked, as it were, independently of the agent's 'interference' – but neither are smiles to be regarded as learnt expressions of those feelings since they are not, primarily, intentional actions. However, there seems to be something problematic about the question itself. It presupposes that we could single out a certain set of facial movements and a certain set of feelings, and then inquire into their correlation. But the whole idea of identifying expressions and feelings independently of one another is questionable. On the one hand, as was suggested above, we would not experience a facial movement as a smile unless the situation was one in which smiling made sense, in one way or another: for example, one in which she might be understood to be pleased, or amused, and so on (and here it would not matter whether the movement was what Ekman calls a Duchenne smile or not). On the other hand, our understanding of what someone is feeling is partly a reflection of the way the feeling gets expressed (coloured, of course, by our familiarity with that particular individual's way of expressing herself). This point is nicely expressed in the following passage by David Cockburn:

> the pleasure that we take in another's joy often involves, or is closely connected with, a pleasure that we find observing the other; and, in particular, observing their facial expression. The parent delights in the

expression on his child's face as she opens her presents. The expression on his child's face, the sound of her laughter, and so on do not simply play the role of *evidence*; the particular way in which he is moved cannot be characterized independently of the pleasure that he takes in her manifestations of joy. (Cockburn 1990, p. 67)

This passage brings another point into focus. If we wish to consider smiles as a phenomenon of human life, our consideration should not be limited to the fact that people will display particular facial movements in particular situations. The fact that others will usually be touched or moved by those movements in ways appropriate to the situation – will be delighted, relieved, encouraged, feel ready to forgive, feel threatened, humiliated, and so on – is as much part of the natural history of smiles as those facial movements themselves. This point is noted by Wittgenstein at the conclusion of the remark quoted above. The questions at the end of the quotation, 'Would this fixed smile really be a smile? And why not?' are the sort of semi-rhetorical question typical of Wittgenstein. His response to them is indirect. He writes, 'I might not be able to react to it as I do to a smile. Maybe it would not make me smile myself.' The suggestion, apparently, is that whether or not we would call this expression a smile – the use of the word, after all, is not so precisely circumscribed, and in fact it does not really matter whether we would call it a smile or not – these facial movements would lack a feature that is characteristic of the situations in which we normally speak about people smiling: they have no tendency to move us in the appropriate ways. Our likeliest response to the fixed smile, I would suggest, would be one of astonishment, maybe even revulsion. (This is not to say that we could not gradually come to respond to it as a smile; we might, e.g., become accustomed to it as the expression of someone whose facial muscles had been injured.)

The concept of a smile and what it may signify does not enter our life through a discovery. Neither have smiles been introduced as a social convention. The word 'smile' is learnt in a setting in which smiles already have a place, in which people smile and respond to smiles without giving the matter much thought. Both the view of smiles as natural phenomena and the view of them as applied conventions, then, are expressive of the same misconception: the idea that smiles can be studied as physical configurations without regard to their significance.[14]

Notes

1. Thus, he sent out a questionnaire to missionaries and others who were in contact with aboriginal tribes, containing questions like the following:

   When in good spirits do the eyes sparkle, with the skin a little wrinkled around and under them, and with the mouth a little drawn back at the corners? (Darwin 1872, p. 16)

2. From a talk given at the Maryland Institute of Art, 4 December 1964.
3. Ekman has also published a new edition of Darwin's book with his own introduction, afterword and commentaries. (London: Fontana Press, 1998.)
4. We are not told whether the joke was a poor one and he smiled politely or whether it was a really good one; in any case it obviously did not crack him up. To judge by the illustration, the smile was rather on the polite side. Anyway, the example makes one realize how hard it is to 'read' an expression from a picture, especially if the person is someone you do not know.
5. Grice considers the case of frowning, which he argues can either be caused by displeasure or be an intentional way of showing displeasure.
6. Even though we may smile when we are by ourselves, smiling is something primarily done in company. In this way too smiles are different from heavy breathing. We usually smile *at* someone. It would even be weird for someone to smile to himself while in the company of others, rather like talking to oneself while others are present.
7. Another obscurity concerns the concept of society. In speaking of 'our society' is Birdwhistell referring to 'Western civilization' or to American society, to the east coast, or possibly to Maryland? The reason this question is simply ignored may be that there is a tendency here to think about cultures as analogous with languages, as constituted by a code through which various human actions get their significance, and which is more or less clearly delimited from neighbouring codes. For one thing, however, this view neglects the fact that no such unified, clearly delimited codes exist: some practices are highly local, others are widespread, some even universal. Thus, what is to count as belonging to *one* culture is not given once and for all, but depends on the context of comparison. And besides, many of the difficulties we may have in finding our feet with people from a foreign culture have nothing to do with codified ways of acting, but are simply due to the fact that their habits of feeling and expression are different. In this regard, the difficulties we may encounter in trying to understand people in a strange culture are similar to the difficulties we may have in coming to understand unusual or eccentric individuals in our own. Robert C. Solomon (2002) makes a related point by drawing attention to the differences in what he calls 'display rules' for different groups of people, say, different classes or genders (p. 119). However, I would suggest that to speak of rules in this connection might give a misleading impression of the degree to which these variations are codified.
8. Notice that Birdwhistell, in the above quotation, puts the word 'smile' in scare quotes. Evidently, he is wavering on whether a certain facial movement is indeed to be called a smile independently of its meaning.
9. The difficulty, mentioned by Goodman, that a Western audience may have in understanding Japanese films, I would suggest, is not due simply to our inability to read their facial expressions but rather to our ignorance of their whole society, including the kind of significance various situations have for those involved, conventions regulating relations between people, and so on, and also to differences in habits of feeling of the kind discussed above (note 6).
10. I have slightly deviated from the translation by C.G.Luckhardt and M.A.E. Aue.
11. Consider the German '*lächeln*' – '*lachen*' (a smile is described as small laughter), the French '*sourire*' – '*rire*' (a smile is a subdued laughter). The relation between smiles and laughter can be compared to the relation between colours. It is part of how we speak about smiles and laughter that there is a transition from one to

the other; just as it is part of what we mean by blue and green that there is a gradual transition from blue to green.

12. As for the notion that we *internalize* modes of conduct and expression, I find the term too vague to be illuminating, although I suppose it would be correct to say that smiling is an internalized response if all this means is that our propensity to smile, the way we smile, and so on, is to some extent shaped by the expressive behaviour of those around us. But this does not mean that learning to smile means coming to do unthinkingly what we had done before deliberately.

13. In this context, Goodman quotes, with approval, the choreographer and director Doris Humphrey:

> Along the way I have often been obliged to teach young men how to make love, and young girls how to be predatory or flirtatious or seductive, and I've had to advise everybody how to express anxiety, alarm and endless other emotional states. They may have felt these things, but the movements for them are complete strangers. (Goodman 1969, p. 49)

Now if young men and girls actually had to wait for the intervention of Ms. Humphrey or her colleagues in order to acquire the ability to make love or to be flirtatious or seductive, humankind should probably long have been extinct. What she seems to be overlooking is the fact that she had to teach the representation of those attitudes *on stage*, not their expression in the stream of life.

14. I wish to thank David Cockburn, Ylva Gustafsson and Michael McEachrane for useful comments on an earlier version of this chapter.

Bibliography

Cockburn, D. (1990), *Other Human Beings* (Basingstoke: Macmillan).

Darwin, C. (1872), *The Expression of the Emotions in Man and Animals* (London: John Murray).

Ekman, P. (2003), 'Darwin, Deception, and Facial Expression', *Annals of the New York Academy of Sciences*, vol. 1000, pp. 205–221.

Goodman, N. (1969), *Languages of Art* (London: Oxford University Press).

Grice, H.P. (1957), 'Meaning', *Philosophical Review*, 66, 377–388. See http://www.ditext.com/grice/meaning.html

Solomon, R.C. (2002), 'Back to Basics: On the Very Idea of "Basic Emotions"', *Journal for the Theory of Social Behaviour*, 32, 115–144.

Webster's Third New International Dictionary of the English Language Unabridged (Chicago, etc: Encyclopædia Britannica, Inc., 1971).

Wittgenstein, L. (1980), *Remarks on the Philosophy of Psychology*, Vol. II (Oxford: Basil Blackwell).

8
Emotion, Expression and Conversation

David Cockburn

1. Introduction

Emotion does not sit easily within the traditional mind–body divide: the divide that (at least on standard readings) finds its purest articulation in Descartes, but that, I believe, continues to have a powerful, and undesirable, grip on much philosophical thinking. In *The Passions of the Soul* ([1649] 1989) Descartes presents a detailed and fascinating placing of emotion within a view of the real self as a unified, rational, mind or soul lodged within the body: the former being the seat of consciousness, the latter an external and alien force to be struggled against in my attempts to think clearly and to act as I should. An emotion, say of fear, being a state of consciousness, is a condition of the soul. It is, however, a condition of the soul that is largely determined by *bodily* forces, and, as such, is characteristically an obstacle to clear thinking. It is, then, bodily processes that generate the feeling and make it resistant to alteration by rational thought. Further, it is those same bodily processes that are *directly* – that is to say, not by way of the emotion – responsible for what we normally, mistakenly, think of as the behavioural, the bodily, 'manifestations of emotion': that are responsible, for example, for the tremor that we hear in his voice or the transformation that we see in his face. One way to characterize my aim in this chapter is to say that I hope to clarify the relation between these two strands in Descartes's thinking: the radical lack of connection between emotion and behavioural manifestations[1]; and the idea that to experience a situation through an emotion is to experience it in a *confused* way – the idea, that is, that an emotion is, by its very nature, an obstacle to clear thinking, rather than itself being a way of thinking (clear or confused) about a situation. I will suggest that we can only attain clarity here by moving away from Descartes's exclusively first personal perspective: by giving central place to the way in which *another's* emotions may enter into my thought about, and relations with, her.

Within more recent philosophy the difficulty in placing emotion within a traditional mind–body divide finds its clearest expression in the topic's almost total neglect within discussion of huge swathes of the central concerns of the Anglo-American tradition: in the idea that the topic of emotion is one that can be left to a few specialists who happen to be interested in that kind of thing. Indeed, I am inclined to suggest that the neglect of the topic is one of the central manifestations of a continuing grip of Cartesianism. However that may be, I hope to suggest that illumination is to be gained from giving the emotions a more central place in philosophy; and, in particular, in our philosophical thinking about our relations with others, and, with that, in our philosophical thinking about language.

I will make one further, related, introductory comment. It is widely accepted that there are certain emotions that can only be ascribed to a being that possesses language. While the point has a number of dimensions I will focus on its application to possible *objects* of emotion. Thus, it will be generally agreed that it makes no sense to suppose that a dog might hope that it will be sunny next Thursday, or feel depressed about the result of the election. Now we can ask: *how* does the possession, or lack of it, of language bear on the possibility of ascribing particular emotions to a creature? We may be inclined to picture it like this: 'It is a precondition of such feelings that one possesses certain concepts: certain temporal concepts, the concept of an election, and so on. But the possession of such concepts requires the possession of language'. I believe that proposals of this form are not simply unilluminating but fundamentally misguided. They are unilluminating in that the term 'concept' as it appears in that line of thought is a fudge in much the same way as Wittgenstein suggested that the term 'mental' is often a fudge: we wheel it in to paper over a gap in our thinking; to mark something we feel to be of enormous importance but that we hope will take care of itself. But further, in its suggestion that 'concept possession' is a *precondition* of undergoing certain emotions, this picture reflects, and reinforces, the marginal, or secondary, position that the emotions have tended to occupy in representations of human life in the Anglo-American philosophical tradition. For the notion of a 'concept' that is at work here is one that involves giving priority to our 'cognitive' relation to a situation over our 'affective' relation to it. I hope that what I say will indicate another way in which we might think of the relation between an individual's possession of a language and the possibility of ascribing particular emotions to her.

2. The bodily expression of emotion

I will begin with a form of behavioural manifestation that is seriously marginalized in Descartes's, and much subsequent, discussion: the bodily expression of emotion. It might be said that we recognize most directly what another is feeling, not in the intentional actions grounded in the feeling, but in her posture, gesture, and, above all, facial expression: the non-purposive bodily expressions in which her anger or fear are manifested. Certainly there will not always be a straightforward answer to questions of the form: was his scream on seeing the tiger an attempt to warn the others or a direct expression of his terror? But while the line that divides 'bodily expression' and 'intentional action' is not a sharp one, it is important to recognize that there is a genuine distinction here: to recognize that the belief-desire psychology that dominates certain areas of philosophy, with its exclusive emphasis on purposive action, involves the marginalizing of something that is central to our life with others.

Much of what we learn about others we learn through their emotional expression: the surprise, anger, joy, dismay that we see in the other's face and general demeanour, or hear in her voice. In the cases to which I will give a central place, this point has two faces: two faces that look in rather different directions. First, we might say that, in contrast with what we learn of others through their *actions*, our recognition in these ways of the other's condition is unmediated. From his bodily demeanour, his facial expression, the tone in his voice, we see straight off that he is angry or afraid; and that he is angry with, or afraid of, *her*. As Wittgenstein remarks: 'The fear is there, alive, in the features' (Wittgenstein 1968, § 537). And second, the sense in which we learn about another through her emotional expression is, or may be, one that, in involving a reference to her *life*, takes us beyond the present instant in a way that stands in contrast with the sense in which we learn about her through her bodily expressions of sensation. I will take these two points in turn.

To say that 'we see straight off that he is angry' is not to deny that, on particular occasions, we can be mistaken about what we think we see: we can misread another's bodily expression, and the other may deliberately suppress or feign particular expressions. What, then, *is* the point of this way of expressing the matter? Here is one way in which we might articulate the point. Since bodily expression, in contrast with intentional action, is not goal-directed, the form that it takes on a particular occasion is not mediated by any beliefs about the best way to achieve a goal. My fear on noticing the bear may lead me to burst into song; but this behaviour is only to be recognized for what it is in the light of my belief that this is the best way to avoid being attacked. By contrast, while I may, in a particular case, have reason to *suppress* my startled cry or the expression of horror in my face, if I do not suppress them no further beliefs need be assumed for them to be recognized as expressions of fear. This is closely connected with the fact that purposive action involves a form of dependence on *context* – in the way in which the context presents practical considerations of which account must be taken in deciding how to act – that is absent with bodily expression. Perhaps the force of these points is most clearly seen in the fact that there is such a thing as mimicking fear or anger as such; and that this involves reproducing the *expression* of one who is fearful or angry.

Another, closely connected, way in which we might articulate the significance of the contrast between 'expression' and 'purposive action' is in terms of the idea that there is a 'conceptual connection' between fear or anger and its expression in behaviour: in terms of the idea that certain patterns of expression are 'criteria' for what another is feeling. This formulation may go with the idea that the key point is of this form: grasping what fear or anger is involves accepting that certain forms of expressive behaviour are, other things being equal, an 'adequate basis for judgements' about how another feels; there is no step, after I have learned what anger is, of noticing that anger characteristically finds expression in *these* ways.

But while I am sure that there is something right in both of those lines of thought, I suspect that what *is* right in them will be seen most clearly if we give central place to the role that bodily expression has in our relations with each other. Bodily expression, and in particular facial expression, has a central place in our interactions with each other: is a central form of our *contact* with others. I respond to the other's smile of pleasure or amusement with a smile. I turn away from the other's angry gaze, or return her friendly or loving gaze. I shrink in the face of the other's manifest hostility or anger, and the other may respond to my shrinking, perhaps with a softening of her expression; as, more generally, she may respond to my timidity with an encouraging smile. In many cases this contact involves an acknowledgement of a world that we share with the other. We exchange a smile at the remark just made, a look of surprise when the guests arrive on time, or a fearful glance when we recognize the danger. What is involved here is, or may be, not simply *noticing* our common response, but a *sharing* of it. We are linked together in our shared response to the situation: this mutual acknowledgement of the surprising or dangerous aspect forms a background to the way in which we carry on together in this situation.

My examples there are all essentially visual: indeed, doubly so. I respond to what I *see* in the other; and what I see centrally involves the other's *look*. The latter point itself has two faces: there is what, in our shared situation, the other looks at, and there are the ways in which the other looks at me. The first of those involves an essential linkage between expression and its context to which I will return. The second is an important aspect of the mutuality of our relations in such contexts: the sense in which the other features in my life, not simply as the object of my response, but as one with whom I am in interaction. More generally, for the sighted, in our culture, the face is a key locus of emotional expression, and, with that, of our interactions with each other. That said, a fuller discussion would require reference to a range of other factors: including gesture, bodily demeanour, gasps and groans, tone of voice. It would require reference, too, to the tactile interactions – the way, for example, in which we may grab each other in joy or horror – that may share the essential mutuality of visual interaction, but whose centrality varies significantly across different relationships and different cultures. It would also require a reference to speech: to which I will return.

If we want to get clear about the importance that emotion has in our lives we must note how, in ways such as these, bodily expression plays an important part in our relations with each other. While I suggested that there is something right in the idea that there is a 'conceptual connection between an emotion and its characteristic expression in behaviour', where that is linked with the idea that another's bodily expression can be an 'adequate basis for judgements' about how she feels, this way of speaking may, in its emphasis on *judgement*, fail to get us to the heart of the matter. One for whom bodily expression had nothing like the significance that it has for us would not simply be one who did not *say* 'He is angry', 'She is afraid', and so on, in the circumstances in which we do. He would be one in whose life the emotions of others did not have anything like the place that they have in our lives. As we might put this, it is in this place that expression has in our personal interactions that we see the *importance* of the connection between emotion and expression – and so see its character as a *conceptual* connection: a connection that, contrary to Descartes's picture, is fundamental to the sense of our talk about emotions. Similarly, while I suggested that the special place of bodily expression, in contrast with intentional action, may be found in the fact that, not being goal-directed, it is unmediated by any beliefs about the best way to achieve her goals, there is a danger of misconstruing the truth in that. It is not that its being unmediated entails that it is a direct revealing of her, and *that* is why we give it – and are right to give it – a special place in our thought about her. For the sense in which we take it to be a 'revealing of her' is not prior to, and independent of, the special place that such expression has in our relations with others. We take such expression to be peculiarly revealing of others *in the sense that* it has this special place – the place that I have tried to characterize – in our relations with them.[2]

3. Expression, context and life

I have been speaking of the sense in which in bodily expression we may, in contrast with intentional action, have immediate *interaction* with – and, with that, unmediated recognition of – another's emotions. I want to turn now to the way in which another's expression may, in contrast now with the expression of *sensation*, be revealing of her in a way that takes us beyond the present instant.

I suggested that purposive action involves a form of dependence on context that is absent with bodily expression. This is not to deny that there are ways in which the latter is dependent on context. While what I see in a face, taken in isolation, may, in a particular case, immediately strike me in a certain way, knowledge of the context may transform, or remove an ambiguity in, what I see. To take an example of Wittgenstein's, what strikes me immediately as a kindly smile in one context (he is smiling down on a child at play) may, in another context (he has just heard of the suffering of an enemy), strike me immediately as a malicious grin (Wittgenstein 1968, § 539). The faces may 'strike me immediately' in these ways to the extent that it may take a great effort for me to acknowledge that what is to be seen in the two faces is exactly the same – in the (rather specialized) sense in which this is so.

On the one hand, then, what I see in her may, taken in isolation from any context, immediately strike me in a certain way; and, with that, may clearly suggest a context of a certain form: for example, that she has just been treated in a wounding way by someone she cares for deeply. On the other, knowledge of the context may play a crucial role in what I see in her. It is, I believe, important to the place that the expression of emotion has in our lives that its relation to context may involve movement in these two different directions. Were it not for the first possibility, there would be no such thing as learning about what is going on through noticing her reaction to it: 'learning', either in the sense that I simply had not noticed the incident to which she is responding, or in the sense that I had not appreciated the aspect of it that her expression draws to my attention. Were it not for the second, 'recognizing what another is feeling' would not be learning about *her* in a sense that I want now to highlight.

Wittgenstein remarks:

> Only surrounded by certain normal manifestations of life, is there such a thing as an expression of pain. Only surrounded by an even more far-reaching particular manifestation of life, such as the expression of sorrow or affection. And so on. (Wittgenstein 1967, § 534)

Our talk of physical pain would not get a grip on a life in which what we think of as bodily expressions of pain came and went with the ticking of a clock. But there is, Wittgenstein suggests, a richer sense in which this is so with sorrow or affection: a richer sense in which there is such a thing as 'seeing that another is sad' only in so far as what we think of as the bodily expressions of sadness characteristically fit, in certain familiar ways, into the pattern of a person's life. Someone who is sad is someone from whom certain forms of behaviour can be expected; and the importance that the facial expression of emotion has in our lives is crucially linked with this. In recognizing as dismay another's facial expression on hearing the news of his brother's success we learn something about *him*; and the sense in which we learn something about him, as we *don't* learn anything about him in recognizing that he has a pain in his toe, is inseparable from the way in which certain other things can be expected from a person with such a face.

This idea of 'other things that can be expected' from one whose response we take in a certain way is closely linked with something of which I spoke earlier: the richness of the situation that is relevant to our characterization of someone's emotion. For the context that is relevant to our identification of what he feels as *grief* or as *shame* is that in which the relevant further behaviour will be played out. Grief on the death of a loved one is a response to the disappearance of one around whom one's life revolved; and the further behaviour that we will expect from someone in whose face we identify deep grief involves, for example, startled confrontations, and attempts to cope, with the hole that is left by what has disappeared from her life.[3]

A final point here before moving on. I have noted the way in which what we see in a face may be dependent on context. There is a sense in which what we see in a face may be relatively *independent* of the character of the face that is also worthy of note. I may see what strikes me in just the same way in faces that, in their basic structure, are very different. Two faces that, in most contexts, would strike me utterly differently suddenly come together in a way such that I want to say that I saw in each of them just the same reaction to a humorous remark or to a dreadful piece of news. This may happen in a way that we find surprising: we would not have expected this face to be capable of expressing just this feeling. And it may happen in a way such that the feeling to be seen in the face completely obscures the underlying character of the face: in this particular instance, the only impression left by a face that would, in other contexts, have struck me with its particular beauty, intelligence or bitterness, is *fear*. As we might put this, the same emotion can find a grip on radically different facial features. This is important to the place that emotion has in our lives. While the *particularity* of others – a particularity in which the face characteristically plays a central role: it is, for example, this face that I long to see – is of fundamental importance to the lives we lead with them, it is also important that *different* people – different in the place that they have in my life, in the basic shape of their lives, and in their physical characteristics – may manifest what strikes us immediately as the *same* emotional reaction to a situation. That things strike us this way is essential to the idea that we share a world with those among whom we live, many of whom are more or less strangers and many of whom have lives that are in deep respects very different from our own.

4. The linguistic expression of emotion

I want to turn now to the linguistic expression of emotion: to the ways in which what a person *says* may be expressive of what she feels. My aim in the present section will be to suggest that we may attain a clearer picture of the character and importance of this by noting both its continuity and contrasts with the non-linguistic expressions of the kind that I have been discussing. I will go on to argue that, in doing this, we see the sense in which, contrary to pictures, such as Descartes's, within which our emotions are obstacles to clear thinking, to feel a particular emotion may be to *recognize* the character of a situation with which one is confronted.

What someone speaks about, and the ways in which she speaks of it, may embody a certain picture of how things are. What I have in mind here is not so much the *beliefs* that are revealed in what she says: that someone asserts that Tony Blair was a marvellous prime minister, or that there is almost certainly intelligent life on Mars, may reveal something important about her, and, with that, may be important elements in a certain picture of how things are. But we learn about another, not only through the propositions to which she is prepared to sign up, but also through the patterns in her speech. A certain view of a third party is expressed, perhaps most directly, in the way in which the speaker returns repeatedly to a particular anecdote about that person, or in the selection of incidents in the other's life around which her talk of him revolves. It is expressed in the way she responds to what others say of him: the way, for example, in which she responds to my drawing attention to an apparently kind action by the other with observations of ways in which the other did, or may, himself benefit from the deed. What may be central here is not the speaker's commitment to a judgement of the form: 'He only did it in order to secure this end for himself'. Even if she would never say such a thing (even to herself), it may be that she systematically sees his 'kind' actions in the light of benefits that he did reap, or might have reaped, from them; and present him in her speech in that way. Similarly, just as the attention of one who is in love is focused in such a way that the beloved's finer characteristics and deeds *strike* her forcefully, while she is prone to overlook – simply not notice – defects that are obvious to others, so her proneness to *remark on* (perhaps endlessly) her beloved's finer points, and, perhaps, to set apparent acts of meanness in the context of difficulties in his life at the time, may be among what reveals most clearly that she is in love.

We learn about another through the patterns in her speech. Perhaps better: learning about, coming to know, another *is* coming to see the patterns in her speech. These patterns may be expressive of, at one end of a spectrum, the kind of person that she is, and, at the other, a fleeting emotional response to her immediate situation. While it may not be very helpful to ask just what stretch of this spectrum is occupied by 'emotion', it is clear that in many cases what is most expressive of a person's emotional state lies simply in what she is inclined to remark on. A proneness to remark on such factors as another's dreadful rudeness, gross inefficiency, or disgracefully slovenly appearance is one of the characteristic marks of anger or contempt; as a proneness to remark on the drabness of life and the dim future prospects is one of the characteristic marks of depression. We might express the point here in terms of the 'tone' of her conversation; a term that may help to highlight that what is at issue is not simply that which might be captured by an accurate transcript of what she said.[4] There is a contrast between, for example, speaking of another's failings in tones of charity and speaking of them in tones of condemnation: a contrast that, in requiring a reference to factors such as tone of voice and the embeddedness of one's words in other forms of expressive behaviour, is not exhaustively characterized in terms of a difference in *what* one says (on a reading of that last phrase that I hope is clear.)

In speaking of what a person says as 'expressive' of her emotions I am consciously making a connection with the non-verbal forms of expression of which I spoke earlier. Much of the remainder of what I say will be an attempt to show that this is an illuminating connection. We can begin by noting the following link. Just as my smile or frown is not (in the case with which I am concerned) an attempt to achieve some goal, so the lover's endless chatter about her beloved's finer points, or the angry man's flow of references to the character failings in the object of his anger, are not (again, in the case with which I am concerned) an attempt to achieve some goal. Much of our unreflective talk is of this form. We go over situations, presenting them in our speech as structured in certain ways. And the importance of an audience – someone to listen and respond to what we say – may have little to do with any goal of the form: letting the other know how things stand. Indeed, the need to talk about something that is on my mind – the need for this form of contact with another – may overrule a clear understanding that it would be much better if nobody else knew what has happened, or how I feel about it.

With this, such talk is 'expressive' of a person's love, jealousy or anger in the sense that a proneness to speak in these ways plays a central role in our readiness to characterize his feelings as we do. It is, in part, in the ways in which he unreflectively speaks of her that we recognize that he loves or is afraid of her – and the particular character of his love or fear. We *hear* his love or fear in his words in the sense that the most direct characterization of *what* he feels may involve, in what we say about *him*, the very words that he employs in speaking of his situation: in reporting what he says about her we are telling how he feels about her. An analogy in one direction would be the way in which in reporting what someone says we may be telling what he believes; an analogy in a rather different direction would be the way we may convey what another felt by mimicking his facial expression.

I noted that we may see what strikes us immediately as the same feeling in faces of very different basic structure. This goes with the fact that we may see the same feeling in faces that, described in terms of the current arrangement of facial flesh, are very different. There are close analogues of these points in the linguistic expression of emotion. In particular, I may hear what strikes me immediately as just the same joy or fear in speech that, described in terms of the sounds produced, are very different. We can think here of a wide range of differences, ranging from differences in pronunciation, through differences in the particular words in which the feeling is expressed, to differences in the language of the speaker.

It is, however, also worth noting in this connection a significant *contrast* with non-linguistic expression. We can imagine someone (and we are, perhaps, all like this up to a point) who could not recognize another's facial expression as a reproduction of what was to be seen in her own face; and we can do so without this casting doubt on whether this really was an expression of fear or grief. If, however, we imagine someone who, systematically, could not recognize what another says as a reproduction of what *she* has said, we will be imagining someone whose 'words' are not at all what words normally are. The fact that, in this sense, what a person says is equally accessible to both speaker and listener is one of the things that goes to make it *saying* something. While I have stressed the spontaneous and unselfconscious way in which our feelings may be revealed in our conversation, it is central to linguistic expression that what may be unselfconscious may also be self-conscious. Thus, it is a fundamental characteristic of speech that another may feed my words back to me, asking, for example, whether I can really mean what I appeared to say. And *this* goes with the fact that if I am really *speaking* I acknowledge that there is a question of getting it right: 'getting it right', not simply in the sense, emphasized in much philosophy of language, of 'uttering propositions that are true', but in the sense of 'portraying things accurately' which is such that I may present an utterly distorted picture of a situation while saying nothing that is actually *false*.[5] This is central to the distinctive forms of engagement with another that are involved in the *linguistic* expression of emotion. I will return to this.

5. My relation to another's words

There is, as we can express this, a conceptual connection between his words and what he feels; and in the life of someone to whom this form of articulation was not available there would be no place for an emotion of just that character. But we can, as earlier, press this further by asking: what is the significance in our lives of our readiness to ascribe to others, on the basis of what they say, the emotions that we do? To answer this question will be to clarify what the conceptual connection amounts to; and to do that will be to clarify the importance of emotion in our lives. In approaching this it will be helpful to distinguish a variety of different ways in which another's emotions may matter to me.

Another's emotional state may, in a particular case, be for me simply a practical consideration to be taken account of when planning a course of action: she is terrified, so she may well do something foolish. That she feels as she does is, in a sense, nothing to me – though I do take her words seriously in the sense that, on the basis of them, I form certain ideas about what is to be expected from her.

In other cases, another's state *does* matter to me. I respond to the other, on account of the resentment in her words, with shame or anger; or, on account of the grief in her words, with sympathy. My shame, anger or sympathy are forms taken by my recognition of the other's emotional state. Further, my response to her, as it is expressed in my behaviour and words, is inseparably linked with that to which I am responding. Thus, much as my fear in the face of her anger may find expression in my shrinking from her gaze, so it may find expression in the ways in which I engage with her angry words: in the way, for example, in which I defend myself against her accusations or attempt to deflect her rage onto someone else. We can add: there is only room for just *that* response in so far as what I am responding *to* is another human being laying out a stretch of my life in a way that casts it in an unambiguously shameful light.[6]

In these two different ways, another may be for me an object of concern on account of the feelings expressed in what she says. But there is something else that another's words may be for me. I may take another's words seriously in the sense of treating them as a serious attempt to articulate how things are. This may involve giving serious consideration to the possibility that things *are* that way: to the possibility that if I am to think straight about what happened I must arrange things in my thought about it as she arranges them in her speech – and, with that, I must feel about what happened as she feels about it. Again, we may talk through a situation that we both face, exchanging articulations of it in ways that involve a shared, and reinforcing, delight or horror in it. In other cases, because of the different relations in which we stand to a situation – because *his* situation is not *our* situation – there is no question of an attempt to reach a consensus in our feelings about it: if I am engaging with another's love or jealousy, while I may try to help him think more clearly, the upshot aimed at is not, generally, that we both think of the object of his feelings in the same way. (I am not to come to see his beloved through the same eyes as he sees her.) In such cases, I may take another's words seriously in the sense, not of taking seriously the possibility that things are as she presents them, but of being ready to engage with them – that is, with her – in a certain way. I may, for example, attempt to correct what seems to me an imbalance in her view of the situation. Perhaps she connects a series of, as I see it, quite unconnected incidents: the connecting thread being, we may suppose, some reference to herself. My taking her words seriously may here involve countering her characterizations: presenting a different arrangement of the same facts, along, perhaps, with the addition of further relevant information. In other cases again I may be more or less baffled by the terms in which another speaks of some person or situation, and my engagement with her is, primarily, an attempt to get some grip on what it *is* that she is feeling. While in some cases of this kind my concern may gravitate towards a concern about *her* in the sense mentioned earlier, in others my inchoate sense of a genuine perceptiveness in her words may push me towards an engagement with them in the hope of clarifying my own thinking about a situation.

Such engagement with another is an important form of, or element in, those verbal interchanges that are most naturally spoken of as everyday 'conversation': where 'conversation' is to be contrasted with purely practical exchanges in which the other serves, for example, as simply a handy source of information, which could be replaced without significant loss by an encyclopaedia or a speaking clock. In conversation we present alternative characterizations of a situation – which may involve rearrangement of agreed facts, reminders of overlooked facts, and the addition of further relevant information – in an attempt, perhaps, to correct what strikes us as another's misunderstanding of the situation, or to reach a better understanding of it ourselves. I believe that any remotely adequate picture of the place of language in human life will give a central place to interchanges of this general kind.

6. Talk and feelings

My relation to the emotions of one who has a capacity for their *linguistic* expression is necessarily different from my relation to the emotions of one who does not[7]: different in that there is a place for those forms of relating to – interacting with – the other that are involved in sharing a language. This goes with the fact that a capacity for their linguistic expression transforms the *range* of emotions that can be ascribed to someone.

We might ask: what is the importance of its possession of language (or: of its possession of 'concepts') for the possibility of a creature's undergoing certain emotions – for, for example, the possibility of a creature's hoping that it will be sunny next Thursday, or feeling dreadful about the sufferings of people in a past war? But while we *might* formulate our question in that way, we will do better to ask: what is the importance of its possession of language for the possibility of our ascribing to a creature the hope that it will be sunny next Thursday, or feeling dreadful about past suffering? We do better to ask this, not because it is not an 'objective' matter whether a particular creature does have such feelings, but because our question here is one about *sense*.

Now we might articulate the point about sense in terms of the notion of a 'criterion'. His words 'If only it will be fine next Thursday', or 'Those poor people', are *criteria* for these feelings; and the sense of our ascription is dependent on our recognition that there is a conceptual connection between such emotions and such verbal behaviour. This connection – the special place of such grounds in the ascription of these feelings, and, with that, the senselessness of ascribing such feelings to non-linguistic creatures – is something that we learn in coming to grasp the sense of sentences of the form 'He hopes it will be sunny next Thursday' or 'He feels dreadful about the sufferings of those people'. But, as in my discussion of non-verbal criteria, we can press this further by asking: what is the *importance* of this 'conceptual connection'. For what is at issue here is not simply our willingness to *say* these things of another, but our *thinking* them: where this includes, centrally, our relating to the other as one who has this emotion. Our question is, for example: how does a recognition of another as feeling dreadful about the sufferings of people in a past war come to something in my life – come, that is, to more than my willingness to utter the words 'He feels dreadful about the sufferings of those people'? To focus the question a little more, we can ask: how does a recognition that the object of his feelings is the sufferings of *those* people come to something in my life?[8] Well, in a particular case, it may be in ways such as this: I discuss with him the physical conditions in which these people were living, the backdrop of the destruction of their whole way of life, the hopes that their situation may just have left open and that might have made their sufferings bearable, and so on. It is, as I am imagining it here, in the ways in which I take up what he says, take it up in conversation with him about these people, that my recognition of *their* sufferings as the object of his feelings finds expression. While we can, of course, imagine other ways in which my recognition may find expression (not only in my relations with him, but also, for example, in the ways I speak *about* him), our question is: take away the possibility of *linguistic* expression of his feelings – and, with that, the possibility of conversation with him about the object of his feelings – and what will be left? While I will not attempt to answer that question – either in the context of the example I have just been discussing, or, more generally, in relation to other feelings about absent objects – in appreciating in particular cases just how little, if anything, will be left we grasp the force of the suggestion that, in such cases, what a person says is a central *criterion* of his feelings: we appreciate the place that *his* talk about the object of his feelings has in the sense of *our* talk of him as feeling what he does.[9]

7. Person-directed and world-directed concern

I have drawn a distinction between cases in which the way another speaks of a situation draws my attention to *her* and cases in which it draws my attention to *the situation* to which she is responding: her words may lead me to look at her through new eyes, or they may lead me to look at the situation of which she speaks through new eyes. The distinction is, however, not as straightforward as that way of presenting it may suggest. This is so if only because a concern about the clarity of a person's thinking is a form of concern about the *person*: my concern, on account of her feelings, about one who matters to me may, in a particular case, be primarily a concern that what she is feeling is wildly inappropriate to her situation.

But I want to explore this a bit further. For the fact that our engagement with another's verbal expression of emotion has, as we might express it, both world-directed and person-directed faces is a fundamental feature of it; an understanding of the relation between them, and an appreciation that these are *poles* towards which our thinking may gravitate, is, I believe, crucial to a grasp of the key position that emotion and its expression have in our lives. This can be illustrated by developing a bit further what I have said about engagement with the other that takes the form of *reasoning* with her.

Just as certain other things can be expected from a person with a face marked by rage or sadness, so certain other things can be expected from someone who speaks of another in terms that are clearly expressive of love, or of an incident in his own life in terms that are clearly expressive of shame. Other things 'can be expected' in the sense that, in the first of these cases, we will be surprised if, in the absence, so far as we can see, of an intervening incident of an appropriate kind, he later behaves towards her with indifference, speaks disparagingly of her, and so on. In the context of *linguistic* expressions of emotion there is, however, a further sense in which other things 'can be expected': what a person says may lay him open to certain demands. Thus, we may rebuke him – either for his earlier words or for his later words and behaviour – if our expectations in the first sense are not fulfilled.

In this sense, among others, taking another's words seriously involves a readiness to connect what he says at one time with what he says and does at other times. The love, shame, anger or fear that is articulated in what he says is, or may be,[10] an expression of ways in which certain things matter to him. His words come from *him* in a sense deeper than that in which a cry of physical pain comes from him in that they connect up with much else in his life; and what I make of his anger now may depend on how far I am able to see it as part of his life: a life, for example, in which this could be understood as something to be angry about. The anger is a condition of the *person* in so far as it connects up with the rest of 'his life' in appropriate ways; and *thinking* of it as a condition of the person involves a readiness to *make* such connections: to make such connections both in the sense of looking for them, and in the sense of requiring them of him. Now one central form of the latter – of *requiring* such connections in my relations with the other – is *reasoning* with him. For such reasoning may – perhaps characteristically does – involve an exploration of whether his immediate reaction to a person or situation is an intelligible expression of what really matters to him. To take as illustration a recent incident in Britain, I may ask whether a person's, or in this case a group of Sikhs', anger at the portrayal, in a play, of a rape in a temple fits into a life in which *this* juxtaposition of sex and violence with their God could be seriously judged to be offensive.

I said: reasoning may involve an exploration of whether his immediate reaction to a person or situation is an intelligible expression of what really matters to him. From *his* perspective the point would, no doubt, be better put: an exploration of whether his immediate reaction is an intelligible expression of *what really matters*. In the case as I have presented it he and I stand in relation to our conversation in ways that are importantly different. In others, where he and I stand in the same relation to the situation that is the object of his feelings, each may stand in the same relation to our conversation. For both, our conversation is an exploration of the character of the situation: an exploration, that is, of how we are to feel about it.

But there is a further point here: a further form of interplay between thinking about *him* and thinking about *the situation*. In my discussion of non-verbal expression I suggested that it is important to the place that the expression of emotion has in our lives that its relation to context may involve movement in two different directions. On the one hand, what I see in her face may, taken in isolation from any context, immediately strike me in a certain way; and, with that, may clearly suggest a context of a certain form. On the other, knowledge of the context may play a crucial role in determining what I see in her face. It is, I believe, an important feature of the place of language in our lives that what another *says* may display an analogous dual relation to context. Another's words 'Those poor people', or 'How could I have said that', uttered in tones of compassion or remorse, may, independent of context (or, at least, relatively so), immediately strike me in a certain way; and, with that, may clearly suggest a context of a certain form. But equally, what I make of his words may be transformed by my knowledge of their context. In considering the latter relation it is, however, important to note that the 'context' of another's words is not necessarily something that, for me, is simply 'given' – as, in a particular case, the bear in hot pursuit is, for me, simply given as the context of another's flight and terror-stricken expression. The context may be not simply 'given' in the straightforward sense that I lack a key piece of information (he has just passed a dreadful road accident). But it may be not simply 'given' in the more interesting sense that it may take work to identify the relevant configuration of circumstances that is the 'context' of what he says: while, in one sense, I have all the information at my disposal, I have failed to pull it together in the way that reveals, for example, the dreadful indelicacy of the remark to which he was responding. Now, and this is the point I want to emphasize here, it may be through the way in which the other goes on to speak of the situation that I come to recognize the light in which he understands it – and perhaps, with that, come to appreciate for the first time a particular way in which it may be understood. In his reaction – in, for example, the lightness with which he relates to what initially strikes me as the small-minded meanness of another's words – I see another humanly intelligible, and perhaps admirable, way of relating to them: another way of taking the one whose words they are. But further, through the way in which the other speaks of a situation, and the non-linguistic behaviour in which his speech is embedded, I may come to acknowledge that this is the way in which the situation *is to be understood*. *His* attitude, as expressed in his speech and behaviour, may reveal to me the situation as one to be thought of with compassion, shame or gratitude.[11]

While I distinguished between an engagement with another's verbal expression of emotion that has as its focus a concern about *her* and one that has as its focus a concern to get clear about the character of *the situation*, my central point has been that the distinction is not the clear one we may suppose it to be. For, on the one hand, there is no such thing as having a clear view of *her* in isolation from having a clear view of her situation; and, linked with that, my concern about her may be primarily a concern about the clarity of her thinking about the situation. On the other, it may be in the ways in which she speaks of it that I see what it *is* to have a proper grasp of this situation.

8. Summary

I said that my concern was to understand the relation between two strands in Descartes's treatment of emotion: the radical lack of connection between emotion and behavioural manifestations, and the idea that to experience a situation through an emotion is to experience it in a *confused* way. We might formulate the first of these ideas in this way: 'What we normally think of as "expressions of emotion" do not come from the *person*, but from his body. And that is to say: such "expressions" have no direct role to play in our assessment of, or engagement with, him'. I have suggested, first, that we may take as our starting point the fact that such expressions *do* have a role to play in our engagement with the other; and second, that it is through this that we see the force of the familiar idea that emotion is not simply an obstacle to clear thinking but may itself *embody* a view of how things are. For in the case of linguistic expressions of emotion, engagement with the other may involve treating his reaction as one with which rational engagement may be in place; and, closely linked with that, taking seriously the possibility that things are as, in his words, he presents them as being. Further, I have suggested that this – the idea of *reasoning* with him – is inseparable from a rich sense in which a particular expression of emotion may come from the *person*. The sense, it may be noted, is one for whose articulation Descartes's mind–body imagery is quite unsuited. For it is to be brought out through the idea that what is felt now is an event in the life of a persisting individual: a life with which the present upheaval may cohere or fail to cohere.

My discussion has focused on *expression*, and my relation to another in the light of her expression, without too much concern about whether what is expressed is *emotion*. While there are no doubt important distinctions to be drawn within the realm of 'expression', the phenomena on which I have focused are tied together by the way in which they resist placing within traditional mind–body dualism, and with that, within the belief-desire psychology that still dominates much philosophical thinking. Such views insist[12] that it takes a desire to shift an understanding of the world – a picture of how things are that is open to reason – into a domain in which others may engage with it. Expression resists placing within these views in that through it – whether this be in the form of a flash of horror on my face, a lightness in my general demeanour over a period of time, or the patterns in my speech – we may be in immediate contact with each other: a contact that, in the case of speech, may involve an attempt to determine, with the other, whether the way she speaks is an adequate articulation of what she is speaking of. To understand the connection between emotion and linguistic articulation – the limitations in the emotions that can be ascribed to creatures lacking language – we need to focus on the way in which speech is a form of contact with others. The ascription of certain feelings to another has its sense within a framework in which particular forms of engagement with the other are possible: forms of engagement in which language has a central place.[13]

Notes

1. I should stress that I am not here referring to the fact that Descartes does not speak in terms of any form of *'conceptual'* connection between emotion and behavioural manifestations. My concern is rather with the way, noted above, in which he appears to deny that, in central cases, an emotion plays any *causal* role in the generation of the associated behavioural manifestations. See Descartes ([1649] 1989), paragraphs 36–38.
2. And so, for example, we cannot expect any *physiological* investigation to establish that Descartes was wrong to think of bodily expression as simply a product of bodily processes, and so as having no bearing on our attempts to understand another.
3. Perhaps I should stress that I do not mean this to be an adequate characterization either of the object of grief or of the ways in which grief may be expressed in behaviour. My aim is simply to highlight a certain feature of the relation between those.
4. The idea of 'an accurate transcript' may, in fact, not capture the contrast that I am concerned to draw here as straightforwardly as my presentation suggests. An accurate transcript of a conversation is, after all, not a series of marks that enables us to reproduce faithfully the noises that were made. 'Accuracy' in this context is a matter of reproducing faithfully what was *said*. This will always involve recording in the *same* way what, as sequences of noises, were significantly different (for example, differences in accent and pronunciation); and may sometimes involve recording in *different* ways what, as sequences of noises, were 'indistinguishable to the ear'.

5. With what authority do I say that this is a condition of what someone does being 'speech'? None; and, with that, I do not insist on this way of putting the matter. What is important here is simply the fact that such an acknowledgement is central to the place that much talk has in our lives.

6. This is not to deny that we may judge that someone's response to a somewhat different situation is, in important respects, of the same form as my response to this one. Our seeing something as the same or as a different reaction is itself dependent on a context of concern. While *my* concern, in this discussion, is with the particularity of the circumstances that are required for there to be a place for a response of a certain form, in other, more everyday, contexts what marks off the particular form of response to another's anger in one situation from that in another may be of no significance. The latter point may tempt us towards a picture in which the character of the response floats free of the circumstances to which it is a response: this, of course, being the picture that it is the purpose of my remarks to resist.

7. There are significant questions, which I cannot take up here, about my relation to, and understanding of, the feelings of one who speaks a language that I do not share. I will remark only that it is integral to the approach offered here that our *starting* point in considering our relation to another's emotions must be the case in which we do share a language with the other.

8. It might be supposed that the reference to 'me' is gratuitous; that the question we need to ask is, rather, of the form: what is the connection between what he is feeling and the sufferings of *those* people? But without suggesting that that would be the *wrong* question, it is important to remember that it is me, or someone, who judges that this man feels dreadful about the sufferings of those people. It is the sense of that ascription that is under discussion: in particular, it is *my* reference to 'those people' in my characterization of his feelings that is our concern here. (Of course, there is also room for a discussion of *another's* reference to my reference to those people in my characterization of the first man's feelings; but I imagine that there would be a fairly rapid falling off of philosophical dividends as we moved up this hierarchy.)

9. Simone Weil reports somewhere that she cannot think of the sufferings of those who died at the hands of the Albigensian 'crusade' in the thirteenth century without weeping for them. Part of what is startling in this account of her feelings is the idea that her life could contain a richness of a kind such that her distress might be unambiguously a distress over their suffering.

10. There are passing eruptions that are more or less disconnected from the rest of a person's life. We might add: the more obviously disconnected the eruption is the more inclined we might be to think of it as either physiologically grounded or pathological.

11. Compare the way in which another's presentation of a geometrical proof may reveal to me that a triangle is to be thought of as a figure whose angles add up to 180o. I want to suggest that the cases are importantly analogous in a certain respect: analogous in the way in which the appropriateness of the way of thinking is not 'detachable' from the way in which it is revealed to me.

12. Perhaps it would be closer to the mark to say: *are committed to* insisting.... . It is, I believe, a noteworthy feature of belief-desire psychology that it is sometimes quietly forgotten in the context of *verbal* behaviour.

13. I am grateful to Ossie Hanfling, Bob Sharpe, Anniken Greve, Camilla Kronqvist, Ylva Gustafsson, Lars Hertzberg and Maureen Meehan for helpful comments on earlier drafts of this chapter.

Bibliography

Descartes, R. ([1649] 1989), *The Passions of the Soul* (Indianapolis: Hackett).

Wittgenstein, L. (1967), *Zettel*, Anscombe, G.E.M. and von Wright, G.H. trans. Anscombe, G.E.M. ed. (Oxford: Blackwell).

——. (1968), *Philosophical Investigations*, Anscombe, G.E.M. trans. Anscombe, G.E.M., von Wright, G.H. and Rhees, R. eds (Oxford: Blackwell).

9
Illusions of Empathy*

Ylva Gustafsson

1. Introduction

How do we understand other people's emotions? In attempting to explain this question, the concept of empathy has become quite a popular subject in both philosophy and psychology.

In this chapter, I will examine how empathy is talked about as an ability to understand other people by using our imagination. My aim is, on the one hand, to bring into question the idea that there is some such thing as a general and neutral method to understand others. On the other, my aim is to question the way in which this method is considered to be of importance for our moral engagement with other people.

To begin with, it is important to note that the concept 'empathy' in philosophy has a formalized and reduced meaning that does not have much in common with our normal use of this word. My discussion in this chapter concerns the philosophical ideas about empathy. In ordinary life when we say that someone is empathic, we often mean that he is a compassionate person. This is not what philosophers usually mean by empathy.

Though there are several different ideas about precisely what empathy is, there are also certain common traits in these discussions. A central idea in most philosophical discussions on empathy is that it is seen as a major folk psychological skill used to explain and predict other people's emotions, beliefs and actions. For instance, Karsten R. Stueber writes:

> Empathy should be seen as the epistemically central, even if at times limited, default method of gaining knowledge of the minds of other individual agents. (Stueber 2006, p. 19)

Gary Fuller writes:

> Here is one way one might try to predict, and perhaps explain, the beliefs, decisions, emotions, and actions of another. Put yourself in the other's

shoes and see what you would do, come to believe, etc. and then go on to ascribe those actions, beliefs, etc. I call this the method of empathy. (Fuller 1995, p. 19)

The empathic imaginative ability is also considered neutral; that is, the empathic method can be used both for good and for bad purposes. Martha Nussbaum, for instance, thinks so:

In short, empathy is a mental ability highly relevant to compassion, although it is itself both fallible and morally neutral.

Does empathy contribute anything of ethical importance entirely on its own (when it does not lead to compassion)? I have suggested that it does not: a torturer can use it for hostile and sadistic ends. (Nussbaum 2001, p. 333)

I aim to question this picture of empathy being a general technique by which we understand other people.

I have divided the chapter into three parts. In the first part, I discuss certain psychological experiments in which one has tried to prove that empathic imagination produces compassion. In the second part, I discuss the idea that we have to see the other person as 'a separate perspective' or as a 'separate mind' to understand her. I try to show that this idea is based on problematic presuppositions about understanding, knowledge and imagination being private, mental and purely epistemological concepts. When it comes to understanding other people these concepts get their meaning in the ways we engage in each other's life, and centrally in our talking with each other. The meaning of these concepts can't be separated from the ways in which we are morally responsible to each other. In the third part of this chapter, I question the idea that empathy is a neutral method of imagination that can be used equally for good and bad purposes. Here I consider the relation between imagination, knowledge and cruelty, and what it means to understand or to be seduced by images of cruelty.

2. Psychological experiments and empathy as a mental tool for compassion

One reason why philosophers and psychologists are interested in empathy is that they want to explain our moral engagement in others, especially compassion. The starting point here appears to be the thought that imagination about the suffering of the other person is essential for feeling compassion. Psychologists have then conducted several experiments to prove that empathic imagination produces compassion. A.I. Goldman (1995), for instance, discusses the following experiment conducted by Ezra Stotland in 1969.

> Ezra Stotland (1969) had subjects watch someone else whose hand was strapped in a machine that they were told generated painful heat. Some were told just to watch the man carefully, some were told to imagine the way he was feeling, and some were told to imagine themselves in his place. Using both physiological and verbal measures of empathy on the part of the subjects, the experimental results showed that deliberate acts of imagination produced a greater response than just watching. (Goldman 1995, p. 199)

The result of these experiments was, as Goldman notes, that the groups that were exhorted to imagine reacted more strongly than the group that was exhorted to watch. Goldman takes this experiment to prove that the mechanism of empathic imagination can produce compassion. As he writes: '[empathy] seems to be a prime mechanism that disposes us toward altruistic behavior' (Goldman 1995, p. 202).

However, what is experiment actually evidence for? It is worth examining more closely what the persons who were asked to watch were told to do:

Watch-Him Condition
    In a few moments you will be watching the actual demonstration. While you are doing so, please watch exactly what the demonstrator does. You are to watch all of his body movements that you can see. Your job will be to watch his leg movements, arm movements, foot movements, head movements, hand movements. You are to notice anything that he does, whatever it is. (While you are watching him, don't try to imagine how you would feel in his place or how he is feeling. Don't think about how he feels or how you would feel. Just watch him closely.) (Stotland 1969, pp. 292–293)

One thing the experimenters apparently have not noticed is the fact that the persons who watch carefully do not have any strong emotional reactions is obviously connected with how they understand what they should do in the experimental situation, they are *asked* to put their feelings aside. Now, actively putting aside one's feelings is not proof of the basically passive, outer or separate character of seeing; it is not evidence of how our ability to see others 'works'.

The idea that we always have a deeper understanding of people when we imagine how they feel than if we simply watch them is an expression of a dualistic way of thinking about human beings. The body is seen as a shell and our feelings, thoughts and beliefs are thought to be inside this shell. So when we look at another person we merely see this corporeal outer shell but when we imagine how he feels we get access to his inner life, so to say. The thought is then that we can only understand other people's emotions, feelings or beliefs by a kind of analogical imaginative process. This way of thinking is also apparent in the way one regards a kind of passive distant observing as a contrast to using one's imagination. However, the former is actually a very sophisticated form of seeing. It is not the normal, basic or the only way of seeing others. It is something the persons are *instructed* to do.

Normally our seeing each other is inseparable from the ways we are engaged in each other. Think, for instance, about the way one might suddenly look a friend in the eyes when he says he is very worried about something. This is a way of showing to the other that one is listening, that one understands that he is saying something important. Or one looks into each other's eyes while laughing at a joke, or one looks angrily at someone, or one sees that a person on a bike falls and one instantly goes to help him, one asks him if he hurt himself and so on. None of these forms of looking or seeing has anything to do with passively observing a bodily shell that is reacting in certain ways; they are responses to the other person and as such expressions of understanding. When the people in the experiment are exhorted to watch carefully, they are actually exhorted to adopt a way of looking at other people's bodies that has nothing to do with what it means to see another person. Ludwig Wittgenstein writes in *Philosophical Investigations*:

> But isn't it absurd to say of a body that it has pain? – And why does one feel an absurdity in that? In what sense is it true that my hand does not feel pain, but I in my hand?
>
> What sort of issue is: Is it the *body* that feels pain? – How is it to be decided? What makes it plausible to say that it is *not* the body? – Well, something like this: if someone has a pain in his hand, then the hand does not say so (unless it writes it) and one does not comfort the hand, but the sufferer: one looks into his face. (Wittgenstein 2001, § 286)

Wittgenstein criticizes here the idea that a bodily feeling such as pain can be understood somehow in itself as being 'purely bodily'. It is in our responding to each other that the concept of pain as well as the concept of body has a meaning.

There are further problems with the experiment that one recognizes if one considers the two other groups that were asked to imagine. They were told the following:

Imagine-Self Condition
In a few moments you will be watching the actual demonstration. While you are doing so, please imagine how you yourself would feel if you were subjected to the diathermy treatment, whether it turns out to be

painful, pleasant or neither. While you are watching him, picture to yourself just how you would feel. (... You are to react as if it were you who will have the experience that is pleasant, painful or neither.) While you are watching him, you are to concentrate on yourself in that experience. You are to concentrate on the way you would feel while receiving the treatment. Your job will be to think about what your reactions would be to the sensations you would receive in your hand. (Stotland 1969, p. 292)

Imagine-Him Condition

In a few moments you will be watching the actual demonstration. While you are doing so, please imagine how the demonstrator feels as he is subjected to the diathermy treatment, whether it turns out to be painful, pleasant, or neither. While you are watching him, picture to yourself just how he feels. (You are to keep clearly in mind that... It is he who will have the experience that is pleasant, painful, or neither. While you are watching him, forget yourself.) While you are watching him, you are to concentrate on him in that experience. You are to concentrate on the way he feels while receiving the treatment. Your job will be to think about his reaction to the sensations he is receiving in his hand. In your mind's eye, you are to visualize how it feels to him to be the demonstrator in this experiment. (Stotland 1969, p. 292)

These two groups were *not* merely, as Stotland and Goldman think, asked to use a certain mental technique. That is, the experimenters thought they were exhorting the test persons to use a neutral mental technique, but they actually urged the test persons to take on the one hand an egocentric attitude and on the other hand a compassionate attitude. This means, of course, that the result that the test persons who were instructed to imagine tended to react more strongly than the group that was instructed to watch is not a consequence of them using a mental technique but a consequence of them understanding the instructions in the experiment in a certain sense. This means that the requests become strangely ambiguous. Their strong reactions do not reveal anything about how we might react in real life since they are trying to fulfil the demands of the experiment.

Furthermore, it is notable that the results of the reactions from the different test groups are measured in *strength*. The results of the experiments were observed through a 'palmar sweating measure', a 'vasoconstriction measure' and a 'questionnaire measure' (Stotland 1969, pp. 284–288). Both of the two groups that were asked to imagine showed stronger palmar sweating reactions and vasoconstriction reactions than the group that was asked to watch. But in what sense does a strong reaction of egocentric nausea have anything in common with strong feelings of pity for another person's suffering? That the 'strong reactions' of palmar sweating or vasoconstriction here express completely different attitudes does not seem to bother the experimenters, the reactions are lumped together as 'strong' or 'weak' on completely irrelevant grounds.

The experiment is also unrealistic in other ways. There is a huge difference between watching a person who has freely volunteered for a painful experiment on the one hand and seeing someone severely ill or badly injured and in severe pain because of it, on the other. Usually pain is not something we can just freely choose to be or not to be subjected to, and it is usually not something we can walk away from when we want to. Strong pain is often connected with serious illness, injuries, several forms of handicap and death. As Wittgenstein writes, 'The concept of pain is characterized by its particular function in our life' (Wittgenstein 1981, § 532). Neither should the persons try to help or comfort the one who suffers; they should observe or imagine but do nothing. In that sense, the exhortations resemble some sort of surreal game. This makes it quite obscure in what sense their observing or imagining can be said to be an expression of understanding that a person is in pain.

There are also some slightly more nuanced ways of making experiments concerning empathy along similar lines as Stotland's experiment. Daniel C. Batson has conducted psychological experiments, the general purpose of which is similarly to demonstrate the relation between empathy and compassion. In Batson's experiment, there are two groups of people both of which are asked to listen to a story where a young woman is in a desperate situation. The woman called Katie Banks is 'a university senior whose parents had recently been killed in a tragic automobile accident. ... Mr. Banks did not have life insurance, and Katie was struggling to take care of her surviving younger brother and sister, ages 8 and 11, while she finished her last year of college' (Batson 1997, p. 499). The first group is asked to

> Try to be as objective as possible about what has happened to the person interviewed and how it has affected his or her life. To remain objective, do not let yourself get caught up in imagining what this person has been through and how he or she feels as a result. Just try to remain detached as you listen to the broadcast. (Batson 1997, p. 499)

The second group is asked to

> Try to imagine how the person being interviewed feels about what has happened and how it has affected his or her life. Try not to concern yourself with attending to all the information presented. Just concentrate on trying to imagine how the person interviewed in the broadcast feels. (Batson 1997, p. 499)

After the official experiment, the test persons are asked if they would like to help the woman by donating a sum of money. The result is that the persons who were asked to imagine were inclined to help while the ones who were asked to observe were not as strongly inclined to help.

A difference between Stotland's and Batson's experiment is that Batson does not distinguish between watching an outer body and having a mental picture of an inner state but rather between certain forms of perspectives; between, on the one hand, trying to remain objective and neutral and, on the other hand, trying to imagine the other person's perspective as well as trying to see similarities with the other. Another difference is that Batson's experiment is not as abstracted from real life as Stotland's experiment is.

However, even if there is a good side to Batson's experiment in the sense that it is not as completely abstracted from human life as Stotland's experiment, he still has, basically, the same problematic idea about empathy being a mental technique we can use to understand others. The general form of the experiment as well as the result of the experiment is the same as in Stotland's experiment. The people who are asked to remain objective and detached do not respond as emotionally and 'compassionately' as the people who are asked not to attend to the details of the information they received but instead to imagine how the woman feels. Batson thinks this proves that our moral understanding is dependent on our using different mental techniques when trying to understand others. But, as in Stotland's experiment, in this experiment, too, the 'objective' group is asked *not* to become engaged while the group that is exhorted to imagine is, again, *not* merely, as Batson thinks, asked to use a certain mental technique, they are exhorted to engage morally in the other person's life. The positive results are an outcome of flaws in the ways the experiment is conducted in roughly the same way as Stotland's experiment.

It is unclear what sort of objective stance the test persons actually are exhorted to take. For instance, when we talk about a judge or a doctor being objective, we mean that the person should try to be fair and considerate. It does not mean that one should merely consider some kind of technical details. Trying to be fair to others involves caring about others, not being inhuman, cold or callous.

The fact that the test persons after the experiment tended to react in ways that reflect the ways in which they were exhorted to react in the experiment does not mean that the experiment somehow would prove that compassion is the result of our using an empathic imaginative technique. It only means that psychological experiments can influence people after the experiment also. Wittgenstein summarizes the tendency to believe in psychological experiments, in a few words: 'The existence of the experimental method makes us think we have the means of solving the problems which trouble us; though problem and method pass one another by' (Wittgenstein 2001, p. 197e).

Here, I have tried to illustrate a tendency among philosophers discussing empathy to be too uncritical when considering certain experiments as proof for their theories.[1] This seems partly to be connected with a belief in empirical research being true in some kind of absolute sense. The thought seems to be that if empirical experiments have positive results they must reveal something true about human reality. But the experiments actually only illustrate how easily an experiment can be formed to reach certain results. Partly, the uncritical belief in these psychological experiments is an expression of how both the experimenters and the philosophers have the same problematic ideas about human understanding as basically being a psychological and mental phenomenon. Martha Nussbaum, for instance, takes Batson's results for granted. She thinks Batson's experiment proves that there is a strong link between empathy and compassion.

> [T]here is sufficient material in the experimental reports to see that there is also a strong relationship between empathy (or, alternatively, the judgment of similar possibilities) and compassionate emotion. If empathy is not clearly necessary for compassion, it is a prominent route to it. (Nussbaum 2001, p. 332)

The way Nussbaum without hesitation accepts the result of the experiment is a reflection of her own theories about empathy as a useful imaginative technique. I will return to her views on empathy later in this chapter.

The thought that we use an imaginative technique to understand others is connected with a psychologizing view of compassion. Compassion becomes something we just *tend* to feel in certain relations, because we see certain similarities with the other or because we become emotionally engaged by using certain mental techniques of imagination. But in what sense does the fact that people *tend* to feel compassion in certain ways show anything about compassion as an expression of true understanding? That is, we can often feel compassion in ways that are an expression of sentimentality or partiality. Talking about this merely as a psychologically positive trait ignores how these reactions can express serious forms of moral blindness for others.[2] This psychologizing perspective on compassion is often connected with generalizing talk about 'altruistic behaviour'.

In a paper on the role of imagination in philosophy and the humanities (2002),[3] Lars Hertzberg says that when we talk about someone being able to imagine another person's suffering we use the word 'imagine' in a moral sense. We say something about his being attentive to others, or fair-minded, of his being neither sentimental nor cynical (Hertzberg 2002, pp. 8–9). Here, one is not talking about what goes on inside his mind or what he feels. One describes his ways of being with others; his ways of acting and paying attention to others in difficult situations.

Hertzberg gives an example of a man who is severely ill and tells a doctor that he wants to die and that his treatment should be stopped. A doctor can feel that there is an uncertainty in how to take the man's words. Does he really want to die or is he merely expressing his desperation? This does not mean that there is one right answer to be found if we managed to read his mind. It is not even certain that the person himself actually knows whether he really means what he is saying.

Hertzberg's point is that it is because the situation is of such a serious nature that one may become uncertain about how to take the suffering person's words. The reason we do not constantly find it difficult to know what people feel or what they mean by their words is not a matter of our usually having more information about others but rather of the situations being harmless and ordinary. The way one attaches importance to the person's words as well as the way one can be uncertain about how to take his words, again, is an expression of one's realizing the serious character of the situation. This reaction in itself is a form of moral awareness of the other, which shows in how one acts, in how one listens to the person, how one might be sensitive to his gestures and so on. The way questions and uncertainty about the meaning of the other person's words come in here are in themselves an expression of a compassionate attitude towards the suffering man.

3. Minds, persons and knowledge

Philosophers who talk about empathy as a matter of seeing the other person's perspective often conclude that it is an essential condition for our being able to understand others that we see them as *separate minds* or as a *separate consciousness* or as a *different stance*. The difficulty then lies in trying to imagine how another person thinks, someone who might think very differently from me. This is a view based on the presupposition that the truth about other people is independent of my attitude towards them. Understanding is seen as a neutral and epistemological concept, as a matter of acquiring certain mental information about others, information the meaning of which is independent of how or why we acquire it. Peter Goldie writes:

> First it is necessary for empathy that I be aware of the other as a centre of consciousness distinct from myself.... Secondly, it is necessary for empathy that the other should be someone of whom I have a substantial characterization. Thirdly, it is necessary that I have a grasp of the narrative which I can imaginatively enact, with the other as narrator. (Goldie 2000, p. 195)

Goldie talks about the need to be aware of the other as a separate centre of consciousness distinct from myself and that I must try to grasp the other person's narrative. In a later paper called 'Emotion, Personality and Simulation' (2002, p. 102), he continues to discuss empathy in roughly the same manner: as an imaginative technique by which we are able to predict and explain the other person's emotions, beliefs and actions. He gives an example of a person who stands in a queue predicting how the woman in front of him might react if he queue-barges in front of her (Goldie 2002, p. 102). Goldie sees this as a typical example of how one can use one's empathic imagination to try to understand another person. The difficulty with this way of understanding is, according to Goldie, that our imagination is easily coloured by our own personality so that we think the other thinks and acts as we would in the same situation. I agree with Goldie that this can be the case. However, I would say that Goldie is still stuck in a more serious problem that has to do with the whole idea about what empathy is and thus the idea about what it means to understand another person.

Goldie tends to talk about our understanding others as if a true understanding of others consisted in a neutral, purely epistemological procedure to read other minds. However, there is an ambiguity in the example. One could say that the person in the example expresses a *lack* of understanding no matter how good he might be at seeing through the woman in question. This is so because the person in the queue is trying to manipulate the woman in front of him. No matter how good he might be at reading the woman's mind he will not have an honest understanding of her. Philosophers discussing empathy have a neutral, epistemological conception of the truth about other people's emotions. This is connected with them thinking that our awareness of other people is an awareness of another 'mind' or a 'separate perspective' or a 'separate consciousness'. Batson's and Stotland's experiments are based on the same idea of understanding others as a matter of seeing through them in some sort of epistemological sense, by using our imagination. One central problem with how one talks about empathy, then, is that one thinks there is some form of factual truth about other people's emotions and that the way we find things out about others does not matter for what our understanding means, for how we talk about this understanding as truthful or as manipulative.[4]

The emphasis on empathic imagination as a form of understanding others is connected with a view of understanding as a matter of reflection. But another person standing calmly in the queue not reflecting at all about the woman in front of him would, as I see it, express a much more respectful attitude and thus a more serious form of understanding the situation than Goldie's manipulating person does by his careful reflections. Sometimes our *not* trying to explain or predict another person's emotions or behaviour is connected with a kind of spontaneous respect for others and a respect for the character of the situation (in the queue you wait patiently like everyone else). This attitude towards the other is more closely connected with what it means to have a truthful relation to another person than the urge to know everything about the other.

One major difference between, on the one hand, the philosophers who talk about empathy and, on the other hand, the examples Wittgenstein gives of what it means to understand other people is that Wittgenstein sees our understanding of each other as centrally having its form and meaning in our relations and encounters with each other. He writes in *Zettel*: 'Being sure that someone is in pain, doubting whether he is, and so on, are so many natural, instinctive, kinds of behaviour towards other human beings'(Wittgenstein 1981, § 545). It is in the form of specific responses to each other that our thinking, doubting or reflecting has meaning.

Wittgenstein thus considers second-person relations to be of great importance for what we mean when we talk about understanding another person. A second-person relation differs from a third-person relation in that it is a mutual relation; the persons confront each other, talk with each other; have some form of mutual relation to each other. However, also a third-person point of view is relational, since you are responsible for your thoughts about the other. One could say that these perspectives are mutually dependent on each other. The meaning your talking *about* a friend or thinking *about* him has can't be separated from the sort of relation you have to him, or from the way you would talk *with* him. Or, to take another example, the meaning of your remembering or not remembering your grandchild's birthday can't be separated from this being your grandchild. Or, the meaning our talking about Iraq or Darfur has is dependent on whether this talk is an effort to reach moral awareness and acknowledgement of what is happening to the people there, or, on the other hand, whether talking about Iraq is merely a way of having a nice dinner chat.

Empathy philosophers often consider a third-person perspective to be the ultimate and basic perspective from which we understand others. In fact, their perspective is not a third-person perspective; it is no perspective on human beings at all but rather a perspective on a theoretical construction, the mind. This has to do with the fact that they distort the third-person perspective into a morally neutral, purely epistemological perspective.

One of the most common ways of trying to understand another person is to *ask* him/her what he/she thinks or feels. And one of the most common things is *telling* others about our worries and our feelings. The way knowledge comes into our understanding of each other's emotions is centrally connected with the way we *talk and engage with each other* rather than finding out things about each other by guessing. This is connected with the central sense in which understanding another person has meaning as a way of sharing each other's thoughts. Talking to each other and engaging in each other's life, trying to comfort, helping, quarrelling, disagreeing, asking, telling, expressing our joys and worries show our willingness or unwillingness to understand each other. This form of our knowledge and understanding is centrally mutual and expressive rather than private and mental.

The way philosophers ignore the role our talking has for the meaning of our emotions leads to a tendency to think that our emotions are basically private mental occurrences (thoughts, attitudes, feelings, states). This way of thinking distorts the role our emotions have in our life as well as the character of our difficulties to understand each other. Our emotions centrally have meaning in our engagement with each other where our talking is one of the main forms in which we engage. For instance, talking about one's feelings is usually not a question of reporting about one's state in the first place (though it might be when visiting a doctor). Our talking has the form of sharing a life, confiding in each other, expressing our opinion, our anger or frustration or worry and so on.

The ways in which we talk about our feelings with each other is inseparable from the character our human relations have for us, inseparable from what it means to be close to another person. The meaning of our words or gestures can't be separated from the ways we are related to each other. A letter or a handshake mean different things depending on the ways we have shared a life and depending on the ways we have talked with each other before. Our ways of thinking about others are also in this sense, as I have tried to say, dependent on the way we approach each other and the way we are related to each other. My keeping my thoughts to myself can thus reveal very much about me, about the character of my emotions and about my relation to another person. That is, my emotions have a certain character *because* I keep them to myself.

Only by seeing that our understanding and knowledge of each other has meaning in the ways we share our lives, can one see the character of our difficulties to understand each other. It is in our inability to acknowledge each other that our difficulties to understand each other lie. Moreover, the thought that our not understanding another person always has to do with our lacking certain information about him or her ignores the aspect that it is usually in our *close* relationships, in relationships where we know very much about each other, that we have the strongest feelings of not understanding each other; the strongest feelings of desperation, anger, contempt and disappointment in each other. From the empathy philosophers' point of view, this becomes a contradiction. The ways we can be callous, self-centred and childish show in how we take each other's words, how we see a meaning in what the other person says and in how we respond to each other. Knowledge plays a lot of different roles in our personal difficulties to understand each other, but it is usually not a *lack* of information that is the difficulty.

Contempt, for instance, is very much an attitude where I think I know who you are; hence I do not need or want to ask you anything. And no matter what you say I turn your words against you as merely affirming what a loser and creep you are. My bitterness, again, can take the form of my clinging to my knowledge of your deceit, never forgetting it, making the memory colour our whole relation. The way I cling to this memory as a jewel reveals the character of my self-centred bitterness.

Compassion, on the other hand, expresses an open form of knowledge. Compassion has a mutual character in how one acknowledges one's presence to the other by talking. For instance, one might say worriedly to a sick friend 'How are you feeling?' This way of talking is one of the more central ways of showing compassion towards another person; it is a way of acknowledging the other person's suffering, a way of expressing warmth and of caring for the other. One *shows* that one cares about another person, one lets him know. The central form of the relation between compassion and knowledge here is not that we have certain general and neutral information of facts which makes us care, but that we let the person *know* that we think about him. Bodily expressions can in this sense, as Wittgenstein also shows,[5] be of great importance as expressions of compassion; that one looks into another person's eyes, that one does not leave a suffering person alone, that one holds the person's hand. Knowledge comes into compassion very much as something one shares with the other, in one's attentiveness towards the other.

Furthermore, compassion often takes the form of a respectful acknowledgement that one does *not* have the authority to say how things are for the other. In *Letters to Malcolm*,[6] C.S. Lewis writes about the difficulty of his grief after having lost his wife. 'You wrote; "I know I'm outside. My voice can hardly reach you." And that was one reason why your letter was more like the real grasp of a real hand than any other I got.' (Lewis 1991, p. 41) Lewis illustrates here how a friend's expression of compassion is expressed in the respectful and honest acknowledgement that grief can be a lonely struggle.

Expressions of compassion are connected with our acknowledging the other's situation rather than with a closed and private form of expert knowledge. It is in this way that the question 'How are you feeling?' has meaning. However, when empathy philosophers talk about understanding other people, knowledge remains a kind of private matter, something that has meaning independently of my relation to the other person, and it remains something that I have authority to decide about as I please.

The idea about empathy is expressive of a perspective on human life as something that should ultimately be possible to explain and understand in all its details. This perspective is very much an outsider's perspective on life, and it easily ignores the way illness, death and other forms of suffering can make us quiet and can make us lose our words. These are situations where explanations would easily be an expression of superficiality.

4. Empathy; cruelty; seductive thoughts and the impossibility of understanding

The philosophical picture of empathy as a useful method for understanding others implies that a callous or cruel person and a compassionate person could think in the same way about another person's suffering. It suggests that both could use the same imaginative technique to understand the other person's mind but then only choose to use this information for a good or a bad purpose. It further implies that a general and neutral psychological ability to imagine all the details of another person's thoughts or feelings is in itself a useful practical ability that is essential for our moral engagement in others. However, C.S. Lewis writes in his *Letters to Malcolm*:

> [The Crucifixion] did not become a frequent motive of Christian art until the generations which had seen real crucifixions were all dead. As for many hymns and sermons on the subject – endlessly harping on blood, as if that were all that mattered – they must be the work either of people so far above me that they can't reach me, or else of people with no imagination at all (some might be cut off from me by both these gulfs). (Lewis 1991, p. 86)

Lewis here reminds us that a certain kind of detailed imagination of things such as torture is not necessarily an expression of insightful understanding or an expression of a true ability to imagine what suffering means. This kind of detailed imagination about certain forms of suffering is rather expressive of a *lack* of imagination. It is a lack of imagination in the sense that it is a lack of ability to be truly moved by human life, the only form of movement being a curiosity for abhorring details.[7] Lewis's way of talking about imagination here does not have to do with our mind or some general cognitive ability to think. He is talking about imagination in a moral sense. One might say that our ability to think shows itself in our reactions to cruelty: not only how we can find it difficult to talk about, but also how we can try to acknowledge cruelty by talking about it, as well as in our trying to help the victims of cruelty. Sometimes being able to imagine and talk about all the gruesome details of torture with ease can be seen as an expression of a superficial attitude towards life, as an inability to think. Even if the detailed imagination of suffering is not an expression of contempt or hate or any other clearly immoral attitude, the interest in picturing the suffering as exactly and vividly as possible may be an expression of blindness.

In his book *Elizabeth Costello* (2003), J.M. Coetzee discusses the relation between imagination and cruelty. He describes how we can become seduced by literature which is seeped in detailed descriptions of torture. His thought seems to be that simply reading such things will, in a sense, make us part of this evil. I think Coetzee says something important here about imagination. He makes us think about imagination not merely as a way of reflecting which does not touch on who we are, and which does not have any moral relevance. The way we imagine things, as well as the way we can be seduced into imagining things, expresses and forms who we are. This does not mean that it would be wrong to reflect on certain extreme forms of cruelty such as cruelties in war or other forms of extreme abuse. That would be an absurd consequence. But, as Susan Sontag[8] notes in her book *Regarding the Pain of Others* (2003), the difficulty lies in being able to describe such atrocities without being seduced by them.

Sometimes there is a tendency to picture cruelty as an expression of talent, sophistication and high intelligence. This is usually connected with portraying extreme forms of sadism. This is, I think, one way of being seduced by cruelty; one regards cruelty as mysterious in an exciting sense. Such things as, for instance, domestic violence then appear too ordinary, too boring, lacking imagination and sophistication and mystery. Martha Nussbaum connects cruelty with intelligence and sadism in this way. She writes:

> In short, empathy is a mental ability highly relevant to compassion, although it is itself both fallible and morally neutral.
>
> Does empathy contribute anything of ethical importance entirely on its own (when it does not lead to compassion)? I have suggested that it does not: a torturer can use it for hostile and sadistic ends. On the other hand, it does involve a very basic recognition of another world of experience, and to that extent, it is not altogether neutral. If I allow my mind to be formed into the shape of your experience, even in a playful way and even without concern for you, I am still in a very basic way acknowledging your reality and humanity ... Consider Hannibal Lecter's treatment of Clarice Starling in *The Silence of the Lambs*. Although Lecter's intentions towards Clarice are entirely malign, and although he might easily be imagined eating her, nonetheless, in his very effort to reconstruct the workings of her mind there is a basic human respect. The evil of utter dehumanization seems worse: for Jews, or women, or any other victim to be treated as mere objects whose experience doesn't matter may perhaps involve a more profound evil than for them to be tortured by an empathetic villain who recognizes them as human. (Nussbaum 2001, pp. 333–334)

My impression is that Nussbaum is greatly confusing things here. First, she is too uncritical of the character of the film *The Silence of the Lambs* (Demme 1991). She does not seem to notice that the portrayal of Lecter as highly intelligent and sophisticated is a way of mystifying cruelty and making it appear fascinating and deep in an obscure sense.

Second, Nussbaum's reflections are an expression of her confused epistemological idea about empathy; she is caught up in an epistemological view on what we mean when we talk about imagination that she oddly assimilates with respect merely because one imagines 'another perspective'. I can't see what this has to do with respect. Neither can I see how her examples of 'empathetic torturers' have anything to do with respect. Talking about respect in this sense distorts the meaning of the word.

Third, Nussbaum's conclusions are connected with her confusing certain moral ways of talking with epistemological and ontological expressions. This can be seen in her saying that when we talk about the Nazis treating the Jews as if they were not human beings (or treating them as objects) we say that the Nazis lacked an empathic capability to imagine the other person's perspective. However, when we talk about cruelty in terms like 'seeing a human being', 'treating someone like an object' or 'being able to imagine', we express ourselves *only* in a moral sense. We are not talking about the cruel person suffering from some sort of epistemological and ontological inability to see the other person's perspective.

Peter Winch, on the other hand, avoids the temptation to see cruelty as exotic. In his essay 'Can We Understand Ourselves?' Winch remarks that he finds it impossible to understand that someone can find football so important that he is ready to kill for it (Winch 1997). Winch is not saying that if he could get more psychological information he might understand such a fascination for football better. Neither is he saying that the football fantast is unusually intelligent and that it is therefore difficult to understand his way of reasoning. His saying that he cannot understand is not an expression of a lack of information or a lack of some psychological skill. By saying that it is impossible to understand he is expressing his horror over the fact that sport can have such importance for people that it leads to violence and murder.[9] Cruelty can have a very simple form and still be impossible to understand. In his paper 'The Limits of Understanding' Hertzberg writes:

> My specific point is this: if I call the activity of the snipers who were shooting the children of Sarajevo incomprehensible, or if I say I do not understand it, this is *not* like saying that I do not like it, or that I find it abhorrent. In fact, I think it would be strange if someone said he did not 'like' the sniping, or that he 'found it abhorrent'. It is as if the distance he is expressing were not deep enough. I should like to say that there is a form of distancing which is the most directly expressed by using words like 'incomprehensible' or 'I don't understand.' It is a reaction to certain forms of evil. (Hertzberg 2005, p. 5)

The sense in which people in wars or in other cases of brutality are treated as if they were not human beings is similar to the sense in which these acts of cruelty may be said to be impossible to understand. These expressions have nothing to do with saying that the cruelty is of a very sophisticated psychological character. Neither do these expressions have anything to do with describing some sort of epistemological problems of the cruel person not seeing the other person's perspective.

Another example of suffering being pictured in an exotic way is a scene in Steven Spielberg's *Schindler's List* (1993). A handsome Nazi officer (Amon Goeth) is looking into a half-naked and beautiful Jewish woman's (Helen Hirsch's) eyes and asks himself 'Is this the face of a rat?' The scene, in my opinion, does not illustrate anything real about the Holocaust but only something about Spielberg wanting to please the audience. It is a way of portraying humiliation and the threat of rape in an erotic light. It becomes one of a billion film scenes portraying a sado-masochistic relation between a man and a woman, a weak and scared beautiful woman in the hands of the powerful and intelligent handsome man. I think that in this scene Spielberg utterly lost touch with the story he wanted to tell about the Holocaust.

Nussbaum, by contrast, considers this a powerful scene which reveals how one can become morally aware of another as a human being through sexual arousal (Nussbaum 2001, p. 320). As in her example with Hannibal Lecter, I cannot see what this example has to do with moral understanding, nor can I see that it shows anything real about cruelty. My impression is that Nussbaum is again too uncritical of the character of the scene in the film, thereby once more accepting an exotic picture of cruelty. She is also caught up in thinking that the Nazis suffered from an epistemological inability to imagine another perspective. These two forms of confusion seem to feed each other.

Knowledge takes many different forms when cruelty is concerned, forms that are not epistemological, and several that express different kinds of blindness. But the blindness does not only appear in a tendency to portray cruelty in an exotic light, it can also consist in our talking about cruelty in neutralizing terms. Consider for instance the way the U.S. government talks about 'interrogation methods' being used in Guantanamo, trying by all means to avoid the word 'torture'. Using neutralizing expressions the government softens down certain images of what is being done to people. It is a corrupt way of trying to make extreme forms of cruelty sound reasonable. The expression 'interrogation method' gives the impression of a well tested and safe technique that the 'interrogation experts' have long experience of using and that produces 'good results'.[10]

Two things may be said of the above example. First, the allusion to knowledge can have a strong role in the form of appearance of expertise and professionalism. This can be extremely effective in seducing people to think that what is done must be right. The expression has the appearance of knowledge since it has a professional and even medical sound, as well as a sound of necessity and authority.

Second, there is no way of describing violence neutrally without distorting what is being done to people. When the U.S. government tries to talk about torture in neutral terms, they are in fact actively diminishing and ignoring what is being done. They are not at all being neutral in their 'neutralizing' use of words. They are playing with slippery expressions. It is, for instance, absurd to make a distinction between what is and what is not torture by claiming that the violence is 'safe' and therefore not torture. It is like claiming that a person has not been raped if she or he was not killed or badly mutilated. In this sense, I also find it misleading to say that empathy is a neutral imaginative method that we can use for good or bad purposes. How can one's imagination be neutral without being corrupt, when it comes to violence?

However, there are examples of writers who describe cruelty and suffering in a way that is completely free from any desire to seduce the reader. This, I think, is the case with Primo Levi's book *If this is a Man* (Levi 2000). Levi has a very unusual down-to-earth way of describing his experience in the concentration camp which in itself is expressive of a deep sense for human life. In this way, he manages to reveal both the unimaginably inhuman existence in the camps and some very special instances of humanity.

The ways we talk about cruelty and violence, the expressions we use when describing specific events, show our sense for human reality. There is not some simple, single epistemological and neutral way of understanding life. And it is a mistake to think that the more details we have about others in some sort of general sense, the more we understand about them. Some detailed descriptions of cruelty have an exotic character. Some descriptions have a neutralizing and callous character. Some manage to give a revealing picture of human life.

Notes

* I am very grateful to David Cockburn, Lars Hertzberg, Mari Lindman, Michael Mc Eachrane, Camilla Kronqvist, Göran Torrkulla and all the people at the research seminar at the department of philosophy, Åbo Akademi University for valuable comments.

1. Not all philosophers who talk about empathy are uncritical of such empirical research. Peter Goldie (2000) is, for instance, critical of Goldman's conclusions about empathy from the experiment.
2. Nussbaum would probably partly agree with these thoughts. She does also think that compassion centrally is connected with our trying to be aware of how we can be blind for others and unfair towards others. The trouble is that she still sees empathy as an expression of a basic form of awareness of other people.
3. Hertzberg's paper is written in Swedish. The title is: 'Om inlevelsens roll i filosofi och humaniora'.
4. In a more recent paper 'Wollheim on emotion and imagination' (2006) Goldie is much more sceptical of the idea that empathy would work. He thinks empathy is problematic because it would be almost impossible to try to take Salieri's perspective towards Mozart (that is his example) since one would have to imagine so much about his perspectives and psychological tendencies to react and think. Instead of empathy Goldie says our normal ways of understanding has the character of our reacting towards the other. I think Goldie is here close to realizing what the trouble is with the idea about empathy, but he still does not really see how deep the problem is. Even if Goldie is sceptical about the usefulness of empathy he does not really see that the whole concept of empathy is based on a certain

kind of conceptual and logical blindness for what it means to have a truthful understanding of another person. It is not merely a difference in degree. The problem is not that empathic understanding is something very difficult to achieve and that we therefore *ordinarily tend* to try to understand others in another more 'reactive' way. The problem is that the concept of empathy is based on deep misconceptions of our relation to other human beings as other minds, and misconceptions that also have to do with thinking that understanding, seeing, thinking are mental and psychological concepts.

5. See the earlier quote from Wittgenstein, 2001, art. 286.
6. Malcolm is generally considered to be a fictional character.
7. An example of such lack of imagination would, for instance, be Mel Gibson's film *The Passion of the Christ* (2004).
8. Sontag does also discuss the way suffering is pictured in media in several very important ways that I am not able to elaborate in this chapter.
9. One could perhaps criticize Winch for making it sound as if liking football inevitably meant accepting the violence at football games. I doubt that Winch meant this. Surely one can love football without accepting the violence, but there is a clear trend in football being connected with violence. Winch shows in his essay that our difficulty to understand does not have to concern distant cultures but can concern our own culture. Our inability to understand other people is thus not necessarily an epistemological difficulty but a moral reaction.
10. See also David Bromwich's article 'Euphemism and American Violence' (2008) where he discusses how cruelty is talked about in euphemistic terms, thereby distorting what is actually being done.

Bibliography

Batson, C.D. (1997), 'Is Empathy-Induced Helping Due to Self-Other Merging?' *Journal of Personality and Social Psychology* 73, 495–509.

Bromwich, D. (2008), 'Euphemism and American Violence', *New York Review of Books*, April 3 2008, LV (5), 28–30.

Coetzee, J.M. (2003), *Elizabeth Costello* (London: Penguin Books Ltd).

Fuller, G. (1995), 'Simulation and Psychological Concepts' in Davies, M. and Stone, T. (eds), *Mental Simulation* (Oxford: Blackwell Publishers Ltd).

Goldie, P. (2000), *The Emotions, a Philosophical Exploration* (New York: Oxford University Press).

—— (2002), 'Emotion Personality and Simulation' in Goldie, P. (ed.) *Understanding Emotions: Mind and Morals* (Aldershot: Ashgate).

—— (2006), 'Wollheim on Emotion and Imagination', *Philosophical Studies* 127, 1–17.

Goldman, A.I. (1995), 'Empathy, Mind and Morals' in Davies, M. and Stone, T. (eds), *Mental Simulation* (Oxford: Blackwell Publishers Ltd).

Hertzberg, L. (2002), 'Om inlevelsens roll i filosofi och humaniora' in *Att förstå inom humaniora* (Helsingfors: Finska Vetenskaps-Societeten).

—— (2005), 'The Limits of Understanding', *Sats-Nordic Journal of Philosophy* 6(1), 5–14.

Levi, P. ([1947] 2000), *If This is a Man: The Truce* (London: Everyman's Library).

Lewis, C.S. ([1964] 1991), *Letters to Malcolm Chiefly on Prayer* (London: Harcourt Inc).

Nussbaum, M. (2001), *Upheavals of Thought* (Cambridge: Cambridge University Press).

Sontag, S. (2003), *Regarding the Pain of Others* (New York: Farrar, Straus and Giroux).

Stotland, E. (1969), 'Exploratory Investigations of Empathy', *Advances in Experimental Social Psychology* 4, 271–314 (New York: Academic Press).

Stueber, K.R. (2006), *Rediscovering Empathy* (Cambridge: The MIT Press).

Winch, P. (1997), 'Can We Understand Ourselves?' *Philosophical Investigations* 20(3), 193–204.

Wittgenstein, L. ([1953] 2001), *Philosophical Investigations* (Oxford: Blackwell Publishers).

—— ([1967] 1981), *Zettel* (Oxford: Blackwell Publishers).

Filmography

Demme, J. (1991). *The Silence of the Lambs*, USA.

Gibson, M. (2004). *The Passion of the Christ*, USA.

Spielberg, S. (1993). *Schindler's List*, USA.

10

The Fiction of Paradox: Really Feeling for Anna Karenina*

Danièle Moyal-Sharrock

> It will be asked, how the drama
> moves, if it is not credited.
>
> Samuel Johnson (1765, p. 502)

'How can I feel compassion for a woman because she felt her life to be so intolerable that she threw herself under a train, when I know at the same time that there is no woman, no intolerable situation, and no train?' – This, in a nutshell, is the paradox of fiction.[1] How can we be moved by what we know does not exist? In the same way, it is irrational for someone to feel sorry for my daughter if they know I don't have one, or feel glad that I won the lottery if they know I haven't, it seems irrational to be moved by the fate of characters, like Anna Karenina or King Lear, we know never existed. Yet our own reactions to fictional characters tell us that we are often thus moved. In this chapter, I claim that the paradox fatally hinges on cognitive theories of emotion that generate positions which phenomenologically and intellectually misrepresent our experiences of art – such as Kendall Walton's *pretend theory* and Peter Lamarque's *thought theory*. I examine and reject these positions, and acknowledge the concept-formative role of *genuine* emotion generated by fiction. I then argue, *contra* Jenefer Robinson, that this 'éducation sentimentale' is not achieved through *distancing*, but precisely through literature's ability to *engage* our emotions. Literature does this, I claim, by its uniquely *perspicuous presentations* of emotional (and other) concepts and the *cognitive pleasure* that such 'presentations' prompt in us.

1. The paradox of fiction

The paradox consists of three premises which, taken individually, seem plausible but are jointly inconsistent:

1. We often experience emotions towards what we know to be *fictional* characters or situations;

2. we can only experience emotions for objects that we believe exist;
3. we do not believe that fictional characters or situations exist.

Therefore, the paradox consists in the claim that we have and yet cannot have emotions towards fictional objects. Philosophers have attempted to resolve or dissolve the paradox mostly by rejecting one of the three premises and claiming either that

1. what we experience towards what we know to be *fictional* characters or situations are *not* emotions; that is, we are not *really* moved;
2. what moves us are not the fictional characters themselves, but
   a) their real-life counterparts
   b) the *thoughts* that they provoke in us;
3. we *can* experience emotions for objects that we do not believe exist.

The third claim is made by philosophers who hold a noncognitive theory of emotion. I am of that ilk and so believe that we can be *really* moved by *fictional characters*, and that this does not generate a paradox – therefore my title: *the fiction of paradox*. But before joining the noncognitive contingent, let us briefly examine the opposition.

2. Kendall Walton: Not emotions, but *quasi*-emotions

> [The actor] on a stage plays at being another
> before a gathering of people who play at
> taking him for that other person.
>
> Jorge Luis Borges (1962, p. 248)

On a *narrow* cognitive theory of emotions,[2] emotions require *beliefs* (in the existence of the object of one's emotion), which are linked to *desires* (that move us to action). On a *broad* cognitive theory of emotions, an emotion need only be accompanied by a propositional attitude; and that needn't be a belief, it can be a thought, a judgement, an imagining. Kendall Walton is a *narrow* cognitivist; he claims that we (ordinary viewers and readers) cannot experience genuine emotions towards fictional characters because we do not believe they exist, and that this absence of emotion is phenomenologically visible in the absence of desires that would be there in actual situations: we do not run away from the monster, attempt to stop Juliet from killing herself or organize a rescue mission to get Robinson Crusoe off his island. There is, then, in the case of our reactions to fictional characters or events, neither *existential endorsement* nor *motivational upshot*. And this absence of the relevant beliefs and desires means, for Walton, that what we experience towards fictional characters cannot be emotions, but *quasi-emotions*: we do not really fear Dracula, pity Anna Karenina, hate Iago and so on, but only experience *quasi-fear, quasi-pity* and so on, towards them.[3] And by this, Walton means that we merely *imagine* ourselves afraid or sad as part of a game of make-believe[4] in which the story is a prop. Walton compares readers and viewers of fiction to children who *play at* being afraid, say, when their father, acting as a monster, runs after them.

So that what we have always considered emotional reactions towards fictional characters or events are for Walton nothing but play-acting: when we are reading Shakespeare's depiction of Juliet's death, we *pretend* to experience sadness; we behave in a way that *imitates* sad behaviour. Walton goes as far as to say that the reader or viewer, in his reaction to fiction, 'is an actor impersonating himself' (1978, p. 311). This is not to say that we don't get 'caught up' in stories and become 'emotionally involved', but this, says Walton, is make-believe emotion which we mistake for real emotion (1978, p. 307). Because quasi-fear is an experience that imitates fear, it is *almost* phenomenologically indistinguishable from real fear and the similarity is such that we fail to recognize the difference. For Walton, then, all readers or viewers of fiction are not merely spectators of make-believe or pretence; they themselves play a game of make-believe or pretence. In short, all *consumers of fiction are actors and self-deceivers.*[5]

But Walton is wrong: other than in its restricted pejorative connotation,[6] fiction is not synonymous with (self-)deception or delusion; nor is it the case that spectators or readers by default *pretend to be moved* by fictional characters. There are, of course, instances when we do pretend to be moved *by* fictional characters – say, when reading to a child, I act afraid of the big bad wolf or simulate ecstatic joy as the glass slipper fits Cinderella; or when someone unaffected by an act of cruelty in a film he is watching with friends feigns repulsion to seem or feel 'normal': such instances are rightly called *acting, pretending to feel,* or *simulating emotion.* And such examples of make-believe emotion should highlight the contrast with the way we ordinarily react to fictional characters. As Lamarque rightly notes, our responses to fiction do not correspond to our paradigm of 'make-believe emotions': children who play at being sad, angry or frightened (1991, p. 165). Walton's children analogy is not a good analogy for art.

In fact, Walton erroneously multiplies processes across the board. Not only does he claim that we are not afraid but merely 'imagine ourselves afraid', but he also contends that because artistic objects do not exist, we only 'imagine seeing' them: and so we only 'imagine seeing' the apple in Cezanne's *Still Life with Apple*, or Dracula in the eponymous film. But this too is misguided: we see the apple and Dracula in a very ordinary sense of seeing – only we see them 'in a painting', or 'in a film'. To *imagine seeing something* is, as for pretending to be moved, a much more deliberate and complicated process: 'imagine seeing' is something I might do if I were blind. Analogously, to *imagine seeing an apple in a painting* is much more contrived than *seeing an apple in a painting*[7]; it does not characterize our standard perception of artistic objects.

Literary characters and situations prompt real, full-fledged emotions that often have prolonged, even life-long, impact. Indeed, so *real* was the fear that Hitchcock's *The Birds* spurred in me when I watched it at the age of nine that I know it to be *responsible* for my still-existent ornithophobia. And what of the emotions provoked by Goethe's *The Sorrows of Young Werther* (1774) which caused so many young men at the end of the eighteenth century to commit suicide?[8] Can we call these 'make-believe'? As Colin Radford writes, our ordinary responses to fictional characters are genuine responses:

> We shed real tears for Mercutio. They are not crocodile tears, they are dragged from us and they are not the sort of tears that are produced by cigarette smoke in the theatre.... Indeed, we may be so appalled at the prospect of what we think is going to happen to a character in a novel or a play that some of us can't go on. We avert the impending tragedy in the only way we can, by closing the book, or leaving the theatre. (1975, p. 70)

Moreover, Walton – and narrow cognitivists generally – is wrong to think that motivational upshot and existential endorsement are essential to experiencing emotion. Let's start with motivational upshot.

2.1   Emotion and motivational upshot

Granted, we do not send for a policeman when Othello kills Desdemona, as we might if we witnessed our neighbour killing his wife – but if we broaden our range of examples, we realize that not all emotions prompted by *real* events involve an inclination to action. Not all cases of fear, for instance, motivate a desire to escape, or to act: I can be lying in the operating theatre in acute fear of the procedure I am about to undergo, but with no inclination or desire to run away, so conscious am I of the good the operation will do me. Nor do real-life cases of pity *all* motivate a desire to comfort: I may feel genuinely sorry for my friend's untimely death or for Socrates' undeserved death, and yet this emotion does not involve any desire to action.[9]

Not having motivational upshot is simply a feature of the ways emotions work in some situations and not in others, regardless of whether the situations are fictional or nonfictional. So that Walton's cleavage between reality- and fiction-directed emotions on the basis of motivational upshot is untenable: an emotion need not motivate us to action to be a *bona fide* emotion. And if motivational upshot does not, in fact, divide the real world from the fictional world, Walton's key argument founders.

It can be said, then, that in his determination to find a solution to an apparent logical problem, Walton misrepresents our *experience* of fiction. As Noel Carroll puts it: 'Walton's theory appears to throw out the phenomenology of the state for the sake of logic' (1990, pp. 73–4) – and for a logic that is unduly restricted by a *narrow* cognitive theory of emotion.

2.2   Emotion and existential commitment

As for claiming that we cannot experience genuine emotions for fictional characters because we do not *believe* they exist (and therefore that they can suffer, love, seek revenge, walk with a limp, lose their eyesight, be miserly or self-sacrificing) – this, I suggest, is to drain the concept of belief of one of its most ordinary and vital uses. There is more to the concept of belief than a propositional attitude towards something we regard as true in the nonfictional world. To say of Desdemona that she is Othello's wife is true, and not to believe that, or to believe she is Iago's wife, is to have seriously misread Shakespeare's play.[10]

This ordinary use of the concept of belief, at least, shows that belief does not require existential commitment,[11] but nor does emotion. Indeed, many *common everyday emotional experiences* do not require existence beliefs. Many of our emotions have to do with the nonfactual, such as fearing a ghost or a burglar when none is there; or fearing a forecast earthquake that does not occur. For his theory to work, however, Walton claims it is not necessary that we believe in the *actual* existence of the object of our emotion, believing in its *possible* existence will do. But, in response to Walton, there are some emotionally stimulating fantasies or daydreams that do not presuppose beliefs in the actuality *or possibility* of their content; for example, 'Suppose I were immortal / invincible / irresistible / Midas / endowed with magical powers that would bring my father back to life ...'.[12] Although all of these nonfictional fantasies can elicit emotion, they are – none of them – grounded on belief or even half-belief, and have no *possibility* ground to stand on.

We can then go on to ask, with B.J. Rosebury, whether such fantasies might not provide a model for an explanation of our responses to fiction which would avoid raising the question of belief at all, and thus circumvent the paradox (1979); but our answer would have to be: not quite. For though such fantasies, by rendering belief unnecessary, render both Walton's make-believe theory and narrow cognitivism otiose, we still have to contend with *broad* cognitivism.

3. Peter Lamarque: Not beliefs, but *thoughts*

Broad cognitivism in the form, mainly, of Peter Lamarque's thought theory[13] – is characteristic of the second type of assault on the paradox, that which consists in rejecting the idea that emotions require *belief* in the existence or possibility of their object, and regarding *thought* as sufficient to stimulate emotion: 'we can be frightened by the thought of something without believing that there is anything real corresponding to the content of the thought. At most we must simply believe that the thought is frightening' (1981, p. 330).

With thought theory, then, we are still within the dictates of cognitive theory, but the requirements are not as stringent. Here, belief is not necessary for emotion; it is, as it were, the thought that counts: 'the fear and pity we feel for fictions are in fact directed at thoughts in our minds', and not at the characters themselves; 'when we fear Othello or pity Desdemona our fears and tears are directed at thought-contents' (Lamarque 1981, pp. 330, 329, 331).[14] What horrifies us in the Dracula movie, for example, is the content of our thoughts 'that Dracula might exist and do these terrible things' (Carroll 1987, p. 56).

So that where, with Walton, we had lost all full-fledged emotions towards fictional characters and events; with Lamarque, we lose the characters and events themselves as objects of our full-fledged emotions. But this, I suggest, is where the thought theory collapses before it even gets off the ground, for it *is* towards characters and events in fiction that readers and viewers speak of having emotions, not towards thoughts. Our emotions are directed at characters embedded in lived situations, not at thoughts or propositions in our minds.[15] As Robert Yanal rightly objects: 'It is one thing to shudder over an abstract thought, it is another to shudder when "Mrs Bates" comes into the bathroom in *Psycho*' (1999, p. 38).

3.1   *Contra* Lamarque: Art is *not* thought

Moreover, what Lamarque must see is that if a thought can fill us with pity, it cannot do so *ex nihilo*; a thought always occurs in a context, and it is the context that determines whether the thought can fill us with pity or not. If the mere thought that 'Anna Karenina is suicidal' could inspire pity, why bother writing novels? Why not dispense with fiction altogether and merely articulate thoughts? Lamarque foresees this objection by speaking of a requirement of *vividness* for the thought to evoke emotion.[16] But what gives a thought its vividness if not the context in which it occurs – that is, the author's depiction?[17]

On a continuum of vividness, the thought 'Anna Karenina is suicidal' – uttered independently of having read or heard about the novel (or without any reference to a real person of our acquaintance named Anna Karenina) – will be at point zero, and so will its emotion-inducing capacity. Add a little more depiction, and the emotion will increase. But no thought or summary or paraphrase of a novel – however vivid – can vie in emotional impact with the novel itself. This is a commonplace, which highlights the essentiality of *form* in literature. F.R. Leavis reminds us of it with regard to his own summarizing:

> My summary has, as of course any summary of theme and significance in *Anna Karenina* must have, an effect of grossness from which one shrinks. The actual creative presentment is *infinitely subtle*, and comes as

the upshot of an *immense deal of immediately relevant drama and suggestion* in the foregoing mass of the book. (1967, p. 28; my emphasis)

And whatever 'causal connection' might exist between our thoughts and the sentences and descriptions in the fiction (Lamarque 1981, p. 334), if our emotions are provoked by those *intermediary* thoughts, they are not the emotions prompted by the work itself, directly and fully. What Lamarque fails to see is that literature is not philosophy; literature does not essentially operate *via thoughts*, but through the 'immense deal of immediately relevant drama and suggestion in the foregoing mass of the book' – only *that* vividness can prompt the kind of emotion felt by readers of the novel. So that if the *vividness* is essential to the production of the emotion, the thought is *not* enough[18]; it is *not what counts*. Indeed, it might be asked why the thought is even necessary. What Lamarque summarily calls 'vividness' is the power of literary depiction, not the power of thought.

3.2   Inseparability of form and content

The power of literary depiction, or what Leavis often refers to as 'dramatic presentation' or 'creative presentment' (e.g. 1967, pp. 18, 28), consists in the *inseparable* conjunction of form and content – that is, of *how* the work of art expresses and *what* it expresses. The meaning (of a novel or in a novel) cannot be prized apart from its form because the formal properties of the novel essentially contribute to its meaning. Try paraphrasing Anna's love, or Shylock's feeling of alienation or Iago's *ressentiment*. The kind of vividness, without which Lamarque's theory dries up and withers, is not to be found in a thought sparked in the reader by a work of fiction, or even in the very sentences of the work, but in the way those very sentences are presented (e.g. as dialogue, narrative, description, meditation, stream of consciousness), and in the literary devices (e.g. metaphor, symbolism, vocabulary, syntax, tone, cadence, silence) and other elements (e.g. irony, suggestion, psychological acuity, action, timing, juxtaposition, tension, mood, plot), that bolster (e.g. contextualize, highlight, compound, characterize, enliven) them,[19] intricately constituting what D.H. Lawrence calls the novel's 'subtle interrelatedness' (1936, p. 528).

The depiction itself is *essential* to our being moved by fictional characters and situations. As Howard Mounce points out, whether or not a character moves us depends on its place in the fiction: we are not simply *told* that Anna is suffering; she is *portrayed* as suffering; and it is the detail and manner of her portrayal within the novel that are crucial to our emotional experience (1980, p. 191). How we respond to Macbeth's realization of what he has done is intimately linked to how he, Lady Macbeth, other characters and events, have been depicted up to that realization, as well as to how he expresses that realization. Context – and, in the case of literature, this largely comprises *form* – is of vital importance; thought is *not* enough.

A related attempt to make sense of the alleged paradox of fiction is to suggest that the objects of our emotions do, in some qualified or attenuated sense, exist – for example, by claiming, as Barrie Paskins does, that the objects of our emotions are not the characters and situations depicted, but their real life analogues: we pity real life people *in the same bind* as those depicted (1977). But here again, the phenomenology of our experience of fiction is overlooked: readers speak of the characters themselves, not people like them, as the objects of their emotion. Of course, there are similarities between Juliet's love and any woman's love, but how many women resemble Juliet in circumstance, intensity and eloquence? And how many people do we know *in the same situation*, or even one similar, to that of Oedipus or Gregor Samsa or Gulliver? As D.Z. Phillips argues, if literary depictions simply served to remind us of similar scenes in real life, we could be reminded of them in other, more economical ways, making works of literature super-fluous (1996, p. 140).

It is not the *thought* of Anna Karenina jumping under the train that is responsible for the reader's emotion, but Tolstoy's *rendering* of that action in the context of his rendering of her life. And this rendering *is* the novel, in all its subtle interrelatedness. Indeed, as we shall now see, no thought at all is necessary to prompt *some* emotions, so that even broad cognitivism can be rejected.

4. Noncognitivism: Emotions do not require beliefs or thoughts

Noncognitivism rejects the supposition that every emotion must be accompanied by a propositional or a cognitive attitude of any kind – neither belief nor thought is, on this view, a necessary condition for emotion. Jinhee Choi's noncognitivist approach to fiction-directed emotion is grounded on instances of what he calls 'cognitively impenetrable emotions' (2003, p. 149), emotions that *cannot* be prompted by cognition.[20] These include emotions evoked by the style of a work as well as perception-based emotions.

It is generally agreed that the formal features of an artwork are an integral part of our experience of that work – try turning off the sound in a Hitchcock film, and see how much of that is responsible for arousing anxiety – and they affect us directly, nonpropositionally and so noncognitively. As Yanal makes clear about cinematic montage: it is nonsentential, nonlinguistic, and we grasp it that way; that is, we do not mentally 'translate' the images of the montage into propositions to stimulate emotion' (1999, p. 117). The same goes for perception-based emotions – emotions that are more involved with the perception of an object than with its significance or relevance (e.g. we are startled at the mere appearance or size of monsters in film before we find out what it is they do; e.g. drink people's blood).

In response to Radford then: there are essentially different ways, and not only a paradigmatic way, of feeling; and our not feeling in the paradigmatic way does not mean that it is irrational or incoherent that we should feel. Philosophers who think there is only one right way to react emotionally and that any other is substandard or incoherent are basing their view on too restricted a diet of examples of the different manifestations of emotion. Why should sophisticated, cognitive emotions be the benchmark against which we measure whether something is or is not an emotion? And why have fiction-based emotional responses been excluded from our diet of examples; or considered as a deviant, rather than a fundamental, part of our emotional repertoire?

5. Emotions in context

The characteristics of our emotions – intensity, motivational upshot and so on – are dictated by the occasion or context, not by whether their object is real or imaginary. And so rather than make a vertical separation between emotions felt towards people and those towards fictional characters, I propose we go horizontal: track *all* emotions on a continuum going from *nil* cognitivity, existential commitment and motivational upshot to *sophisticated* cognitivity, existential commitment and motivational upshot. The same emotion, say fear, can, *or not*, be due to cognitive or propositional representation, involve existential commitment and action: I can be afraid *of* Dracula's sudden appearance on the screen (noncognitive) or *because* I believe the dentist will hurt me (cognitive); I can be afraid though I know Dracula does not exist or because I believe there is a burglar in the next room; I can be afraid and stay put, or be afraid and run. A continuum would eliminate the implausible discontinuity between our reactions towards fiction and our reactions towards real people and events – eliminating a difference *in kind* between the pity we feel for Anna Karenina and the pity we feel for someone we know; as well as any necessary difference in degree. I can feel more pity for a very dear friend than I do for Anna Karenina, but I can also feel *less* pity for a real person than I do for Anna:

> It is not improbable – maybe even likely – that a person reading Tolstoy's novel will feel more intensely for Anna Karenina (whom he takes to be fictional) than for a real woman whose plight resembles Anna's and which he has read about in the morning's paper. (Yanal 1999, p. 96)

I feel King Lear or Shylock or Willy Loman much closer to me than most *real* people I know. They step off the page and into my life and, when described by great writers, I feel closer even to some minor characters than to my postman, whose existence I don't doubt. I feel more for the death of Desdemona, who I know does not exist, than for the death of my neighbour's sister who does, because I *know* Desdemona far better: I know her psychology, her situation, her feelings; I am made to share her story and live it with her. The *story* here – but also, the way it is related: as a 'structured representation'[21] – are essential. If a travelling salesman came to my house and recounted his problems to me, I would not feel for him as I do for Willy Loman simply because the salesman's recounting of his story cannot vie with Arthur Miller's psychologically eloquent, sensitive and powerful rendering of a life through the subtle interrelatedness of dialogue, metaphor, symbolism, irony and so on. The contrast drawn by Leavis in *The Living Principle* is between 'enacting' and 'telling'; between depicting something so that it seems 'before our eyes' or 'done', and something 'merely told' about or related (1975, pp. 146–8).

The impact of the literary medium on the *quality* of the emotion experienced should not be lost sight of. My husband recounts his experience in a battlefield during the Vietnam War where his emotion reached a peak of *intensity* he had never before experienced, but subsequently reading Tolstoy's rendering of warfare in *War and Peace* and in *The Sebastopol Sketches* prompted in him a *depth* of emotion about combat, which he had never before experienced. The lived emotion had been an utterly animal emotion, whereas 'reliving Vietnam with Tolstoy' spurred a deeper, more reflective emotion – one with a dense, cognitive layering – informed by the genius of a great creative writer. Both, however, were emotions.

Not only does literature provoke genuine emotion, great literature prompts some of the finest, richest emotions we will ever experience. Not many of us experience the intensity of love Juliet and Romeo feel for each other, and for those who do, it is hardly also experienced in the kind of enlightening psychological and poetical atmosphere equivalent to that of Shakespeare's play. As Dammann aptly puts it: 'We can be moved by fictional events, by imaginary events, and by real events, but it is for the first of these to shed light on the other two, not the other way round' (1992, p. 20). The penetration of a great creative genius is such that life learns from fiction.

What Aristotle says about tragedy – that it promotes understanding or cognition – can be said of all great fiction. And tragedy as well as great fiction do this only inasmuch as a *story* (or *plot*, as Aristotle had it) is essential to them. As Amelie Rorty writes: 'While there is sorrow, grief, loss, pain in life, there is *tragedy* only when the actions and events that compose a life are organized into a story, a structured representation of that life' (1992, pp. 3–4; my emphasis). It is this *structured representation*, a representation through an artistic medium, that affects our emotions in such a way that an exceptional kind of understanding – one rarely experienced without the mediation of literature – takes place. As Dammann remarks: 'Fiction moves us because, not in spite of, the fact that it is fiction' (1992, p. 20).

Talk here of understanding and, specifically, of 'cognition' should not be confused with cognitivism or with thought theory. I am not saying that the emotions require cognitive activity to occur, but that literature imparts greater understanding or, in a broad sense: cognition. I use the term 'cognition' half-heartedly because, while I *do* want to suggest that what we reap from great literature is a robust kind of understanding which generates new beliefs, I do not want to suggest that it is constituted by, or generates, new justified true beliefs. I remain mindful of Frank Cioffi's resistance to any alliance of literature with knowledge: there are, he reminds me, differences between, say, learning German verbs and reading a novel; and in our reaching out for a work of literature, 'it is the experience itself and not its epistemic aftermath that we seek and cherish' (personal communication). Yet, as I shall argue below, one of the most important pleasures we obtain from great literary works is that of enhanced understanding – what Aristotle describes as a kind of *cognitive pleasure*.[22] *Contra* Lamarque, literature cannot be reduced to thought, but it is of course conducive to thought. Perhaps Leavis's 'The tale itself *is* the thought' (1976, p. 121) both renders the indispensability of form to the content of literature, whilst also indicating the kind of 'thought' here in question.

6. Literature and concept-formation

Where lived experience will often produce raw emotion, the emotion generated by a great creative work will be more reflective, more refined and nuanced. This is not to say that lived experience *cannot* produce pondered emotion, but a great creative writer will show us and our human condition to ourselves with infinitely greater lucidity than we are capable of. For all the horror that documentaries and history books on the Holocaust convey, it is through Kafka that I came to fathom its Existential resonances. Through works like *The Trial, The Judgment, In the Penal Colony*, the concepts of absurdity, alienation, contingency and arbitrariness took shape for me, and shed their desolate light – but a light nevertheless – on gas chambers, on mass and random killing, on human cruelty and indifference. Through Kafka, the horror became articulate.

Similarly, only through literature – indeed, years of focused reading of poetry and fiction – was I initiated into the enigmatic concept of *ennui*. It is not, however, only sophisticated or esoteric concepts that literature helps us acquire and deepen, but also more ordinary ones: love, war, injustice, bureaucracy, mental illness, jealousy. We discover ourselves and our world through experience, yes, but *in words*; and what better words than those of literature? As Leavis writes:

> Nothing important can really be said simply – simply *and* safely; and by 'safely' I mean to ensure that the whole intuited apprehension striving to find itself, to discover what it is in words, is duly served, and not thwarted. It takes a context, often a subtly and potently creative one, to do that. (1976, p. 122)

Literature is an inestimable source of understanding, but not of the kind that can be meaningfully conveyed in propositions or thoughts. Literature exemplifies what Martha Nussbaum calls 'the ethical relevance of circumstances' (1990, p. 37), and more generally I would say, their *cognitive* relevance.

Both Aristotle and Leavis regard literature as a civilizing tool. It procures an enhanced understanding of, *inter alia*, emotions. It does this, not only by the quality of its depiction, but also by the range or quantity of depicted experiences[23] which would otherwise remain unknown to readers. Not only can reading Stendhal and Tolstoy take us to different climes, it can also take us to different times, and it can do so through the art of two of the most perspicacious individuals ever to have lived. This unrivalled aptitude of literature to make available to us a range and depth of concept-formative and civilizing experiences unavailable to us in life is part of the force of D.H. Lawrence's claim that the novel is one of humanity's greatest discoveries – greater than Galileo's telescope or Marconi's wireless (1968, p. 416).

Breadth, depth and intensity of emotions in great works of art profoundly colour our lives such that to speak of 'make-believe' is idly derogatory. Without literature, our experience of *life* is reduced. Experiences provided through great works of art become a part of our emotional make-up as much as our personal experiences do. Much of the rich texture of our emotional range results from these literary experiences. Acquiring great literature is the ultimate step in acquiring language; our own emotions will find clearer and deeper articulation for it. Art is a major interpersonal channel for enculturation and concept-formation; in grasping through literature what it is to love or hurt or hate, something is being done to us which consolidates our experiences in our culture.

7. Emotions and literature

There are several strands to the relationship between literature and emotions. The two principal ones are literature's aptitude to make us *experience* emotions, and its related aptitude to *enlighten* us about them. I agree with Jenefer Robinson that great literature[24] depicts emotions better than anything else can; and therefore, that great literature promotes our understanding of emotions:

> if we really want to understand emotions in all their uniqueness and individuality, if we want to follow the progress of an emotion process as it unfolds, if we want to understand how different elements of the process feed into one another and interact, and how the streams of emotional life blend and flow into one another, then we would do better to stay away from the generalizations of philosophers and psychologists, and turn instead to the detailed studies of emotion that we find in great literature. (2005, p. 99)

Moreover, Robinson argues that great literary works 'need to be experienced emotionally if they are to be properly understood'; 'learning from a novel is a matter of responding to it emotionally' (2005, pp. 102, 192). So that the education we receive in reading the novel consists 'not just in the fact that it may eventually lead to new beliefs, but also in *how* it does so' (2005, p. 157); and exactly how it does so, Robinson claims, is by *controlling* or *taming* the emotions. This is where we part company.

In fact, Robinson is taking away with one hand what she gives with the other: 'without appropriate emotional responses, some novels simply *cannot* be adequately understood' (2005, p. 107); but on the other hand, the formal features of a work help keep the emotions at bay. On Robinson's view, literature, by the mere fact of being literature and not life, has a dampening effect on the emotions, on our involvement in the novel (2005, p. 203) but, more pointedly, a literary work's formal devices (use of imagery, sentence structure etc.) act as 'coping mechanisms' or defence mechanisms (e.g. *avoidance or distanciation, denial, intellectualization or pointing to a moral*), enabling us to *cope* with troubling content:

> Reading literature always has the potential for creating anxiety or uncertainty, but literature, unlike life, often provides us with the coping strategies that we need to deal with its deep and possibly troubling content. The formal or structural devices in a novel allow us to cope with its themes and ultimately to derive pleasure from the very fact that we have successfully coped with a piece of reality. (2005, p. 219)

So that, on Robinson's view, literature throws a security blanket on our emotions, and this explains why we are not dejected by a Shakespearian sonnet on death but get pleasure from it: 'the poem has enabled us to cope emotionally with the reality of death' (2005, p. 226) and this gives us pleasure. It seems then that Robinson is trying to create a gap between fiction and the emotions – to produce an unnecessary security blanket between the reader and his literature-prompted emotions. But what is the point of that? The point is that it furnishes Robinson with a way of resolving the paradox of tragedy: the distancing explains why people enjoy tragedies despite their often bloody and macabre subject-matter. Note that the pleasure envisaged here by Robinson is an exclusively psychological pleasure, not an aesthetic or *cognitive* one.

The problem with Robinson's view is that this psychological pleasure-as-relief is too specialized to fit into a more general account of the pleasure we get from literature. Not all fictional situations that prompt pleasure are troubling: we get pleasure from the union of Jane Eyre and Rochester because of its *affirming* power; and in such cases, the pleasure cannot be due to our *coping* with a painful emotion.[25] Moreover, we get pleasure from situations that are not emotional: say, the revelation of Gwendolyn's character through George Eliot's initial *physical* description of her in *Daniel Deronda*; or from Birkin's few remarks on an African statuette, in *Women in Love* – remarks that kindle and engage our own reflexion on the question of the universality of art. No need for coping mechanisms here, no sense of having triumphed over painful material (2005, p. 226), and yet fictional pleasure is at its highest. The pleasure – or even an important part of the pleasure – literature procures cannot be due to our ability to cope with the painful emotions it depicts if that pleasure can occur independently of those painful emotions and, indeed, independently of any depicted emotion. Therefore, Robinson would need an explanation different from that of successful coping to account for the pleasure we get from nonpainful material.

Instead, I suggest that the pleasure we experience in all the cases mentioned above – Shakespeare's sonnet, Eliot's character description, Lawrence's aesthetic passage – is an aesthetico-*cognitive* one. A pleasure resulting from our *enhanced understanding* of the world, of our human condition, of a concept and so on through its *artistic presentation*. Whether the fictional representation is pleasant or painful, its artistic presentation – if successful – will always prompt *cognitive pleasure*: the pleasure that comes from the satisfaction of enhanced understanding. This is Aristotle's message. Literature does not act as a coping but as a *cognitive* mechanism; the pleasure we experience is not from having escaped, but from having confronted and understood:

> we take pleasure in contemplating the most precise images of things whose sight in itself causes us pain... the explanation lies in the fact that to be learning something is the greatest of pleasures not only to the philosopher but also to the rest of mankind...; the reason of the delight in seeing the picture is that one is at the same time learning – gathering the meaning of things.(*Poetics* IV, 1148b11–16)

Contra Robinson, I suggest form is here, not to distance us, but to take us in, to absorb or engage us. Literature both evokes and provokes the emotions. When reading a novel, we are not victims of our emotions, as Robinson would have it; we want to have them. Robinson, it seems, shares a Platonist suspicion of the emotions, where these need to be controlled, tamed, lest they overwhelm us and wreak damage. The crucial pleasure we get from literature is not due to its having helped us suppress or cope with our emotions, but to its having helped us understand them (as it does also nonemotional concepts) by *revealing* them – through its unique interrelatedness of form and content – clarified and *cognitively* enhanced. And by *revealing* an emotion, I mean that literature (1) *perspicuously presents* the emotion, played out in particular, textured circumstances; and (2) through this dramatic presentation uncovers *some of the nature (or concept) of that emotion*, thereby prompting *cognitive pleasure* which signals (3) our enhanced grasp of that emotion. *Cognitive pleasure* is a multifaceted pleasure and, at its most sophisticated, results not only from the grasp of meaning, but from our awareness and admiration of, the inextricable interplay – indeed, interdependency – between that meaning and the form that conveys it.

Aristotle, not Plato, is to be trusted here. Aristotle does not regard the emotions as intrinsically harmful. Relatedly, note that the exact meaning of *catharsis* is under debate; its traditional interpretation as psychological purgation (of undesirable emotion) or as moral purification has been challenged by philosophers who see it as related to intellectual clarification. As Leon Golden writes, for Aristotle, 'the essential pleasure of art is an intellectual one derived from learning about human existence through the medium of art' (1973, p. 476). My disagreement with Jenefer Robinson may be profitably formulated in terms of our discrepant interpretations of *catharsis*. Unlike Robinson, I do not take the pleasure we get from literature as resulting from having successfully coped with an emotion, but – as *Poetics* IV makes clear – from seeing and understanding something as never before. Herein, also, lies the solution to the paradox of tragedy.

Whereas Jenefer Robinson suggests that form acts as a security blanket, I want to stress that form is essential to the revelatory nature (and therefore to the concept-formative impact) of literature. The *perspicuous presentations* that *are* great literature generate a more perspicuous understanding of the concepts presented, and this is signalled and encouraged by our *cognitive pleasure*.[26] I call it *cognitive pleasure*, leaving the term *'aesthetic pleasure'* to qualify the more general satisfaction afforded by the disinterested appreciation of form not invested by content[27] (e.g. that of a beautiful face or the smoothness of marble). In *cognitive pleasure*, aesthetic form is internally linked to the occurrence of a *cognitive* experience.

8. Conclusion

As we have seen, emotion is not conceptually linked to existential commitment: we have emotional responses to dead people and past events as well as to impossible situations, and these can be more intense and motivational than our emotional responses to real people and actual situations. *Really* feeling for Anna Karenina does not result in irrationality or paradox. Pitying Anna Karenina is not only essential to understanding Tolstoy's novel and therefore to a better understanding of ourselves and our emotions, it is also *pace* Radford, the most rational, consistent attitude we could have towards her.

Attempting to reduce fiction to thought, as Lamarque does, amounts to reducing it to paraphrase, and that leads to the view that literature is trivial or meaningless. Attempting to reduce our emotions for fictional characters to *quasi*-emotions – that is, to contend that we cannot rationally pity Anna Karenina or cry for Romeo – is to suck the very life out of what we mean when we say 'I pity ...' and to demote one of our most intensely emotional experiences to the shedding of crocodile tears. Walton's claim that our emotional responses to fictional characters is make-believe comes from his misreading the nature of our phenomenological responses to these characters, and amounts to his demeaning and minimizing the invaluable role of literature in our lives. It is a poor account of literature that sees it as playing second fiddle to daily life in the expression and provocation of emotion, but it is a downright mediocre one that sees it as no player at all.

Notes

*I am greatly indebted to John V. Canfield, Frank Cioffi, Laurence Goldstein, Ylva Gustafsson and Michael McEachrane for their comments on earlier drafts of this paper.

1. As succinctly formulated by Jenefer Robinson (2005, p. 143).
2. Cf. Derek Matravers for the distinction between a 'broad cognitive theory' and a 'narrow cognitive theory' of the emotions (2006, p. 254).
3. Cf. Walton (1978, pp. 308, 312; 1997, pp. 43, 47).
4. 'What makes it make-believe that Charles is afraid rather than angry or excited or upset is the fact that his quasi-fear is caused by the belief that make-believedly he is in danger' (Walton 1978, p. 311).
5. On the other hand, Peter Lamarque's simulation theory, which I shall not discuss in this chapter, sees the author as a pretence artist: 'Fiction is essentially a form of pretence, though pretence without intended deception, as in a charade or a child's game'; 'The writer of fiction does not assert facts, he pretends to assert facts; he does not describe events, he pretends to describe events; he does not refer to people, he pretends to refer to people. Furthermore, because he only pretends to make assertions in fact he makes neither true nor false assertions' (1981, p. 332). But here Lamarque distorts what we ordinarily mean by 'pretence', and unwarrantedly limits what we mean by 'description'; the author is not pretending to describe, he is describing (a scene, a character etc.). Rather than say: 'He pretends to describe events, people etc.', Lamarque had better say: 'He describes pretend-events, people etc.' or, better, 'fictional events, people etc.', and even that seems to me superfluous where it is clear that the 'he' is an author.
6. As when we say of someone deluding themselves that they're 'living in a fictional world'.
7. This misleading multiplication of processes is similar to Lamarque's, in note 5 above.
8. The 'Werther effect' is the term used to designate these *copycat suicides* which resulted in a ban of the book in several places. As for less elevated reactions:
   > A Halloween health warning was today slapped on a horror flick that is so gruesome viewers have fainted. Emergency services have so far attended three cinemas after one man and four women fainted at a torture scene in new movie *Saw III*. One of the women was so traumatised that she needed hospital treatment. (*The London Paper*, 30 October 2006, p. 7)
9. What is missing in some cases, suggests Robert Yanal (1999), is *opportunity*:
   > Motivators need opportunity, and it may be that fiction arouses emotion with motivational force but with little or no opportunity to exercise it....I may even wish I could comfort King Lear as he cradles his daughter, a wish

that I acknowledge can't be satisfied in reality, but that presses itself none-theless. Is this so different from a wish to tell a person now dead that one loves him? (p. 61)

10. For a compelling argument as to the propriety of calling fictional statements 'true' or 'false', see A.P. Martinich and A. Stroll's excellent *Much Ado about Nonexistence: Fiction and Reference*. The authors argue that the word 'true' has, like other words, various criteria of applicability. The criterion for applying truth to statements in fictional discourse is not the same as the criterion for applying it in nonfictional discourse, but any observation of people's speech about fiction shows that there is a large consensus as to how truth should be applied to fictional statements. The reason we speak of fictional truths (and falsities) is that there are *fictional facts* (here the word 'fictional' is not to be understood as a negator word), which make fictional statements true (or false). Because criteria of applicability are different, there is no problem in holding that fictional facts can both be factual and known to be incompatible with natural facts (Martinich and Stroll 2007, pp. 8, 23–29). Martinich and Stroll thereby give philosophical back-bone to what many philosophers have rightly maintained, but left unargued; for example, Harold Skulsky (1980): 'The claim that Becky Sharp finally married William Dobbin is subject to refutation (without incongruity) by the warranted counterclaim that in Chapter 67 of the *novel*, Thackeray arranges matters otherwise' (p. 6).

11. This ordinary use of believing *that*; but believing *in* (which is often synonymous with faith or trust, and can also denote *blind* faith) also does not require existen-tial commitment; for example, 'I believe in an afterlife', 'I believe in (his) love', 'I believe in democracy'. For a discussion of the polysemy of belief, see Moyal-Sharrock (2005/2007, pp. 188f.)

12. B.J. Rosebury first suggested these emotionally stimulating fantasies (1979, p. 128) be used as an argument against the cognitive theory of emotion.

13. Cf. especially Lamarque (1981).

14. Lamarque admits as thoughts 'everything we might consider as mental contents, including mental images, imaginings, fantasies, suppositions, and all that Descartes called "ideas"' (1981, p. 329).

15. Michael Weston's stance is close to thought theory; he takes the object of our emotions towards fiction to be 'a conception of life' (1975, pp. 85–6). So that our emotions are not addressed to the fictional character and situations, but to cer-tain truths or ideas about life which the narrative evokes.

16. 'The propensity of a thought to be frightening is likely to increase in relation to the level of reflection or imaginative involvement that is directed to it. There are two points here: thoughts can differ among themselves with respect to *vividness* and our reflection on thoughts can be graded with respect to *involvement*' (Lamarque 1981, p. 330).

17. Lamarque concedes that 'there must be both a *causal* and a *content-based* connection between the thoughts in our minds and the sentences and descrip-tions in the fiction' (1981, p. 334), but he does nothing to explicate these con-nections or say how the thought-contents are 'identifiable through descriptions derived in suitable ways from the propositional contents of fictional sentences' (1981, p. 335).

18. Which is perhaps why Lamarque adds – to no avail, in my view – that 'it is often not so much single thoughts that are frightening...as thought clusters' (1981, p. 330).

19. Occasionally, dialogue, discussion or thought might, as Leavis says about a passage in *St Mawr*, 'in a wholly dramatic way, bring to the point of explicitness the essential work of implicit definition that has been done by image, action and symbolic presentation' (1955, p. 243), but note that 'the affirmation *merely* brings to explicitness what [Lawrence's] art has affirmed pervasively and cumulatively' (p. 256; my emphasis), and that such occasions are rare, and certainly not essential to the deployment and communication of, say, any conceptual, emotional, moral or Existential point. Again, about a passage in *Women in Love*: its 'local explicitness *merely* picks up what has been done in drama, imagery, and poetic organization' (1955, p. 175; my emphasis).

20. That is: 'the transformation of information into a propositional form that is accessible to thoughts and beliefs' (Choi 2003, p. 149).

21. Cf. Amelie Rorty passage below (p. 174)

22. In *Poetics* IV; more on this below. The expression 'cognitive pleasure' is commonly used by Aristotelian scholars to denote the delight experienced in the understanding or insight Aristotle believes we get from art. The word 'cognitive' should be understood here in the general sense of 'learning – gathering the meaning of things' and I shall henceforth italicize the words 'cognitive' and 'cognition' when thus using them so as to distinguish this use from their narrower association with propositional knowledge.

23. For Camus, in *The Myth of Sisyphus*, the consciousness of our human contingency makes the present override the future, and the quantity of experiences override their quality (cf. J. O'Brien translation, Penguin 1981, pp. 59–62).

24. By 'great literature', Robinson has in mind – and I concur – the kind of morally serious, realistic works cited by F.R. Leavis in *The Great Tradition* (1960). For 'not all novels invite...serious sustained emotional attention. There are bad novels that try to teach us something and fail, there are genre novels that merely aim to entertain, and there are novels that are more like intellectual puzzles or games' (Robinson 2005, p. 159). In the 'serious' category, I would, however, also include nonrealistic works such as those of Kafka and Borges.

25. If, in spite of Robinson's unilateral discussion of troubling content, she means distancing to apply also to emotions spurred by non-troubling content, then one must wonder why a coping mechanism is needed at all. Who would not want to share, fully, Wordsworth's burst of joy in his encounter with the daffodils ('I wandered lonely as a cloud ...')?

26. *Cognitive pleasure* is not exclusively generated by great literature – understanding a pun, a witty remark or an ironical act outside of fictional contexts will also generate it; nor, of course, is it the only kind of pleasure afforded by literature.

27. Unlike Scruton, for whom aesthetic pleasure is constitutively *cognitive* (cf. for (1979), pp. 72ff).

Bibliography

Borges, J.L. (1962), 'Everything and Nothing', *Labyrinths: Selected Stories and Other Writings* (New York: New Directions).

Carroll, N. (1990), *The Philosophy of Horror or Paradoxes of the Heart* (London: Routledge).

—— (1997), *The Journal of Aesthetics and Art Criticism*, Vol. 46, No. 1 (Autumn, 1987), pp. 51–59.

Choi, J. (2003), 'Fits and Startles: Cognitivism Revisited', *JAAC* 61(2), 149–57.

Coleridge, S.T. ([1817] 1985), *Biographia Literaria* in *Samuel Taylor Coleridge*, ed. by Jackson, H.J. (Oxford).

Dammann, R.M.J. (1992), 'Emotion and Fiction', *BJA* 32(1), 13–20

Golden, L. (1973), 'The Purgation Theory of Catharsis' *JAAC* 31, 473–9

Hjort, M. and Laver, S. (eds) (1997), *Emotion and the Arts* (Oxford: Oxford University Press).

Johnson, S. ([1765] 1963), 'Preface to Shakespeare' in *Johnson: Prose and Poetry*. Selected by Mona Wilson (London: Rupert Hart-Davis), 489–529.

Lamarque, P. ([1981] 1994), 'How Can We Fear and Pity Fictions?' in Lamarque & Olsen, 328–36.

—— (1991), Review of K.L. Walton *Mimēsis as Make-Believe*, *JAAC* 49(2), 161–6.

Lamarque, P. and Olsen, S. H. (eds) (1994), *Truth, Fiction, and Literature: A Philosophical Perspective* (Oxford: Clarendon Press).

Lawrence, D.H. (1936), 'Morality and the Novel' in McDonald, D. (ed.) *Phoenix: The Posthumous Papers of D H Lawrence* (New York: Viking), 527–32.

—— (1968), 'The Novel' in *Phoenix II: Uncollected, Unpublished and Other Prose Works by D.H. Lawrence*, ed. Roberts, W. and Moore, H. T. (London: Heinemann), 416–26.

Leavis, F.R. (1955), *D.H. Lawrence: Novelist* (London: Chatto & Windus).

—— (1960), *The Great Tradition* (London: Chatto & Windus).

—— (1967), 'Anna Karenina' in *Anna Karenina & Other Essays* (London: Chatto & Windus).

—— (1975), *The Living Principle: 'English' as a Discipline of Thought* (London: Chatto & Windus).

—— (1976), *Thought, Words and Creativity: Art and Thought in Lawrence* (London: Chatto & Windus).

Martinich, A. P. and Stroll, A. (2007), *Much Ado about Nonexistence: Fiction and Reference* (Lanham: MD: Rowman & Littlefield).

Matravers, D. (2006), 'The Challenge of Irrationalism and How Not to Meet It' in Kieran, M. (ed.) *Contemporary Debates in Aesthetics and the Philosophy of Art* (Oxford: Blackwell), 254–64.

Mounce, H.O. (1980), 'Art and Real Life', *Philosophy* 55, 183–92.

Moyal-Sharrock, D. (2005/2007), *Understanding Wittgenstein's on Certainty* (Basingstoke: Palgrave Macmillan).

Nussbaum, M. (1990), *Love's Knowledge: Essays on Philosophy and Literature* (Oxford: Oxford University Press).

Paskins, B. (1977), 'On being Moved by Anna Karenina and *Anna Karenina*', *Philosophy* 52, 344–7.

Phillips, D.Z. (1996), 'Aesthetic Values' in *Introducing Philosophy* (Oxford: Blackwell).

Radford, C. (1975), 'How Can We be Moved by the Fate of Anna Karenina', *The Aristotelian Society* Suppl. Vol. 99, July, 67–80.

Robinson, J. (2005), *Deeper than Reason: Emotion and its Role in Literature, Music & Art* (Oxford: Clarendon Press).

Rorty, A.O. (1992), 'The Psychology of Aristotelian Tragedy' in A. O. Rorty (ed.) *Essays on Aristotle's Poetics* (Princeton, N.J.: Princeton University Press), 1–22.

Rosebury, B.J. (1979), 'Fiction, Emotion and "Belief": A Reply to Eva Schaper', *The British Journal of Aesthetics* 19, 120–30.

Scruton, R. (1979), *The Aesthetics of Architecture* (London: Methuen).

Skulsky, H. (1980), 'On Being Moved by Fiction', *Journal of Aesthetics and Art Criticism* 39, 5–14.

Walton, K. ([1978] 2004), 'Fearing Fictions' in Lamarque & Olsen, 307–19.

—— (1997), 'Spelunking, Simulation, and Slime: On Being Moved by Fiction' in Hjort & Laver (eds) Emotions and the Arts (Oxford: Oxford University Press, 1997), 37–49.

Weston, M. (1975), 'Can We be Moved by the Fate of Anna Karenina?' in *The Aristotelian Society* Suppl. Vol. 99, July, 81–93.

Yanal, R.J. (1999), *Paradoxes of Emotion and Fiction* (University Park, PA: Penn State University Press).

11
On The Pursuit of Happiness

Duncan Richter

Happiness is a concept that links the philosophy of psychology with ethics. It is often thought of as an emotion, hence psychological, but also as the ultimate goal of life, and so ethical. Perhaps some psychological concepts are sharply defined, but Wittgenstein's mature view of ethical concepts is that they are, so to speak, blurry. He writes in *Philosophical Investigations* § 77 that 'if you look for definitions corresponding to our concepts in aesthetics or ethics' then you are in the same position as someone trying to draw a sharply defined picture that corresponds to a blurry one. You can draw what you like, but you cannot claim that it is definitively correct. A similar conclusion about happiness is reached by Nicholas White in his *A Brief History of Happiness*: 'If having a concept of happiness requires that it meets a high standard of clarity, then you might well say that we don't really have a concept of happiness, or at least that it certainly doesn't show itself in the history of philosophy' (2006, p. 162). I think that this view is right, and will try to explain why. I also think that this is important. Daniel M. Haybron, one of the leading contemporary philosophers working on happiness, has written recently that 'it is hard to see how we could possibly claim to understand human welfare without having any clear notion of what happiness is' (2005, p. 288). Later in the chapter, I will discuss the implications of what I have to say about happiness for questions about what we should do to promote our welfare or live a good life.

Before going any farther, though, I should address a concern that might already have arisen. Is there such a thing as the concept of happiness? Haybron concedes that happiness might not be 'a unitary phenomenon' (2005, p. 289). Is happiness understood as something like *eudaimonia* not simply a different concept from the emotion of joy or the experiencing of something pleasant? I think that the answer is both 'Yes' and 'No', and this is relevant to my claim that the concept of happiness is blurry. Of course, there is a difference between pleasure and *eudaimonia* or flourishing. One is a sensation and the other is a quality of one's life. But they are not wholly distinct concepts, since any claim that one can be *eudaimon* despite a complete lack of pleasure is counterintuitive. Such claims have been made, and might be true, but they always call for some explanation. They are *prima facie* paradoxical. I will assume, therefore, that such notions as pleasure, joy and happiness are members of one family, and will treat them as such, under the broad heading of happiness. This assumption is not meant to simplify misleadingly, or to imply that there are no important distinctions to be made within the family. Joel J. Kupperman, for instance, makes a nice distinction between joy and happiness in connection with the 'inner glow' ascribed by Buddhists to those close to Nirvana. We can speak of such people as experiencing bliss or joy, but 'It would have seemed very odd, and entirely out of character, if Buddha had said "I'm very happy".' (Kupperman 2006, p. 42). Despite such differences, the concept of joy is intimately related to that of happiness. It is not a mistake for Haybron to treat being joyful, as he does, as a paradigmatic case of happiness (see Haybron 2005, p. 290). Because there is a family of concepts that connect with and disconnect from each other in various ways, what matters is the map of crisscross links, not the particular label ('happiness', 'joy', 'bliss', etc.) that we apply to any one point in the network. I will not provide such a map here, but will try to give reason to doubt that happiness is a neatly bounded, easily defined concept.

Another concern I should perhaps address here is what exactly I mean when I talk about ethics. Wittgenstein does not really define what he means by the term, except negatively by saying that it is something that cannot be expressed or talked about, something concerning 'absolute value', words which, he says, have no meaning. My concern, though, is with questions about how one should live, about how happiness or a happy life can best be achieved. Aristotle believed that one would be much more likely to achieve such a life if one had an ideal of it, a target, clearly in view. From a Wittgensteinian perspective, I shall argue, this is something of a hopeless task. Happiness is not a clearly defined concept, and so one cannot set it as a target that is clearly in focus. Aristotle recognized this to some extent, acknowledging that ethics is not a precise science, but he still seems to have thought that the happy life can be described in enough detail to give people something to aim for. Agreement on what exactly constitutes the happy life, however, has been hard to come by. From a Wittgensteinian perspective, this should not be surprising.[1] Happiness can only ever be a blurry goal.

What follows is not a sharp definition of happiness, but a sketch of a blur. The point is to elucidate this important concept, and to do so by drawing on what Wittgenstein wrote about it. So I hope that some contribution to our understanding of Wittgenstein will also be made by this chapter. An additional goal is to make clear some of the difficulties involved in developing philosophical theories, especially in ethics, that centrally involve the concept of happiness. This chapter is not really about ethics, but its value might be more obvious if what it says is brought into contact with some recent ethical discussions. Since, as I will try to show, happiness is not a neatly bounded concept, no theory can use it precisely without importing a partial understanding of happiness. Precision requires some editing, and this cannot be done without omitting something that some people might regard as important. In this sense, at least, ethical theories involving precise notions of happiness cannot be justified objectively, as some moral theorists would like them to be. This should become clear in the discussion that follows.

The concept of happiness appears to cover a spectrum from lofty, mysterious ideas such as Aristotelian *eudaimonia* and the Christian notion of blessedness down to an almost physiological conception of pleasure, closely related to the concept of pain. Pleasure and pain seem to be most obviously connected in this physical way when we think, as Arthur Schopenhauer (1969) does, that 'Teeth, gullet, and intestinal canal are objectified hunger; the genitals are objectified sexual impulse; grasping hands and nimble feet correspond to the more indirect strivings of the will which they represent' (§ 20, p. 108). Pleasure would then simply be the satisfaction of some physical desire, pain its thwarting. Wittgenstein showed the concept pain to be really quite mysterious though despite its familiarity. That is, he gave good reason to think of pain what Augustine thought of time: as long as no one asks me, I know what it is, but if someone asks me, then I am at a loss. To the extent that pleasure is the counterpart of pain, what goes for one should go for the other.[2] But pleasure is not simply a sensation in the way that pain seems to be, and there is more to happiness than pleasure. This is something that John Stuart Mill, for instance, seems to have had in mind when introducing his notion of 'higher' pleasures. Mill has been much criticized for this problematic notion, though.[3] More generally, there are problems of how we can use the language of this world to talk about matters that are thought to be higher or otherworldly, and of how we can talk at all about worldly but 'inner' states or processes. These problems interested Wittgenstein greatly, throughout his life, as we shall see.

In the first part of the chapter, I will briefly attempt a tracing of the picture of happiness that emerges from an examination of what Wittgenstein writes about it throughout his career. We shall see, however, that his early remarks on happiness are so few, opaque and far-between, that it is more useful to concentrate instead on his later work and his mature conclusions on the subject of happiness. In the second part, we will see, I think, that the concept of happiness really cannot be defined, but that it is still worthwhile to try to sketch what we can of it. For instance, it is doubtful that a concept that cannot be defined could ever be understood or mastered by a machine, so we might demonstrate something about the nature of the creatures that use such concepts, something, that is, about ourselves, in the process of our investigation. I make no precise claims, though, about what my rather imprecise sketch will show. My interest is not in the relation between humans and machines, nor primarily in ethics, so much as it is in the concept of happiness itself and what Wittgenstein thought about it.

1. 'Live happily!'

In his *Notebooks 1914–1916*, Wittgenstein struggles both to think straight about the problems that concern him and to express satisfactorily the thoughts that he has. This makes it difficult to interpret what he says fairly. In the midst of some remarks on good and evil wills, he writes: 'It seems one can't say anything more than: Live happily! [*Lebe glücklich!*]' (Wittgenstein 1979, p. 78e). On the next day, though, he adds '*It is clear* that ethics *cannot* be expressed!' So his view is apparently either that 'Live happily!' is all that one can say, even though he feels that this is not enough, or else that even the words 'Live happily!' do not really express what he means. Either ethics cannot be expressed in words at all, or else they can be expressed only to the limited extent of saying 'Live happily!' (Perhaps ethics could be expressed in behavior, in how one lives, but it is not clear what 'expressed' would mean if there were nothing there that could be put into words.)[4]

One thing that seems clear is that the concept happiness is especially important to Wittgenstein at this time. Despite his claim that ethics, which in these notebooks concerns the relation between the will and the world, cannot be expressed in words, he nevertheless continues to wonder and write about the relation between spirit, character, and will, on the one hand, and physical objects on the other. He wonders on p. 84e whether an angry (*böse*) face is angry in itself or merely empirically connected with bad temper. This kind of question comes up again in much later work, which I will explain in Section 2.

Similar remarks about happiness and ethics to those found in the *Notebooks* appear in the *Tractatus*. Remark 6.421 says that 'It is clear that ethics cannot be expressed.' Despite this, remarks from 6.4 to 6.43 certainly look as though they say various things about ethics and value. For instance, 6.41 says that there is no value in the world and that, if there were, it would be without value. Ethics is said to be higher, to be transcendental, to be one with aesthetics. In 6.43 we are told that if good and bad willing change the world then they must do so by, as it were, making the world larger or smaller, and that therefore 'The world of the happy is a different one from that of the unhappy.' This sentence is fairly baffling on its face. How can there be more than one world, especially since Wittgenstein writes at the beginning of this book that the world is everything that is the case? How can we make sense of the idea of more than one everything that is the case? It seems that remark 6.43 can only be understood as something like a conclusion from the previous few remarks. We have no hope of making sense of it unless we consider its context. But those preceding remarks tell us repeatedly that they and their ilk (i.e. remarks about ethics and value) cannot exist: their content is such that it cannot be expressed. We can make some excisions, setting aside what is most puzzling, and understand what is left, or *feel* that we understand, but no more than this, as far as I can see. If what Wittgenstein is writing about here is ethics, then we might agree with him that ethics cannot be expressed. It at least seems hard for him to express intelligibly what he has in mind.

If we were to accept that ethics cannot be expressed in words, that what we mean by 'ethics' must be something above or beyond this world and beyond the reach of mere words, then we might still be left with a desire (if we had it in the first place) to say something like the anti-egoistic, approximately Schopenhauerian things that Wittgenstein wrote about ethics and happiness in the *Notebooks*. That is, we might still have a desire not to settle only for what can be said according to the *Tractatus* (i.e. nothing). It is almost as if what remains is the, by now quite self-conscious, desire to deny desire, or the will to insist that it is bad to will or to insist. Perhaps such self-consciousness of self-contradictory willing could effect an end to itself. The bad will, seeing itself clearly in reflection, might lose its bad character. If so, then the *Tractatus* really might be 'a machine for becoming decent'.[5] But this is very obscure.

Let us return to 6.43 and make the best sense we can of it. What can we say about whatever it is that distinguishes the world of the happy from that of the unhappy? Assuming that there is only one world, the 'everything that is the case' of *Tractatus* 1, then the world of the happy can only be different from that of the unhappy in a peculiar sense. It is the same world, yet its character is different. It is, so to speak, bigger, its limits having been expanded, but it is not literally bigger, and the world no more has limits than language does. A limit of the world, or an instance of whatever we might be tempted to call a limit of the world, would not be part of the world.[6] It would not be part of everything that is the case. Therefore, it would not be the case. The idea that we can conceive of a limit of the world is an illusion. Talk about some people living in a smaller world than others, tempting as it might be, can really tell us nothing. It might well express how we and others feel, but it is uninformative (and so perhaps self-indulgent[7]) and imprecise. A precise explanation of the difference between the happy and the unhappy would have to consist in statements of objective facts, most likely about their behavior (how much they smile, for instance). It is hard to see how these facts could involve value judgments, unless one valued things that might be measured objectively, such as amounts of money or friends. This, presumably, is the kind of worldly value that really has no value, as Wittgenstein sees it. (Not that he would not value friendship, but that its value would be missed by someone who thought that it could be measured by counting heads.) As far as happiness is relevant to ethics, is a valuable goal for one's life, it cannot be put in words (or thoughts). Or so Wittgenstein seems to think in the *Tractatus*. Precisely why he thinks this, and whether we should agree with him, is not very apparent, however.

It might help us understand why someone might think that the meaning of happiness cannot be captured in words if we consider a contemporary example of someone who believes in an evaluative, indefinable sense of happiness. Philippa Foot conceives of happiness as 'the enjoyment of good things' (2001, p. 97). It follows from this view that happiness is bound up very closely with virtue, without being simply identical with it. That is to say, Foot regards it as possible that one might behave virtuously without deriving any pleasure from doing so, but also that enjoyment only counts as *happiness* if it is enjoyment of *good* things. Mere enjoyment, she might say, is a value without value. Like Wittgenstein, she does not want to try to define happiness precisely. In *Natural Goodness* she reaches the conclusion that, 'happiness is a protean concept, appearing now in one way and now in another' (Foot 2001, p. 97). This is a Wittgensteinian thing to say, and it reveals a serious problem for anyone trying to develop a theory of virtue according to which goodness is defined in some relation to what makes for a happy life. We cannot derive useful rules for life from a protean concept any more than we can from one that transcends the world we live in.

In contrast with Foot's view, Rosalind Hursthouse argues that happiness is not an obscure concept but is, rather, essentially connected with a very familiar phenomenon that she calls 'the smile factor' (1999, p. 185). 'If [a man] never enjoys himself in the straightforward way evidenced by the smile factor then, though his life may be the life of continence, it cannot be the life of virtue' (Hursthouse 1999, p. 186). This is compatible with Foot's idea that happiness is enjoyment of good things. Foot and Hursthouse would agree that without enjoyment in a straightforward sense one cannot be happy. However, Hursthouse defines *virtue*, not just happiness, in terms of such enjoyment. A virtuous person would then be guaranteed happiness, in a straightforward sense, at least for part of his or her life. Hursthouse's ethics, then, allow for value that has genuine value within the world.[8]

That is one view of ethics, but it is obvious that others are possible. The early Wittgenstein, for one, would presumably disagree with it. It is also clear that other conceptions of happiness are possible too, however problematic they might be. It has been maintained that one can be happy even on the rack, and the unconventional views about who is blessed found in the Sermon on the Mount and about a dissatisfied Socrates being happier than a fool satisfied that we find in Mill's *Utilitarianism* are quite familiar. Hursthouse's view, then, is perfectly legitimate, but not uncontroversially true with regard either to her conception of happiness or to her ethical stance. Wittgenstein's view that worldly values lack value is not one that we have to share, but there seems to be something arbitrary about whether we take Wittgenstein's view, Hursthouse's or some other view. Various definitions are available to us but none of them is clearly, objectively correct.

This comes out in Wittgenstein's 'Lecture on Ethics'. Here again we see some familiar themes. 'There are no propositions which, in any absolute sense, are sublime, important, or trivial' (Wittgenstein 1993, p. 39). 'Ethics, if it is anything, is supernatural and our words will only express facts...' (Wittgenstein 1993, p. 40). The essence of ethical and religious talk is a kind of simile, but a real simile can be put in other words, while these cannot. That is to say, I can perfectly well say of someone that he is happy if his drug deal has been successful and he has used the proceeds to buy some slaves. Look at the smile on his face! If, though, I want to deny that this is *real* or *true* happiness, then one might wonder what I mean. I might mean that it will not last, or that the gamble of living outside the law is not prudent. But if I mean something else, something ethical or 'higher', that I do not count an emotion bearing all the hallmarks of happiness as happiness if it arises in such a way, then I am changing the concept of happiness, using it in a different way, or at least imposing my own definition on it.

Another example might help to make this point clear. Haybron writes that 'A shallow cheeriness has its merits, but if that's the best that can be said for your emotional state then it is questionable whether we could sensibly deem you happy' (2005, p. 303). This is quite right. It is questionable, but not undeniable. Haybron has in mind 'the vacant cheeriness of a shopping mall addict who finds his life agreeable but has no occasion for real joy or fulfillment' (2005, p. 303). It is not hard to notice an apparent value judgment here implicit in such words as 'vacant' and in Haybron's (seeming) attitude toward shopping malls. Such judgments are understandable but also debatable. What we count as happiness is, in part at least, a value judgment. Different judgments can lead to different conceptions of happiness and different uses of the word 'happiness'. The standard understanding and meaning of happiness could therefore change over time if one kind of value judgment became more, or less, widespread than others.

There is nothing wrong with this. Wittgenstein never says that we cannot change concepts, or try to do so, at least, and he would be wrong if he did. Now imagine someone asking me who really is happy in my sense, and in reply, I give a list of martyrs. Why do I want to use the word 'happy' to describe these people? There is something about the existing, standard concept of happiness that I want, but not its literal or naturalistic meaning. I want a kind of simile that cannot be translated into another, more prosaic kind of language. This is what Wittgenstein calls nonsense in the 'Lecture on Ethics', although he insists that he respects it deeply. Neither the later Wittgenstein nor I would call it nonsense to describe a martyr or Socrates dissatisfied as happy, but there is something problematic about such descriptions. There is some bending of the concept happiness here, which it is flexible enough to allow. Because of this flexibility, we can define virtue or happiness in such a way that they are necessarily connected. But because this requires something other than a straightforward application of the concept, we do not have to do so. Conceptual analysis alone will not yield such a definition of ethics, virtue or happiness except, perhaps, as a possibility, an option for us to consider. Unbiased analytic philosophy will not lead to a hedonistic or eudaimonistic ethical theory of any substance. For that, one must take a stance, adopt a certain attitude, and philosophy as Wittgenstein understood it will not do this for us.[9]

The concept of happiness is connected with many others, such as pleasure and flourishing, none of which can be defined easily if at all. They are intimately, but not necessarily essentially, connected with such patterns of behavior as (sincere) smiling. It is doubtful that even smiling can be defined completely and precisely, giving necessary and sufficient conditions such that a robot might be able to use them to pass a modified Turing test of emotional recognition. Rather, happiness appears to be a pattern discernible as running through our form of life. It takes a certain kind of attitude, a certain way of looking at things, to make out such a pattern.

This goes two ways. A certain kind of attitude or attunement to the world is required for one to be able to grasp the concept of happiness, and happy people will themselves have a particular kind of attitude or attunement. Haybron writes:

> To be happy is not merely to have experiences of a certain sort; it is also to be configured emotionally in certain ways. Indeed, one's whole *psychic* disposition seems altered. One is prone to take greater pleasure in things, to see things in a more positive light, to take greater notice of good things, to be more optimistic, to be more outgoing and friendly, and to take chances more. One is also slower and less likely to become anxious or fearful, or to be angered or saddened by events. *One confronts the world in a different way from the unhappy.* ... When you're happy, everything is different. (Haybron 2005, p. 310; emphasis in the original).

Among the things that differ depending on how one confronts the world seems to be happiness itself. Hence, for instance, from Bertrand Russell's book on happiness we learn not only some sensible advice but also something about Russell himself. It is telling, or seems so to me, that Russell lists love along with food and shelter as one of the 'simple things' that are indispensable to most people's happiness (1933, p. 242). Could someone with much understanding of love regard it as simple? Would someone more monogamous than Russell agree with him that, 'The happy man is the man who lives objectively, who has free affections and wide interests, who secures his happiness through these interests and affections and through the fact that they, in turn, make him an object of interest and affection to many others' (1933, p. 244)? One's account of who really is happy is surely likely to be informed by one's values or general outlook on life. An objective account of happiness is not easy to come by.

The concept of happiness is connected also with such concepts as reward and punishment, since a reward must be something likeable and a punishment unpleasant in some way. There is a strong link connecting such notions as happiness with those of good and bad, but these seem to be no more definable than happiness is. Certainly, Wittgenstein appears to have thought so. He is reported to have said that, 'The use of the word "good" is too complicated. Definition is out of the question' (Bouwsma 1986, p. 42). In that sense we cannot say what is good and what is bad in terms both general and uncontentious. We can give examples, some of which will be more controversial than others, but that is about all. Therefore, we cannot make ethics objective in a way that we might want to without redefining or reconceiving it.

What does all this show? I hope to have shown three things in this section: that happiness is a concept of fundamental importance to the early Wittgenstein, closely connected with ethics; that he regards it as a serious problem how we can talk about such things as happiness, except in an unsatisfying, behavioristic or materialistic kind of way; that he reaches no clear solution to this problem in his early work. We have also seen the seeds of an idea that he would develop later, and to which we shall return: that of a special kind of simile, something that appears both profoundly important and nonsensical.

2. Happiness later

Wittgenstein's later work says almost nothing at all about ethics, but happiness crops up relatively often in one form or another. In *Remarks on the Philosophy of Psychology Volume I* he asks:

> § 858. How does one realize that the expression of joy is not the expression of some bodily pain? (An *important* question.) (Wittgenstein 1980b)

My response, and I assume most people's, would be that there really is no such realization. It simply does not occur to us to wonder, in normal circumstances, what a smile expresses. With babies, we might wonder whether a smile is the result of gas and not a real expression of mood at all, but we have to be taught to wonder about such things. Babies do not wonder what smiles mean. They (generally) react. Some babies will be oblivious to some smiles, and some will cry rather than smile back, but there is a tendency for people to smile back, to respond positively to a smile. These shared natural tendencies allow us to get along, to feel that we understand one another (not necessarily erroneously!). They are the basis of understanding, not a product of it.

Again, in the same volume of remarks Wittgenstein writes:

> § 926. One tie-up between moods and sense-impressions is that we use the concepts of mood to describe sense-impressions and images. We say of a

musical theme, or a landscape, that it is sad, cheerful [*fröhlich*] etc. But naturally it is much more important that we use all the concepts of mood to describe human faces, actions, behaviour. (Wittgenstein 1980b)

It is not on the basis of any theory that I would say that a musical theme was cheerful, any more than I have a theory that tells me which jokes are funny. Similarly, people's facial expressions and behavior, and my reactions to them, can be grouped together in various ways, ways that can be given names. Happy behavior goes with, and generally comes from people with, happy faces. (Compare *Remarks on the Philosophy of Psychology Volume II*: '§ 570. Grief, one would like to say, is personified in the face. This is essential to what we call "emotion".' Wittgenstein 1980a) This is about as simple as truths get, but it is hardly simple to say in what 'happy behavior' consists.

In this connection, we might also consider the following from *Remarks on the Philosophy of Psychology Volume I*:

> § 927. Consciousness in the face of another. Look into someone else's face and see the consciousness in it, and also a particular *shade* of consciousness. You see on it, in it, joy, indifference, interest, excitement, dullness, etc. The light in the face of another. (Wittgenstein 1980b)

We do not *realize* that others have minds. 'I am not of the *opinion* that he has a soul' (Wittgenstein 1958, p. 178). We see it, as we see that they have this or that mood. And, as the world appears different to the happy and to the unhappy, faces appear differently to different people. What looks like cheerfulness to one will appear as insolence to another, and there is no simple, objective means to distinguish one from the other. Indeed, it takes a certain kind of attitude to see anything of such a kind as cheerfulness or insolence. If we are indifferent to the attitudes of those around us, whether because we just do not care at all or because we have other things on our minds, then we will (often) not notice them. If we did notice that something was going on on someone's face but did not react to it in any particular way, then we would have a hard time calculating what mood was being expressed by, for instance, measuring the movements of skin around the mouth and eyes. There are no criteria for translating such measurements into ascriptions of mood.

Attributing emotion or mood to a person on the basis of his or her expressions and behavior is quite similar to judging the character of the world on the basis of history, or one's own history. The facts alone do not do it (assuming we can make sense of the idea of 'the facts alone' here.) At least partly, we react.[10] And what we react to is a perceived character or spirit, which can in turn be characterized in a variety of ways. Hence

> § 853. It is important ... that there are all these paraphrases! That one can describe care with the words 'Ewiges Düstere steigt herunter'.[11]

I have perhaps never sufficiently stressed the importance of this paraphrasing.

Joy is represented by a countenance bathed in light, by rays streaming from it. Naturally, that does not mean that joy and light *resemble* one another; but joy – *it does not matter why* – is associated with light (Wittgenstein 1980b).

Emotions can be endlessly characterized, associated with countless other things. To some these associations will mean nothing, but most of us get at least some of them. Otherwise, we might never be able to communicate about emotion at all. There are close connections between the abilities to understand poetry, ethics and religion, and emotion. These are connected closely also with the ability to understand words used in what Wittgenstein called a 'secondary sense'.[12] A word is used in a secondary sense when it is not used in its literal sense, and yet, precisely because of this primary sense, no other word will do. Wittgenstein speaks of wanting to say that Tuesday is thin, for instance. This would be a use of 'thin' in a secondary sense. We might also think of words like 'hot' and 'cold' when used to describe colors (red and blue, perhaps) as being used in a secondary sense. Some uses of words that the early Wittgenstein would have called nonsensical are counted by the later Wittgenstein as uses of words in a secondary sense. This is significant, given that he earlier said that all attempts to speak or write ethics and religion were nonsense. Indeed, the examples he gives of 'nonsensical' uses of words in attempts to put ethics and religion into words, such as talking about wondering about the existence of the world or feeling absolutely safe, seem to fit the idea of secondary sense very well. This connection between poetic understanding and ethics is what makes one inclined to agree with Wittgenstein when he suggests that ethics and aesthetics are one, or that psychology can never be a science. Moods and attitudes seem to be captured much more finely in poetry than they could ever be by some kind of numerical measure of utilitarian hedons (hypothetical units of pleasure) or dolors (hypothetical units of pain).

In Volume II of Wittgenstein's *Remarks on the Philosophy of Psychology* we see a return to the world of the happy, the undirected (or is it omni-directed?) rejoicing in everything:

§ 322. ... If I go for a walk and take pleasure in everything [*mich über alles freue*], then it is surely true that this would not happen if I were feeling unwell. But if I now express my joy, saying, e.g., 'How marvelous all of this is!' [*Wie herrlich Alles ist!*] – did I mean to say that all of these things were producing pleasant physical feelings in me?

In the very case where I'd express my joy like this: 'The trees and the sky and the birds make me feel good all over [*geben mir ein herrliches*

Gefühl im ganzen Körper]' – still what's in question here is not causation, nor empirical concomitance, etc. etc. (Wittgenstein 1980a)

An expression of joy in everything is not about physical sensations. Nor is it a report on one's psychological state. And if I say that the birds' singing gives me a glorious feeling, I am not making a causal claim about some empirical phenomenon, but telling you what I feel good about. (At least that is the case in this example. Under psychological examination, I might report that the trees, etc. make me feel good. The very same words that Wittgenstein uses could be used to describe one's psychological state, but then one would not be expressing one's joy. A report is not an expression.) What I say is an expression of feeling, a reaction to the world that cannot be translated into a report of facts. And, since all of us do not react the same way, and since these reactions seem to be at the basis of our ability to get along with each other, we do not always manage to get along. This comes out in the following remarks:

> Frequently one will say: I do not *understand* these people. [Cf. Wittgenstein 1958, II, xi, p. 223f]
> One also says: I don't understand this person's joy and sadness. And what does that mean? Doesn't it mean that as I understand the words he is actually not sad and not happy? And now what does it mean to say: Maybe exactly the same thing is going on within him as within me, only it is expressed differently? (Wittgenstein 1980a, p. 28e.)
> 'One knows when someone is really happy.' But that doesn't mean that one can describe the genuine expression. – But of course it is not *always* true that one recognizes the genuine expression, or knows whether the expression is genuine. Indeed there are cases where one is not happy either with 'genuine' or 'sham'. Someone smiles and his further reactions fit neither a genuine nor a simulated joy. We might say 'I don't know my way around with him. It is neither the picture (pattern) of genuine nor of pretended joy.'
> Mightn't his relation to a person with normal feelings be like that of a colour-blind person to the normal-sighted? (Wittgenstein 1980a, p. 61e)

Understanding others' moods is like understanding philosophy or another language or culture: we do not always know how to find our way about. In simple cases, such as Socrates' pleasure at rubbing his leg where the fetters had been chafing, we know where we are. But we are capable of a great range of expression, in our behavior and in our language, and not everything is readily comprehensible to everyone. There are various ways in which one might struggle to understand another person, and as Wittgenstein suggests, this can happen by struggling to understand another's happiness or sadness. To the extent that I cannot understand this or that person's happiness, I also cannot claim to understand happiness itself. There are kinds of what we might be tempted, or unsure whether, to call happiness, that lie above or beyond the simple foundations of our mutual understanding. That is not to say that we ought to avoid sophisticated conceptions of happiness, but the more sophisticated (or simply unusual) one's sense of happiness, the less the chances are that others will be able to understand it. There are not unmistakable, objective facts of the matter as to what emotion or mood people are experiencing that lie hidden behind their faces. 'Happiness' and 'grief' are not the names of chemical events or substances, although, of course, we could apply these words only to people whose brains contain particular chemical reactions, just as we can by the same token call happy only those who worship our God. It is, to some extent, up to us what sense we give to these words.[13]

It is hard to see how any such decision to give the word 'happiness' this or that meaning could possibly be value-neutral. Yet this is what is being attempted in the name of positive psychology. The word 'positive' here is intended to contrast with the negative focus of much psychology, which attends to psychological disorders far more than to happiness and well-being. However, positive psychology also aims at being positive in the sense of being strictly descriptive, not value-laden or normative. This is emphasized in a recent attempt to expand positive psychology's definition of happiness by Eranda Jayawickreme, James Pawelski, and Martin E. P. Seligman of the Positive Psychology Center at the University of Pennsylvania (2008). The authors want to be scientific, positive rather than normative, and to discover or identify the best ways of becoming happy, but they struggle to avoid importing value judgments of their own. Admirably, they reject simplistic theories of happiness in favor of a more pluralistic one, which includes four components: happiness attained through pleasure, happiness attained through engagement in absorbing activities, happiness attained through living a meaningful life and happiness attained through achievement of goals sought simply for the sake of their achievement (such as winning at cards or amassing wealth). The authors make clear their own evaluation of these kinds of lives, but point out that their aim is to identify ways in which people find happiness or well-being, not to endorse either the seeking of happiness or any particular way of doing so.

Tensions arise in pursuit of this aim though. The very notion of a meaningful life, for instance, seems problematic from a supposedly purely empirical viewpoint. Jayawickreme et al. deny that a 'subjective state of meaning' is either necessary or sufficient for something to count as meaningful (2008, p. 9). Instead, a valuable life (such as Abraham Lincoln's) is to count as a meaningful life, even if its subject is too melancholy to recognize it as such. For this reason, they say, 'meaning is assessed by some combination of societal judgment, factual consequences, and subjective state' (Jayawickreme et al. 2008, p. 9). Ethical (or simply evaluative) ideas about which lives are meaningful hardly seem likely to be excluded from either the societal judgment referred to here or from the process by which it is decided what combination of such judgment, factual consequences and subjective states are to be used to determine meaning. It seems that the 'Authentic Happiness theory of happiness' (2008, p. 1), *pace* Jayawickreme et al., cannot be 'just a description' (2008, p. 17).

This comes out too in the authors' account of why their theory of happiness is preferable to simpler ones. They list four reasons. The first is that a machine designed to induce pleasure would not thereby provide what many people would count as true happiness. Judgments about what is and is not true happiness, though, seem to be normative, not positive. Jeremy Bentham identified happiness with pleasure, and it is not a scientific fact that he was wrong. The second reason given is that we should take seriously Wittgenstein's dying claim to have had a wonderful life, despite the fact that he was 'very dysphoric' (Jayawickreme et al. 2008, p. 22). Again, this is surely an evaluative judgment about whether Wittgenstein was truly happy (where *truly* is a normative concept). The third reason is that people who do not have strong feelings will be discriminated against by policies designed to maximize positive feelings. Those who feel more (either positively or negatively) will count for more in the hedonic calculus. Once more, this is quite clearly a normative judgment. It is not a scientific, empirical, merely positive claim that such discrimination would be bad. Finally, 'over and above these' reasons, Jayawickreme et al. think that simpler, subjective well-being accounts of happiness are 'morally and politically imprisoning' because 'happiness is plural and not the playground of privileged extroverts' (2008, p. 23). This, they say, is 'just about the only place where we are at all consciously prescriptive' (Jayawickreme et al. 2008, p. 23). It is not, though, the only place where prescriptive judgments influence their work. This does not make it bad work, but it does make it less purely descriptive than they mean it to be. If they do discover the most efficient way to become happy, this way will not recommend itself to those who want (what they think of as) happiness but who have different values. Any account of what happiness is will depend on certain value judgments, or else will have to be hazy enough to lend itself to a great variety of ethical outlooks.

Happiness, as a concept, is blurry and elusive. This is recognized not only by Wittgenstein but also, for instance, by Daniel Haybron. He understands happiness as a kind of emotional condition, importantly related to, but not identical with, mood. It is not, he argues, the same thing as pleasure or satisfaction with one's life. Despite having made such distinctions, though, his 'account remains confessedly vague' in several ways (Haybron 2005, p. 309). Wittgenstein's work suggests that any account of happiness is likely to be either partial or vague. This is not to say that happiness is a meaningless concept or an illusion of some kind. It is still important. We can pursue it. Perhaps we inevitably do pursue it. But we cannot really aim at this blur, as if it stood clear, objective and independent of us like a target. There are different, but related, conceptions of happiness, and we can neither aim at them all at once nor, without being partial, pick out just one. Nor can we realistically hope to derive from the very general concept of happiness rules for living that will spare us the need for careful attention, sensitive perception and fallible judgment about what we ought to do.[14]

Notes

1. This is not to say that Aristotle and Wittgenstein are in direct disagreement here. The disagreement is perhaps more of emphasis or attitude. Aristotle is well aware of the kind of problem that Wittgenstein might point out to him, but he aimed nevertheless to do constructive philosophical work on how one ought to live. Wittgenstein, who claimed never to have read a word of Aristotle, was pessimistic about the possibility of such a project.
2. Wittgenstein refers to pain as 'the connecting link' between delight (he mentions joy and enjoyment too) and what we would normally call sensations. See Wittgenstein (1967, § 485).
3. By Wittgenstein, among others. See Bouwsma (1986, p. 60).
4. Alfred Nordmann (2005) develops the idea of expression through 'music, actions, performances, gestures, and lives' (p. 171 ff).
5. In a letter to Engelmann dated January 16, 1914 (the twelfth letter in Engelmann, 1967) Wittgenstein wrote: 'If you tell me now that I have no faith, you are *perfectly right*, only I did not have it before either. It is plain, isn't it, that when a man wants, as it were, to invent a machine for becoming decent, such a man has no faith.'
6. See Wittgenstein (2003, 5.631–5.632). The 'thinking, presenting subject' is a limit of the world, not something that would be included in a list of things in a description of the world as I found it. Indeed, it would not even be mentioned in a report on this world. And yet the *Tractatus* is a kind of report on the world, and it does talk about this subject.
7. It is tempting to oppose the seemingly Gradgrindian insistence on dealing with nothing but facts that can be read into, for instance, the spirit of logical positivism. But in an atmosphere of windy nonsense (the kind of thing attacked as meaningless in George Orwell's essay on politics and the English language, or as bullshit in Harry Frankfurt's celebrated essay) it might be refreshing. It might even be considered a necessity if the nonsense reached an unbearable level.
8. This paragraph and the one before it are adapted from material in Richter 2007, pp. 182–184.
9. For more on this idea see McManus (2006), chapters 13 and 14, and chapter 4 of Richter (2004).
10. It is tempting to compare what Friedrich Nietzsche writes about judgments on the value of life in § 2 of 'The problem of Socrates' in *Twilight of the Idols*, that they cannot be true but must be considered only a symptoms of either health or sickness in the one making the judgment. Both Wittgenstein and Nietzsche surely had in mind Schopenhauer's rather negative evaluation of the world of experience when they wrote about such judgments.
11. 'Eternal dark climbs down', from Goethe's *Faust*, part two, act V, midnight.
12. For more on the meaning of 'secondary sense', see Wittgenstein (1958, p. 216).
13. In saying that we could speak in this kind of way (calling happy only those with a certain brain chemistry, or a certain religion, for instance) I am noting a logical

possibility, not suggesting that it would be quite all right if we did so. If the decision to do so were based on philosophical confusion about what science can discover, or on narrow-mindedness, then this would not be all right in my view. P.M.S. Hacker (2007) writes that: 'It is an illusion that scientific discovery can disclose what the words we use, such as 'gold' and 'water', 'fish' and 'lily', *really* mean. For what a word means is determined by convention, not by discovery – although, of course, discovery may be elevated into convention by agreement on a new rule for the use of a word' (p. 46). This is why it is both possible and possibly a mistake to call people happy only if their brains are in a particular condition.

14. I am very grateful to Ylva Gustafson, Camilla Kronqvist and Michael McEachrane for their patience and constructive criticisms of earlier drafts of this chapter.

Bibliography

Bouwsma, O.K. (1986), 'Cornell, July 1949', *Wittgenstein: Conversations, 1949–1951*, Craft, J. L. and Hustwit, R.E. (eds) (Indianopolis, IN: Hackett), p. 42.

Engelmann, P. (1967), *Letters from Ludwig Wittgenstein with a Memoir* (Oxford: Blackwell Publishing).

Foot, P. (2001), *Natural Goodness* (Oxford: Clarendon Press).

Hacker, P.M.S. (2007), *Human Nature: The Categorical Framework* (Oxford: Blackwell Publishing).

Haybron, D.M. (2005), 'On Being Happy or Unhappy', *Philosophy and Phenomenological Research* LXXI(2), 287–317.

Hursthouse, R. (1999), *On Virtue Ethics* (Oxford: Oxford University Press).

Jayawickreme, E., Pawelski, J. and Seligman, M.E.P. (2008), 'Happiness: Positive Psychology and Nussbaum's Capabilities Approach' accessed 28 January 2008 online at http://www.dpo.uab.edu/~angner/SWB/Jayawickreme&al.pdf.

Kupperman, J.J. (2006), *Six Myths about the Good Life: Thinking about What Has Value* (Indianapolis, IN: Hackett).

McManus, D. (2006), *The Enchantment of Words: Wittgenstein's* Tractatus Logico-Philosophicus (Oxford: Clarendon Press).

Nordmann, A. (2005), *Wittgenstein's* Tractatus: *An Introduction* (Cambridge: Cambridge University Press).

Richter, D.J. (2004), *Wittgenstein at His Word* (London: Continuum).

—— (2007), *Why be Good? A Historical Introduction to Ethics* (New York: Oxford University Press).

Russell, B. (1933), *The Conquest of Happiness* (Garden City, NY: Garden City Publishing Company, Inc.).

Schopenhauer, A. (1969), *The World as Will and Representation* Volume I, translated by Payne, E.F.J. (New York: Dover Publications Inc.).

White, N.P. (2006), *A Brief History of Happiness* (Oxford: Blackwell).

Wittgenstein, L. (1958), *Philosophical Investigations*, translated by Anscombe, G.E.M., 2nd edn (Oxford: Basil Blackwell).

—— (1967), *Zettel* edited by Anscombe, G.E.M. and von Wright, G. H., translated by Anscombe, G. E.M. (Oxford: Basil Blackwell).

—— (1979), *Notebooks 1914–1916*, edited by von Wright, G.H. and Anscombe, G.E.M., trans. Anscombe, G.E.M. (Chicago: The University of Chicago Press).

—— (1980a), *Last Writings on the Philosophy of Psychology Volume II*, edited by von Wright, G.H. and Nyman, H., translated by Luckhardt, C.G. and Aue, M.A.E. (Chicago: The University of Chicago Press).

—— (1980b), *Remarks on the Philosophy of Psychology Volume I*, edited by Anscombe, G.E.M. and von Wright, G.H., translated by Anscombe, G.E.M. (Chicago: The University of Chicago Press).

—— (1993), 'A Lecture on Ethics,' in Wittgenstein, L., *Philosophical Occasions 1912–1951*, edited by Klagge, J.C. and Nordmann, A. (Indianapolis, IN: Hackett Publishing Company).

—— (2003), *Tractatus Logico-Philosophicus*, translated by Ogden, C.K. (New York: Barnes & Noble Books).

12
Our Struggles with Reality

Camilla Kronqvist

> *Es ist Unsinn*
> *sagt die Vernunft*
> *Es ist was es ist*
> *sagt die Liebe*
> *Es ist Unglück*
> *sagt die Berechnung*
> *Es ist nichts als Schmerz*
> *sagt die Angst*
> *Es ist aussichtslos*
> *sagt die Einsicht*
> *Es ist was es ist*
> *sagt die Liebe*
> *Es ist lächerlich*
> *sagt der Stolz*
> *Es ist leichtsinnig*
> *sagt die Vorsicht*
> *Es ist unmöglich*
> *sagt die Erfahrung*
> *Es ist was es ist*
> *sagt die Liebe*
> Erich Fried

Is it so that the long held suspicion against emotions in philosophy stems from the difficult questions it raises about reality? The above-quoted poem by Erich Fried reminds us that accepting the reality, or realities, of emotion asks for the acceptance of there being, at times, quite diverging accounts of what has happened or what a situation is. It involves the acknowledgement that we do not always share the same kind of life but sometimes live in quite different worlds. Taking the lead from Wittgenstein's *Tractatus* we may conclude that 'The world of the happy is quite another than that of the unhappy' (Wittgenstein 1993, § 6.43).[1]

Considering the rigidity of the *Tractatus* and the views about language and logic that Wittgenstein testifies to there, it is surprising that such a notion should find its expression there. It marks the work, as well as his thinking—this is equally true of his later works, if not even more so—off from what has often been considered to constitute philosophical thought: the commitment to a certain picture of reason as the means for bringing to the surface the underlying structure of language or the world. As Allessandra Tanesini says, 'Philosophy is often understood as the discipline concerned with reason's self-understanding. It involves a rational investigation of the limits of reason itself' (Tanesini 1999, p. 212). The more successful attempts to give emotions a respectable position in philosophy—in cognitive theories in particular—have also emphasized their connections with rationality. It is in virtue of their *rational* character that philosophy is advised to pay due attention to the emotions. The picture of rationality as the key to understanding human life is complicated in many respects, and the following discussion should show at least some ways in which it can be seen to be illusory.

My aim in this chapter is to show how some strands of this kind of commitment to rationality enter into philosophical discussions of idealizations in love. It reveals a preference for statements that can be generalized as well as universalized, assigning to language the role of representing reality that Wittgenstein criticized so strongly. I approach these notions by scrutinizing the claim that the perspective of love inevitably constitutes an idealization of the beloved or of life itself: in other words, that it mainly serves to register a private, subjective response which does not attend to how things actually are. I contrast this with the view, brought out by philosophers such as Iris Murdoch and Simone Weil, that love involves the recognition of the reality of other people.

I argue that the philosophers who regard love in its entirety as an idealization build on too narrow a conception of the concept of 'reality'. 'Reality' mainly figures as an epistemological concept in these accounts, leaving out the moral character of the ways in which the words 'reality' and 'real' are used in the discussions of Murdoch and Weil, as well as in many of our conversations about what is 'real' and what is an 'ideal'.

1. Love and idealization

A recurrent concern in the philosophy of love is the wish to explain the kind of extraordinary seeing that characterizes love. Taking one's point of departure in Stendhal's description of love as involving a process of *crystallization* – a psychological process, in which imagination adds perfections to the image of the loved one, in the same manner that a twig dipped into the water at a salt mine becomes encrusted with salt – one asks, how is it that the lover can find beauty in a face that most people would consider quite bland? What truth can we assign to statements such as 'You are the most beautiful girl in the world' where there clearly is no general agreement as to who deserves that title? Irving Singer, in his three volumes on love, makes a distinction between the appraisal and bestowal[2] of value to approach different historical conceptions of love, finding love to be a creative response to the beloved, in which 'people bestow value upon one another over and above their individual or objective value' (Singer 1984, p. 6). He, and many others with him (cf. Armstrong 2002; Solomon 1990) do not simply agree with the claim that 'love is blind'. Their formulations rather go to show that love involves a fantasy, that the lover has an 'over-active imagination' (Solomon 1990, p. 176) or a 'creative eye' (Armstrong 2002, p. 55).

My problem with these notions is not primarily with the suggestion that loving relationships may and often do involve idealizations. Rather idealizing or embellishing either myself or you, or our relationship, is a constant temptation in love. It is a particularly striking aspect of falling in love and the kind of admiration of the other that often goes with it: I am mesmerized by you and see only the good things about you; I project what I wish for you to be into you, and see only what I want to see; I try to be what I think you want me to be. This temptation to idealize is as alive in the different ways of romanticizing the relationships of love in different circumstances, as in the mystification of the relationship between the genders. Think only of self-help books such as Men Are from Mars, Women Are from Venus (Gray 1992) or of religious zealots emphasizing the biblical 'male and female He created them'.

What troubles me is rather the suggestion that we could make sense of the notion that love *as such* involves an idealization – and not just that this may be a characteristic of a particular love. It is true that I may come to regard my love or my ways of viewing you as mistaken or illusory, thinking that I was living a fantasy. But this is not a mistake that is internal to loving *per se* but something that is better described as a *failure* in my love. Idealizations can be said to form not only a constant temptation for love but also a *threat* against it. Furthermore, this depiction of love ignores the roles the distinction between what is 'real' and what is an 'ideal' in itself has in our conversations about love. Contrast, for one thing, the former descriptions of love as an idealization with Simone Weil who writes, 'Love needs reality. What is more terrible than the discovery that through a bodily appearance we have been loving an imaginary being.' (Weil 1977, p. 359). Our talk about love does not only concern the beauty or wonders in it, but a great deal of it also emphasizes the ways in which we may come to know someone in love, such as the demand to 'love you as you are'.

If we want to see what sense it may have to speak about idealizations in the context of love, my suggestion is that we turn to sayings such as these. The philosophers discussing love and idealization attend to an important question; 'What is truth or fiction in love?' By trying to give a general answer to what is 'real' and what is an 'ideal', however, they misconstrue the roles that this distinction have in our life, as well as the *different* kinds of contrasts we make with the words.

In the following section, I want to question the idea that there is a privileged position from which we could judge whether love *in its entirety* is an idealization. Rather, I will argue that the philosophers taking this stance fail to describe love in that they try to judge it by standards that are not applicable to it. They take a distinction that has meaning *within* certain practices and use it to judge a practice as a whole. Their suggestion seems to be that certain linguistic practices are 'more in contact with reality' than are others, and that they, therefore, enable us to draw a general distinction between what is 'real' and what is not. They fail to notice that the different distinctions between what is real and what is not are those made by us *in* language.

The standard against which love is judged to be an idealization appears to be borrowed from the natural sciences. True statements are considered to be those which correctly describe certain facts of the world (since only factual statements may have truth-value),and the ideal is to find a neutral position from which to represent these facts in language. What is considered to be true in that sense is not dependent on the time or place of the utterance of a statement, nor on who utters it. The truth of a statement solely depends on its correspondence with reality.

This notion of truth, however, is only intelligible in relation to a very limited range of cases. Even then we should be attentive to what role we give to words such as 'fact', 'truth' and 'reality' in our discussion so that we do not turn them into some kind of philosophical 'super/meta concepts'. Certainly 'reality' and 'truth' are concepts that have a fundamental role in our life and in philosophy, but there are many problems involved in assigning to 'reality' the metaphysical role of, for example, grounding our linguistic practices. To quote Peter Winch (1970, p. 82): 'Reality is not what gives language sense. What is real and what is unreal shows itself *in* the sense that language has.'

I can hardly do justice to Winch's remark here, but I want to bring out the following points: When Winch speaks about the relation between reality and language, he is making a grammatical point, not a metaphysical one. Contrary to idealists or realists he is not trying to say anything about what reality is or is not. For instance, he is not making an idealist claim that reality is constructed in language. Rather he is pointing out the internal relation between language and reality and the impossibility of separating the two. Against realism, he reminds us that language is not a reflection of reality, nor is reality something that determines the sense of language. Rather it is in language that we distinguish what is 'real' from what is not.

My argument, then, is that the roles talking about 'truth' and 'reality' may have in conversations about love are different from the ones it may have in scientific discourse. If we do not remain clear about these differences when philosophizing about love, we risk misrepresenting what it is we are doing when we speak about 'truth' in the different cases. To complicate matters, however, I want to add that the different uses to which 'reality' and 'truth' are put in our different practices are not completely separable. I criticize philosophers for using too narrow a conception of 'reality' to capture what is at stake in different practices, but the only conclusion we may draw from this is not just to broaden our vocabulary to encompass different concepts of reality. A consideration of the role the concepts 'real' and 'truth' have in our life may also lead us to reconsider the ways in which they can come into play within the practice of science.[3] In what ways is it the same concept that we use in different situations?

What is at stake in this struggle is in that sense not only the philosophical failure to recognize the different uses of a concept, but also differing conceptions of what our life means. Not only science, philosophy or rationality may propose to tell us what is real, the poem by Fried suggests that it is only love and not reason (or Reason) that says, 'It is what it is.' Here, one should also remember that words such as 'reality', 'real', 'realistic' are in many situations what W.B. Gallie (1962) called 'essentially contested concepts'.[4] In other words, even if we share a general agreement about the meaning of these concepts, and thereby what role it will have in our life to accept to regard our situation in the light of them, there will inevitably be disagreements about their application in given situations. In certain situations we may dispute whether a certain description of a situation captures what is 'real', and, thus, should play a prominent part in our thinking and acting. Think, for instance, of the ways in which someone can put emphasis on being a 'realist' in making political decisions, and also of the cynic's conviction that he sees the world as it really is.

2. The spirit of truth in love

The philosophers who regard love as an idealization give expression to quite general sentiments when they say, 'mostly we don't have all that many virtues or have them only to a limited extent; people in general are simply not terribly lovable' (Armstrong 2002, p. 46), or, 'They are what they are. Why should they be loved for it?' (Singer 1984, p. 14). Along with the extreme idealizations of romantic love, or as a natural consequence of it, there is a widespread cynicism concerning love, which may well tempt us to think these philosophers are right.

Against this background, it is inviting to perceive sayings such as 'You are the most beautiful girl in the world', as subjective, idealizing responses that do not convey the 'individual or objective value' that 'a community of human interest' may assign to persons (Singer 1984, pp. 3, 6). Now, undoubtedly seeing beauty in this fashion has a deeply personal character. It is central to these statements that *I* respond to *you* in this way. Nevertheless, the ways in which the beauty that I see is dependent on me is not to be taken as an expression of what I say being 'merely subjective' in the sense that it is impossible to speak about truth in this connection. Rather I will argue that it is only by considering what *kind* of statement this is, that we can gain clarity about what it means to speak about truth in this case. There is, as it were, no *general* viewpoint from which we can determine whether people, or particular persons, are beautiful or not, nor any *general* standard of truth against which we can decide whether such statements have truth-value.

In the natural sciences there is a clear sense in which my subjective responses (bias) may (unintentionally) distort the results I reach in my experiments and lead to a misrepresentation of what has happened. Here the need for being able to repeat an experiment and report results that anyone could agree upon is significant for *what* kind of practice the scientific investigation is. Our different practices of telling someone he or she is beautiful, however, are a different matter.

First of all, the fact that there is no general agreement about who is beautiful does not give us occasion to think that the one who sees beauty where others do not necessarily is making a mistake. As we will see later in the discussion the sense in which we may be said to mistake ourselves about the true beauty of someone is also of another kind than mistaking oneself about some facts. Furthermore, in the context of love, there is a question not only about whether one speaks the truth, in the sense that what one says conveys the true state of affairs, but whether one *is true to one's words*, and furthermore *true to each other*. The heart of the deception in a scene of seduction, as it were, does not lie in the seducer's failure to represent reality correctly. Many may agree that the one who is being seduced is attractive in a more general sense, this may even be the reason for the seducer to try to seduce her. The deception of the seducer rather lies in his not being in his words. His words are not the expressions of love and devotion they pretend to be but a means of seduction.

Compare this to Weil who, in a comment on Plato talking about the love of truth, says,

> Love of truth is not a correct form of expression. Truth is not an object of love. It is not an object at all. What one loves is something which exists, which one thinks on, and which may hence be an occasion for truth and error. A truth is always the truth with reference to something. Truth is the radiant manifestation of reality. Truth is not the object of love but reality. To desire truth is to desire direct contact with a piece of reality. To desire contact with a piece of reality is to love. We desire truth only in order to love in truth. We desire to know the truth about what we love. Instead of talking about love of truth, it would be better to talk about *the spirit of truth in love*.

Pure and genuine love always desires above all to dwell wholly in the truth whatever it may be, unconditionally. Every other sort of love desires before anything else means of satisfaction, and for this reason is a source of error and falsehood. Pure and genuine love is in itself spirit of truth. (Weil 1978, p. 242, emphasis added)

This sense in which we may talk about living in truth, as opposed to living a lie in love, is quite distinct from saying that we should only say things that correctly represent reality. 'To desire contact with a piece of reality' in the way Weil identifies with love is not simply, or only, to want a scientific explanation of the constituents of the world. The way in which Weil speaks of reality clearly belongs to a moral context.

This is equally true of Iris Murdoch, when she says, 'Love is the perception of individuals. Love is the extremely difficult realisation that something other than oneself is real. Love, and so art and morals, is the discovery of reality' (Murdoch 1997, p. 215). Here, Murdoch brings together notions that are not generally supposed to match. She speaks of arts, morals and love, and she speaks of reality. Even more, she claims that these have something to do with each other. Set against the background of a scientific understanding of reality, this is undoubtedly a strange claim. Why would it be difficult to get hold of reality? And what does it have to do with love? To make sense of this claim it is important to recognize that in speaking about 'recognizing the reality of the other' Murdoch is making a moral point. The difficulties to come to grips with reality that she is describing are moral difficulties.

If one considers the question of who you are as a psychological question, it is easy to think that my difficulties of coming to know you are primarily constituted by the complexity of mapping out the myriad of thoughts, wants, wishes and emotions which may be thought to constitute your psyche or personality. The quote by Murdoch, however, invites us to reconsider the question, suggesting that my difficulties of knowing both others and myself are of a different kind than the difficulties of spelling out the complexities of the mind. The quote also invites us to reconsider our notion of reality, by reminding us that 'beauty', 'goodness', 'love' are as much part of our conversations about 'reality' as are rocks, atoms, minerals and houses.

If anyone is puzzled by the suggestion that the word 'reality' can be said to belong to a moral context, it may help to remember that someone may speak of the need to be 'reminded of what is real' or consider certain aspects of her life as less 'real' than others. Think, for instance, of the star who coming home to his children says: 'This is what's real. All that fame and fortune is just an illusion.' One may of course argue that this kind of talk is only metaphorical, but then one has already subscribed to a certain conception of 'reality' that forces one to take certain actual uses of the words less seriously than others. If, however, we want to deepen our understanding of this concept, we need to take these kinds of statement about reality as seriously as we do scientific formulations. This is also an invitation to allow our thinking about these concepts to change depending on what we learn by doing so.

Simone Weil, whose writing also inspired Murdoch, comments: 'Belief in the existence of other people as such is love' (1977, p. 359). Now, philosophical discussions about the existence of other people and the external world have often taken place against the background of the Cartesian meditations about certain knowledge and how far it may extend. Focusing largely on epistemological questions, they ask, 'What can we know and how do we know it?' However, even if it is possible to counter the doubts of the Cartesian sceptic and the kind of philosophical solipsism he represents, by showing in what way his position is untenable, we have not yet countered a different kind of solipsism, or rather loneliness, that may plague people.[5] As we will see, there are ways of 'living a dream' or entertaining illusions about the world that do not concern the existence of other minds or of the world.

What it means to 'face the truth' or 'confront reality' in this sense, and this is the sense in which I think both Murdoch and Weil are speaking, is rather connected with our lives *with* other people. Here, the fact that other human beings inhabit my world, and that 'my' world is a world I share with them, is a constitutive feature of the kinds of problems I may experience. Here we are not dealing with a doubt about the reality of others as much as we are dealing with a *blindness* to them, and, what follows from this, a blindness to myself, since it is in relation to others that I become aware of my own reality and the meaning of my actions.

Consider a wife who does not seem to fully acknowledge that her husband is untrue despite the overwhelming evidence. She dismisses friendly attempts to bring up the subject. She cannot bring herself to utter or even think the words 'cheating' or 'infidelity'.[6] The full extent of what has happened has not, as one says, sunk in. Or think of the cheating husband who turns down any attempt to regard his affair as harmful to either his wife or his marriage without noticing that this denial may be as harmful as his cheating. He says, 'This is my own business. It doesn't concern her.' Or, 'Our marriage was dead anyway' – as if his having an affair was not yet another step to killing it.

In these cases it is clear that we cannot separate what it is to face reality from the moral difficulties the wife and husband may have in accepting to regard what has happened in the light of cheating. This involves owning up to what both of them may have done to create the problems in their marriage or how they have failed to solve them, as well as asking for forgiveness and forgiving. What is more, what they continue to do, and how willing they are to come to terms with what has happened, constitutes what will be the reality of their marriage, and of what happened. Did his cheating mean the end of their marriage? Did they go on living together suppressing what had happened? Or did it provide an opportunity for them to rekindle their relationship and open up to each other and to forgiveness?

3. Pictures of beauty

For Murdoch, my struggles with reality and coming to recognize another person mainly involve a form of 'unselfing'. My problems with seeing other people is largely an outcome of my difficulties of overcoming myself and attending to them. Now, it is quite easy to think of situations in which I become so wrapped up in myself and what I am doing that I do not take notice of what happens to you. My self-concern prevents me from grasping the meaning of what has happened to you. I do not see you or listen to you although you are sitting right in front of me. What I want to focus on, however, is how idealizations may constitute a similar kind of self-absorption and blindness to the realities of other people. This should also help to spell out why it is misleading to regard love in its entirety as an idealization.

The example I have in mind is the unhappy marriage of Rosamond and Lydgate in George Eliot's *Middlemarch*. From the start this relationship is filled with idealizations, dreams, wishes and expectations, concerning each other and concerning what married life will be. It is fair to say that the disastrous consequences of that marriage to a great extent grew out of these. On Lydgate's part this comes to show in the way he is taken in by Rosamond's enchanting manner. He finds her to be 'grace itself; she is perfectly lovely and accomplished. ... Rosamond Vincy seemed to have the true melodic charm'. (Eliot 1994, p. 93).

From Rosamond's perspective, their beginning infatuation plays out the love story she had scripted long in advance:

> a stranger was absolutely necessary to Rosamond's social romance, which had always turned on a lover and bridegroom who was not a Middlemarcher, and who had no connections at all like her own ... And here was Mr. Lydgate suddenly corresponding to her ideal, being altogether foreign to Middlemarch, carrying a certain air of distinction congruous with good family, and possessing vistas of that middle-class heaven, rank; a man of talent, also, whom it would be especially delightful to enslave: in fact, a man who had touched her nature quite newly, and brought a vivid interest into her life which was better than any fancied 'might-be' such as she was in the habit of opposing to the actual. (Eliot 1994, pp. 115–116)

Rosamond's and Lydgate's idealizations run on many levels, reaching from their hopes and wishes for what the other should be to ideas about what married life should mean in their middle-class society with its respective images of, the appropriate roles for women and men, husbands and wives. This final aspect is especially clear in many of Lydgate's musings about femininity and the functions of a wife, which to him was largely a question of adornment. 'That is what a woman ought to be: she ought to produce the effect of exquisite music' (Eliot 1994, p. 93). Their romanticized picture of marriage, however, comes to a bitter end as Lydgate's financial problems grow. Looking for support and understanding in his wife, and not just for a pleasant sight, he is repeatedly disappointed. The only understanding Rosamond has to offer him is the way she thinks he has failed her. She cannot forgive him for not being the one she thought she married; the man who was going to give her a life full of pleasantness.

There are hopes that Rosamond's and Lydgate's two worlds would meet, and glimpses of this possibly happening, but the two never fully reach an understanding of each other. In the concluding remarks of the book, we are told that the two never came out of considering the other a burden.

A possible reason for why beauty has been so distrusted through philosophy is probably linked with the part that the concept of beauty, or perhaps rather a picture of beauty, plays in the idealizations involved in relationships such as the one between Rosamond and Lydgate. Both these lovers are captured by a picture of what the other person *should be* like, which is attached to a certain understanding of what beauty consists in: perfection, harmony, a pleasure to the eye.

I speak of a *picture* of beauty here to distinguish between two different senses in which 'beauty' (as a concept) may enter our conversations about love. This distinction is related to the distinction that is often made between someone's *inner* and *outer* beauty. Still, I think such a formulation is misleading, not the least because it implies that someone's inner beauty is in some ways less accessible than what one may call a person's outer beauty. It is not, as it were, that we can locate 'outer beauty' in some facial features, whereas the 'inner beauty' is rather located in some inner qualities, such as a generous personality. On the contrary, one could say that the inner beauty is as much there in the face of the other, in her smiles and eyes as in the case of outer beauty, if not even more. It is something I can be said to see or be struck by in her. Her features are something on which I want to dwell.

Perhaps we would be better advised to say that the distinction between 'inner' and 'outer' rather serves as a moral reminder, not to be too taken in by *appearance*, to be *dazzled by looks,* but to attend to other aspects of people than the *initial impression* they make on us. It is a reminder of the ways in which our understanding of 'beauty' may deepen; we may raise questions as to whether something that at first glance appeared to be beautiful was truly beautiful and may also find beauty in someone who by general standards is considered not to be beautiful. Compare this to a point made by Cora Diamond, who writes:

> [O]ne might, for example, meet George Eliot, and find oneself, during the encounter, recognizing her to be beautiful, but not beautiful as one had understood what beauty was. She, that magnificently ugly woman, gives a totally transformed meaning to 'beauty'. Beauty itself becomes

something entirely new for one, as one comes to see (to one's own amazement, perhaps) a powerful beauty residing in this woman. She has done something, something that one could not at all have predicted, to the concept of beauty. In such a case, she is not judged by a norm available through the concept of beauty; she shows the concept up, she moves one to use the words 'beauty' and 'beautiful' almost as new words, or as renewed words. She gives one a new vocabulary, a new way of taking the world in in one's words, and of speaking about it to others. (Diamond 2005, p. 125)[7]

As I understand Diamond, this transformation of the concept of 'beauty' cannot simply be grasped by reference to the realization that George Eliot possessed a remarkable 'inner beauty'. Although expressions such as 'Beauty comes from the inside' give some indication towards the way in which our conception of beauty may change, they still leave us with the idea that the sense in which Eliot is ugly according to ordinary standards remains intact and is only contrasted by an invisible kind of beauty, the one from inside. Diamond's example rather points to the ways in which I may come to question the relevance of any standards. I see beauty in what I previously judged as ugly.

If I allow an emphasis on the exterior, appearance or perfection rule my understanding of 'beauty', I use the concept as a standard against which I judge the people that I meet. In that way, I distance myself from them as well as from what I may learn about beauty from them. In coming in contact with someone's beauty in the way described by Diamond, however, my concept of beauty is transformed by what I learn from the other. I may, for one thing, come to see the beauty that I see as internally related to the goodness she embodies to me. Through this I may also come to question whether 'good looks', understood in a general sense, could be said to reveal to us anything about what beauty truly is. In this, I let myself be transformed by what I learn through my meeting and being with other people.

In this deepening or transformation of the concept of beauty, I move from the standards that may be given to me within my community towards the question of what meaning 'beauty' may have for me. I move, as it were, from the 'collective (norms)' to the personal. The deeper meaning of 'beauty', then, is not to be found in what everybody thinks. Rather we lose the meaning that speaking of 'beauty' may have in these cases if we attempt to reduce it to that. This is not to say that 'beauty' gains a private meaning for me, which is hidden from everybody else, but that my understanding is dependent on and constituted by my particular response to a particular individual. Through this personal understanding, I may also myself contribute to the meaning that 'beauty' has in my community.

It should come as no surprise that whereas I think that the understanding of beauty that comes to show in the latter case is expressive of love, I do not think so of the first case. Rosamond's and Lydgate's failures in love find expression in their holding on to their images of what the other should be rather than respond-ing to the demands that their relationship with each other makes on them in the face of their new situation. Their idealizations are expressive of a preoccupa-tion with themselves that blinds them to the meaning other people could have for them. (As, we might add, the preoccupation with what concepts should mean, often due to our commitment to one philosophical theory or another, blinds us to the variety of meanings they have in our life with other people.)

4. The reality of other people

This kind of preoccupation with oneself is particularly clear in the case of Rosamond. Her idealizations of what life should be extend as much to her-self as to her husband. Conflating exquisite manners with what is good and right, or assuming the two to be the same, Rosamond's life is all about appearance and being the pleasant woman she takes herself to be. The promise that her interest in Lydgate would take her out of the 'fancied "might-be" ... she was in the habit of opposing to the actual', is not fulfilled. Convinced by her own virtue of always being in the right, there is nothing that Lydgate says that reaches beyond the image she presents of herself.

The novel only presents us with two incidents in which her façade breaks. Both of them concern another couple in the novel, Will Ladislaw and Dorothea Casaubon, and a situation in which Dorothea catches Will and Rosamond in what appears to be quite inappropriate circumstances. At this point in the novel, Will is someone about whom Rosamond has begun to entertain romantic fantasies as Lydgate has begun to bore her. Will, how-ever, is completely devoted to Dorothea. At the moment she walks in on him and Rosamond, he is actually telling Rosamond that Dorothea is the only woman in his life, although they cannot be together – a clause in the will of Dorothea's first husband would leave her moneyless if she remarried. Dorothea, on the other side, had come to speak to Rosamond about Lydgate's situation. She was convinced that she could encourage Rosamond to have the same kind of trust in him that she felt. Nevertheless, she misreads the situation and rushes out. Afraid that he has lost the only thing he had from her – her good will in thinking of him – Will lashes out at Rosamond. 'I had no hope before – not much – of anything better to come. But I had one cer-tainty – that she believed in me. Whatever people had said or done about me, she believed in me. – That's gone!' (Eliot 1994, p. 740).

> Rosamond, while these poisoned weapons were being hurled at her, was almost losing the sense of her identity, and seemed to be waking into some new terrible existence. ... What another nature felt in opposition to her own was being burnt and bitten into her consciousness ... her little world was in ruins, and she felt herself tottering in the midst as a lonely bewildered consciousness. (Eliot 1994, pp. 740–742)[8]

After Will has gone, she falls back fainting, and when Lydgate comes back to find her in this distraught state he believes it is the effect of Dorothea's coming to speak with her.

The second encounter takes place when Dorothea realizes her initial intention of speaking with Rosamond about Lydgate. At first, suspicious of her visit, Rosamond is astounded by the other woman's wholehearted openness and mildness, the way she speaks 'from out the heart of her own trial to Rosamond's' (Eliot 1994, p. 756):

> It was a newer crisis in Rosamond's experience than even Dorothea could imagine: she was under the first great shock that had shattered her dreamworld in which she had been easily confident of herself and critical of others; and this strange unexpected manifestation of feeling in a woman whom she had approached with a shrinking aversion and dread, as one who must necessarily have a jealous hatred towards her, made her soul totter all the more with a sense that she had been walking in an unknown world which had just broken in upon her. (Eliot 1994, 756–757)

'[U]rged by a mysterious necessity to free herself from something that oppressed her as if it were blood-guiltiness', Rosamond then tells her about what happened between her and Will, confessing that Will had never had any love for her (Eliot 1994, pp. 758–759).

Both events portray Rosamond in a situation that is new to her. For a moment, at least, she wakes up into a reality where other people are not only pawns in her games but human beings with lives and feelings of their own. Will's desperation at having lost Dorothea's faith in him reveals quite a different way in which other people may matter to one, than any of her own relations.[9] His refusal to act upon her misery by comforting her (which Lydgate always did) imprints in her most clearly that she too has done something wrong.

In this scene, as in the following one with Dorothea, we clearly see how Rosamond's realization of the reality of other people is internally connected with recognizing her own reality. Suddenly struck by their independent being, it is impossible for her to hold on to the images she had made of them and of herself. No longer can she think of 'other people's states of mind...as material cut into shape by her own wishes' (Eliot 1994, p. 739). No more can she consider herself an innocent victim of other people's malice. She is forced to act responsibly, to speak for herself and to recognize what light is reflected on her by their actions and her own.

The blindness towards other people which finds expression in Lydgate's and Rosamond's differing searches for beauty is twofold. Again taking our starting point in Weil's claim that, 'Belief in the existence of other people as such is love' (1977, p. 359); we could say that they are blind both to the fact that other people are *other* than themselves and to the fact that they are *people*.

There are numerous ways in which we may make ourselves images of other people, by idealizing them or romanticizing our life with them. This is apparent not least in the mystification of the difference between the sexes, and the weight one gives to upholding such a difference. Just think of the often feverishly held conviction that 'men and women cannot ever understand each other', or the consequent fear to even try to understand each other as that might rob the relationship of all the 'magic'.

However, to stress a point that Emmanuel Lévinas has repeatedly made, there is no need to *turn* you into another. *You are always other than me.* Contrary to what the above-mentioned accounts would have us think, however, your otherness is *not* an insurmountable obstacle to our understanding each other. Quite the contrary, speaking about understanding in the first place is expressive of the recognition that we are separate people. This obvious insight – you are never me – may be taken as pointing us to at least two different aspects of human life. First, and this is the more shallow point of the two, it is a reminder that however much information I may have about your past or your plans about your future, I cannot deduce your future thoughts and actions from these facts. The facts about you, as it were, accumulate through your life. The second more important point is rather a point about what it means to understand another human being. We could say that knowing and understanding another person cannot be reduced to merely having information about her.

According to such a picture of what it is to know a person, our knowledge about him may primarily increase by learning more facts. Now, it is true that in many situations I may be said to learn to know you better by learning new facts. But if we, by contrast, consider what it may mean for my understanding of you to deepen, this does not necessarily have to involve learning any new facts. What may change is rather the way in which I relate to the 'facts', the meaning I come to see in them or the different kind of emphasis I lay on them. Think, for instance, of the ways in which Dorothea's first impression of Rosamond and Will's meeting as a romantic rendezvous changed when she recognized that the romantic interest was solely on Rosamond's side. Better yet, we could say that my understanding *manifests* itself in what I come to regard as the facts of the situation. Dorothea saw Lydgate's financial problems as a *misfortune* whereas Rosamond considered them a *betrayal* of her.

This is also one reason for rejecting to speak about the ways in which we may understand and misunderstand each other in love solely with reference to different facts. Facts, to put it boldly, do not explain our understanding. Speaking of facts has a place only in conversations where we already share an understanding of what it may mean to understand certain things in the situation as facts. The difficulty Dorothea had of conveying her perspective on Lydgate's situation to Rosamond was not merely a problem of conveying the right facts, but rather the struggle of awakening in Rosamond a similar response to his situation as the one she experienced; responding to it as a wretched situation and recognizing what it, and the lack of understanding Rosamond had shown him, had made of that man. It was the struggle of encouraging Rosamond to respond to her husband with love.

The last points anticipate the other form of blindness to people I mentioned, being blind to what it means for others to be people. Jean-Paul Sartre (2003) insisted that we cannot reduce human beings to their 'facticity'. In Martin Buber's (2004) vocabulary, a similar point is expressed in the thought that even if it is possible to give a description of you as an '*it*', this does not account for the significance it may have to meet you as a '*thou*'. There is a sense in which people go over and beyond any descriptions we may give of them. Thinking that we could reduce them to one description is a way of denying their reality, turning them into objects.

These insights led Luce Irigaray to suggest that a more appropriate expression than 'I love you' would be 'I love *to* you', pointing at the direction my love takes rather than at its object (Irigaray 2004, p. 14).

> Far from wanting to possess you in linking myself to you, I preserve a 'to', a safeguard of the in-direction between us – I Love to You, and not: I love you. This 'to' safeguards a place of transcendence between us, a place of respect which is both obligated and willed, a place of possible alliance. You do not, then, find yourself reduced to a factual thing or to an object of my love, and not even to an ensemble of qualities, which make you a whole perceptible by me. Instead I stop in front of you as in front of an other irreducible to me: in body and in intellect, in exteriority and in interiority. (Irigaray 2004, p. 14)[10]

In the light of this, we could say that the tragedy of Rosamond and Lydgate's marriage lay in its never having been a true meeting between people, neither of hearts nor of minds. Quite contrary to the above-mentioned fear that in love one may come to know each other too well, their misfortune was that they never really came to know each other in the first place. Certainly, they became well acquainted with each other's weaknesses and conduct, but they did not come to understand each other in the sense that is internally related to love.

There are, as it were, two uses of 'knowing' in play here, we may call it a *transitive* and *intransitive* sense. Speaking about knowing in the transitive sense encompasses the facts I might be said to know about someone. The intransitive sense rather points to the 'nothing in particular' character of 'I know him.' This is the sense in which knowing someone cannot be separated from being *in contact* with someone, or *being there for* someone.[11] Just remember how 'I know what you're going through' can be uttered as a way of showing compassion. This second sense of knowing someone, I would say, is internally related to love.

I cannot emphasize enough the sense in which being alive to the realities of other people involves a constant struggle. Directing the kind of loving attention to people that is involved here, as Murdoch says in one place, is 'an endless task' (1997, p. 317). Recognizing what it means for you to be 'your own person', or to have an existence that is independent of mine, is not something I do once and for all. Time and again I have to beware of withdrawing into my own perspective, or of turning you into an object of my own desires, wishes and expectations. That I often fail in this does not lessen the demand. Rather it strengthens it.

5. Summary

My initial aim was to show, first, how set against a certain pre-conception of 'language', 'rationality' and 'reality', the understanding of love, or even the language of love, regarding the beloved as beautiful, could be regarded as constituting an idealization. Through a discussion of the different roles that 'truth' and 'reality' may have in our life, I then hoped to show how this conception of both 'truth' and 'reality' reveals itself to be a philosophical ideal that is not only unattainable, but illusory. It expresses a commitment to the idea that we could give a systematic, unitary, description of 'reality' which does not attend to the different ways in which the concept is used. In that it fails to do exactly what it was supposed to, that is reveal to us the world as 'it is'.

It is up to you as my reader to decide whether I have succeeded in bringing out this point with sufficient clarity. If, however, you agree with me that the notion of rationality as a means of laying bare the structure of reality is a confused one, I want to suggest that it may be more helpful to return to the roots of philosophy – at least etymologically – and consider what it means to understand it as a form of love. What kind of repercussions could such a shift in our thinking have for our self-understanding as philosophers?

My discussion of *Middlemarch* showed some ways in which my idealizations may constitute a blindness to the reality of another human being in love, and suggested that coming to see you as you are, and recognizing your reality, is better described as an act of love. This is not to say that it consists in any actions or attempts to see you as something in particular. Rather it involves a constant struggle to free myself of certain pre-conceived notions, images and idealizations of what you should be. Something similar could be said of philosophy. Our philosophical ideals about 'reality' may well serve to blind us from what it *really* means to offer a description of the reality made up of human beings.

Rather than attempting to force the world into our picture of it, Wittgenstein suggested that the task of philosophy should be to attend to it. The attitude to life that is expressed in his remarks and in his philosophy has often been described in negative terms. Diamond (1991) speaks of the moral dimension of his philosophy in its avowal not to exercise one's will over the world or to try to control it. In more positive terms, however, I wonder if we are not also entitled to say that his philosophy is expressive of a love of life. It is a reminder that only when we release ourselves from certain pre-conceived pictures of what language is, and how it relates to the world, is it possible for us to see both language and our life as they are.[12]

Notes

1. This is not meant as a commitment to relativism. I think that Wittgenstein's philosophy, with its emphasis on nothing being hidden, the ways in which we see emotion in the other's face, and so on has offered us an overwhelming rejection of scepticism which often seems to be a part of relativist positions. Especially in his remarks about our reactions to other people's emotions there is a strong emphasis on the sense in which language is essentially shared. My only point is that emphasizing this aspect too much may lead one to neglect the different kinds of gaps there may be between people.
2. By 'appraisal' he means the 'objective value' that a 'community of human interest' assigns to something, for example a house. This value is connected with the significance certain facts may have for prospective buyers. He also speaks of individual appraisals, which are rather connected with the individual's different interests and desires and how well an object can satisfy them. 'Bestowal', by contrast, is not concerned with 'objective value'. It describes the subjective or emotional value something gets for me independently of its appraised value, say if the house I grew up in becomes dear to me (Singer 1984, pp. 3–4). Love, for Singer, is a case of bestowal. We may, however, be fooled into thinking of it as a form of appraisal.

   In caring about someone, attending to her, affirming the importance of her being what she is, the lover resembles a man who has appraised an object and found it very valuable. Though he is bestowing value, the lover seems to be declaring the objective goodness of the beloved. It is as if he were predicting the outcome of all possible appraisals and insisting that they would always be favorable.

   It is as if he were predicting the outcome of all possible appraisals and insisting that they would always be favorable.

   As a matter of fact, the lover is doing nothing of the sort. (Singer 1984, p. 12)
3. Think, for example, of the ways in which aesthetic reactions and a personal interest in questions may play a role in science (Cf. Wickman 2005).
4. W.B. Gallie (1962) introduced the notion that some concepts 'are essentially contested, concepts the proper use of which inevitably involves endless disputes about their proper uses on the part of their users' (p. 123). Although there is a general agreement that, for example, goodness should be furthered, you may dispute my description of an action as good.
5. Dilman (1987) speaks about our difficulties to care about other people as 'affective solipsism' (pp. 109–111).
6. Cf. Cockburn (2003),

   While the fact is staring her in the face, Mary never says 'My husband is having an affair'. Is she prepared to say it? Well, one question that needs to be asked about this is: prepared to say it when and to whom? (To the radical translator, with his tape recorder, visiting her country from a far off land?) That aside, there may be a quite straightforward, and fairly general, sense in which she is not prepared to say it. Indeed, she cannot even bring herself to think it: her thoughts veer away from the evidence and from any topic that has potential links with her husband's affair. And yet we can see in her demeanour towards her husband, and, perhaps, in adjustments at other points in her life, a recognition of his infidelity. And we suspect that under certain kinds of pressure she would verbally acknowledge what is going on. (p. 154)

7. Diamond's example is a free interpretation of how Henry James once described Eliot in a letter.
8. Dilman (1987) discusses the same example in more detail (p. 115).
9. Even if Raimond Gaita (2004) usually gives other kinds of examples when speaking of the way we sometimes 'see that something is precious only in the light of someone's love for it' (xxiv), this could also be taken as an example of that.
10. I am not completely at peace with Irigaray's proposal. It works as a reminder not to be fooled by the surface-grammar of 'I love you' into thinking that it depicts the same kind of relation as 'I like ice-cream'. Still, if we consider the important task of philosophy to be to remind us of the different uses we may make of 'I love you', it becomes more difficult to see of what help it can be to us. We do not need a 'to' to recognize that the words may be used as a gesture, reminiscent of an embrace, a promise, a plea or a confession.
11. Compare Dilman (1987), chapter 8.
12. I would like to thank Lars Hertzberg, Ylva Gustafsson, Michael McEachrane and David Cockburn for helpful comments on previous versions of this article.

Bibliography

Armstrong, J. (2002), *Conditions of Love: The Philosophy of Intimacy* (London: Penguin Books).

Buber, M. (2004), *I and Thou* (London: Continuum).

Cockburn, D. (2003), 'Language, Belief and Human Beings' in O'Hear, A. (ed.) *Minds and Persons*. Royal Institute of Philosophy Supplement: 53 (Cambridge: Cambridge University Press).

Diamond, C. (1991), 'Ethics, Imagination and the Method of Wittgenstein's Tractatus' in Heinrich, R. and Vetter, H. (eds), *Bilder der Philosophie: Reflexionen über das Bildliche und die Phantasie* (Wien, München: Oldenburg Verlag), 55–90.

—— (2005), 'Wittgenstein on Religious Belief: The Gulfs between Us' in Phillips, D.Z. and von der Ruhr, M. (eds), *Religion and Wittgenstein's Legacy* (Aldershot, Burlingham: Ashgate).

Dilman, I. (1987), *Love and Human Separateness* (Oxford: Basil Blackwell).

Eliot, G. (1994), *Middlemarch* (London: Penguin Books).

Gallie, W.B. (1962), 'Essentially Contested Concepts', in Black, M. (ed.) *The Importance of Language* (Englewood Cliffs, NJ: Prentice-Hall), 121–146

Gray, J. (1992), *Men Are from Mars, Women Are from Venus: A Practical Guide for Improving Communication and Getting what You Want in Your Relationships* (New York: Harper Collins).

Irigaray, L. (2004), 'The Wedding between Body and Language' in Irigaray, L. (ed.) *Key Writings* (London, New York: Continuum).

Murdoch, I. (1997), 'The Sublime and the Good' in Conradi, P.J. (ed.), *Existentialists and Mystics: Writings on Philosophy and Literature* (London: Chatto & Windus).

Sartre, J-P (2003), *Being and Nothingness* (London and New York: Routledge).

Singer, I. (1984), *The Nature of Love: Vol. 1 Plato to Luther* (Chicago: The University of Chicago Press).

Solomon, R.C. (1990), *Love: Emotion, Myth & Metaphor* (Buffalo, New York: Prometheus Books).

—— (1993), *The Passions: Emotions and the Meaning of Life* (London: Hacket).

Tanesini, A. (1999), *An Introduction to Feminist Epistemologies* (Malden and Oxford: Blackwell Publishers).

Weil, S. (1977), 'Criteria of Wisdom: Love' in Panichas, G. E. (ed.), The Simone Weil Reader (New York: David McKay Company Inc), pp. 357–359.

Weil, S. (1978), *The Simone Weil Reader* in Panichas, G.E. (ed.) (New York: David McKay Company Inc).

Weil, S. (1987), *The Need for Roots* (London: Routledge and Kegan Paul).

Wickman, P-O. (2006), *Aesthetic Experience in Science Education: Learning and Meaning-Making as Situated Talk and Action* (Mahwah, N.J.: Lawrence Erlbaum Associates).

Winch, P. (1970), 'Understanding a Primitive Society' in Wilson, B. R. (ed.) *Rationality: Key Concepts in the Social Sciences* (Oxford: Basil Blackwell).

Wittgenstein, L. (1977), *Über Gewissheit-On Certainty* (Oxford: Basil Blackwell).

—— (1993), *Tractatus Logico-Philosophicos* (London: Routledge & Kegan Paul).

13

Extreme Aversive Emotions: A Wittgensteinian Approach to Dread

Rupert Read

1. Outline

In this chapter, I aim to characterize the extreme aversive emotion of psychotic and quasi-psychotic psychopathology that I will call 'dread'.

More specifically, my objective is to indicate a 'deep-grammatical' difference between (respectively) what we can term (1) *fear* (2) *anxiety* and (3) *dread*, using as a starting point not so much the usual Heideggerian and Kierkegaardian reference-points, but rather (a) various remarks of Wittgenstein's such as his wonderful *apercu* about the impenetrably extreme emotions of a young child, and (b) Louis Sass's 'Wittgensteinian' reading of psychotic psychopathology.

To flesh out (b) a little further: I will understand such psychopathology as frequently manifesting what I am calling *dread*, and as resulting, very roughly, from an inability to dissolve metaphysical problems which come to obsess one to the point of such dread being very present, where it is almost entirely absent in (say) Descartes' *Meditations*. I will take dread (as in psychotic psychopathology etc.) as a kind of paradigm of what I am interested in: extreme aversive emotions.

Thus, I will urge that Wittgenstein and Wittgensteinian investigation of the 'pathological emotion' of dread [(3)] (an emotion far stranger than fear or sadness or grief [(1)] and stranger even than 'merely neurotic' anxiety or depression [(2)][1]) establishes its nature. (And, following Sass, I shall at points add parenthetically that, perhaps surprisingly, this investigation points to that nature as being somewhat akin to the supposedly only rational nature of (non-Wittgensteinian) philosophizing itself.)

2. My central argument: suffering from a loss of world?

People seeking philosophical illumination or perspicuity as to the nature of dread – as to what is going on when someone experiences not just fear (which we can all understand preternaturally), nor even just persistent anxiety (whose understanding can challenge some of the more well-balanced among us, but which most of us can eventually attain to understanding), but *extreme* or 'radical' anxiety – typically look to Kierkegaard or Heidegger. And those are very good places to *start* looking. But these great philosophers do not in my opinion go *far* enough to enable the radically aversive to be, in the end, understood as best we can understand it. What I wish to do here is to outline briefly how (having understood) *Wittgenstein* (and Wittgensteinians) can shed a somewhat distinctive light on the (*extremity* of) 'extreme aversive emotions'; and can do so in a way that avoids the dubious theoretical commitments common to mainstream approaches in philosophy of the emotions, such as those of 'Cognitive Science', and sometimes also those even in the subtler work of the likes of Heidegger and Agamben (see Hutchinson's chapter in this volume, and his book on the same topic (2008), for a fine detailing of the kind of thing I mean here).

In short, the key argument I will make in what follows, building on Wittgensteinian thinking, is that dread is best understood as involving not (as 'ordinary' anxiety or depression does) a different *weltanschauung*, but something more extreme: a *kind* of *loss* of *welt*. That is, a felt *weltverlust*, or a perceived and (and this is natural, and critically-important) at-times-overwhelmingly feared *loss of world*.

3. Suffering from a different world

To start with, let us recall a remark from near the close of Wittgenstein's *Tractatus Logico-Philosophicus* (6.43, Ogden/Ramsey translation; emphasis mine):

> If good or bad willing changes the world, it can only change the limits of the world, not the facts; not the things that can be expressed in language.
> In brief, the world must thereby become quite another. It must so to speak wax or wane as a whole.
> *The world of the happy is quite another than that of the unhappy.*

Put that alongside a relatively-little-known passage from *Culture and Value* (1998, p. 4; emphasis mine), from 1929:

> Anyone who listens to a child's crying with understanding will know that psychic forces, terrible forces, sleep within it, *different from anything commonly assumed*. Profound rage & pain & lust for destruction.

As it were the world of the young child is quite another than that of the adult. In Part II of my book applying Wittgenstein (2007), I interpret William Faulkner's *The Sound and the Fury* as showing this profoundly different emotional life, its torments and furies, through brilliant conceptual artifice; and, more crucially for our present purposes, I suggest there at some length that this is a useful object of comparison for the task of understanding something at least as profoundly different: the mind of one caught in the profound suffering of serious mental disorder.[2]

Thus, my suggestion thus far is that the *world* (in roughly the *Tractatus's* – all-encompassing – sense of that word) of those suffering from more or less psychotic dis-ease truly is at the least quite *profoundly* another than that of those who do not.

4. Retreat from the lifeworld

This species of 'profundity' is (to say the least) hard to grasp. The hermeneutic task of understanding the cognitive and emotional states (the 'world') of those suffering from 'schiz spectrum' disorders or from the harsher of the affective disorders (i.e. severe depression, some serious anxiety-conditions, etc.) can be significantly harder even than the deeply challenging task of understanding a 'primitive society', or understanding outmoded science (e.g. Thomas Kuhn on Aristotelian physics). The worlds of the Azande, or of Aristotelian physicists, deeply different and distant though they are, are far 'closer' to our normal world than is the 'world' of those in the grip of dread. Winch's Evans Pritchard's remarkable Azande, and the long-dead and irrecovably unavailable Aristotelian worldview are yet closer to being live options for us not in the grip of dread. For it is not just, as Winch and Kuhn have rightly taught us, that the world 'waxes and wanes as a whole', in ways beyond what is commonly assumed (where what is commonly assumed focuses often upon the hope that we can come to understand the 'primitive' or the outmoded through understanding a different set of (allegedly false) beliefs). Rather, the very sense of security offered by the notion of 'world' itself starts to give out. The world 'wilts' on one, or thrusts itself upon one in ways that no world should.[3] This is why psychopathology is sometimes gestured at through such wonderful gnomic terms as (e.g.,) 'the unworlding of the world'. (I return towards this chapter's close to why such gnomisms are *necessary*.)

The key experiences of derealization and depersonalization are, for instance, I would suggest, profoundly *paradoxical*, and profoundly *resistant* to understanding. To experience the world, and yet not experience it *as* real world; or to experience the world and yet lose the sense that there is any self, any person at all who is having the experience... An actually experienced *epoche*, the bracketing of things that are presuppositional to – through-and-through presumed in – our normal experience; there are no words for this, no thoughts for it.

Louis Sass (1992, 1994) suggests that we can come to have *some* understanding of such experiences, of the crumbling of the world itself, through understanding the rational psychopathology of philosophical illusion.[4] That is, through Wittgenstein's delicate, inhabitative, dialogical understanding of the attractions to one of nothingnesses that masquerade as somethings: forms of words/thoughts which flicker for us between different senses, and so as yet actually have no sense at all. Sass suggests that the rational procedure by means of which one gets oneself convinced of solipsism, or ends up wanting to utter an inarticulate sound, is directly analogous to the paradoxical hovering between senses that characterizes some schizophreniform and the like experience. The logic of Sass's argument is that 'derealization' is (among other things) a name for what it would be to try, absurdly, to take sceptical doubts about the 'external world' seriously. And a good deal of schizophrenia can be understood better than ever before as a lived/felt logical working through of (the contradictions of the nonsense that is) 'solipsism'.[5] Sass sets out all this in marvellous detail, recounting anecdata, interpreting 'schizy' works of art, presenting clinical case studies – giving rich detail and examples that I will pass over here, but that are strongly recommended to the reader interested in taking study of these matters further.[6]

More recently, Sass (2007) has extended his reading of schizophrenic and some other psychotiform pathologies, to help understand how they manifest paradoxes and contradictions of emotionality: especially, the so-called 'Kretschmerian paradox' – the extraordinary, seemingly-impossible *fact* that schizophrenia-spectrum patients can *simultaneously* experience both exaggerated *and* diminished levels of affective response. I would add that similar phenomena appear at some of the worst recesses of depression: A state can be reached which is at the same time both non-aversive and as aversive as could be: both detached/devoid of feeling and as intensely psychologically painful as imaginable (or rather, seemingly: *more than* is imaginable... This again is a paradox that seemingly is sometimes lived by the psychopathologically afflicted).

Perhaps the word 'recess' in the previous sentence is not just coincidental. In my 'The Lord of the Rings: A Philosophical Reading' (in preparation[7]), I suggest something which is central to what I want to set out in the remainder of this chapter: that a common feature of a number of extremely aversive psychological conditions is a *retreat* (though that may make the phenomenon sound more *willed,* more reactive and independent, than it is[8]) from 'the lifeworld'. Withdrawal from others, from life – from 'the natural attitude'.

What is perhaps in common between (what are otherwise very different) the sufferer from a bad panic attack, for whom the reality of her surroundings temporarily fades or withdraws; the kind of extremely depressed person just mentioned, who feels herself in a black pit or black hole, somehow devitalized and walled-off from life and from other people; the person going through the paradoxical experience of derealization, knowing the world to be real and yet absolutely not feeling able to believe that it is[9]; and the paranoid schizophrenic continually trying to systematize an understanding of her threatening 'world', in which the assumed background ontology that we are consensually used to is no longer reliable...what is perhaps in common between these four, is such '*retreat*'. As Sass intimates: dread results, roughly, from an inability to dissolve the deeply problematic nature of such experiences. In Descartes' *Meditations*, one gets no sense of such dread; of the extremely aversive effects of feeling as if one is subject to systematic delusion, or losing one's mind.[10] Descartes' is as it were a purely – excessively – rationalist account of doubt...He splits the emotions, the 'soul', from the mind, in a way that makes it impossible to understand the felt reality of doubt. The way in which absence of world is *internally related* to the emotional experiences I am presenting in the present paper. Wittgensteinians are bound by contrast to highlight this sense: the lived, embodied force of feelings of disembodiment, or of psychological confusion without redress.

5. Dread as absence of world

It is too easy, then, it is insufficient, to say: fear has an object, whereas radical *angst* or dread does not.[11] That what makes the difference between something we can all understand – fear *of something (real)* – and something hard to fathom – fear of...nothing in particular (*viz.* lasting anxiety states) – is the self-perpetuating attraction of the 'strategem' of retreat as a way of sealing oneself off against the 'threat' offered by objects-in-general.[12] There is something quite right about this insight; but it is yet too easy. The hermeneutical challenge is – still – *harder*. For the different psychopathologies sketched in the preceding paragraph do not fail the reality test – they do not simply get the world wrong.[13] And while they are in part based, I believe, in a thoroughly would-be self-protective manoeuvre, of fearing all kinds of possibilities that do not normally bother people much or at all,[14] their phenomenology goes self-defeatingly beyond that. Their nature lies perhaps in the profoundly different *kind* of world that they present, phenomenologically? No; better, and harder still in the absence of a reliable, stable world *at all. That* is the *possibility* – a paradoxical (non-)place in 'logical space', hitherto all-too-little-noted in the history of thinking about emotion, reason and mind – that I wish to be outlining the nature and consequences of, in this piece. One is seemingly deprived of the world, of ordinary access to and natural presence in it, in one way or another. And one is almost certainly further cognitively/morbidly absorbed, terrified or depressed by this, which hardly helps (and explains part of the difficulty in emerging from serious psychical disorder)...The difference is, roughly, between *objectless* fear or sadness – that is, ordinary 'neurotic' anxiety or depression – and a *generalized objectlessness*.[15] A non-inhabitation of a world in which there reliably are objects at all.

No suitable object of comparison which itself is capable of relatively straightforward stable statement, presentation and appraisal is suitable, for this possibility. Winch, after undermining our presumption that we know how to 'place' Zande magic (i.e. as primitive science) had recourse to the object of comparison of *Christian prayer*, to help us see the Azande; Kuhn helped us see Aristotelian physics by first taking us as far from the Newtonian conception as it was possible to go, and giving us another world(-view). The problem of what I am calling extreme aversive cognitions and emotions is harder. An object of comparison which illuminates by similarity must in the present case be an 'object' which constantly shape-shifts. The situation is worse even than just objectlessness, *for that too is/sounds by nature static*. It is not that what I am calling 'dread' is fear without an object; it is that it is the *absence* of a stable world in which to place anything so 'harmless' or sane as a fear. One *has withdrawn from the world*; or again, the world has withdrawn from one.

Dread, a Wittgensteinian approach has helped us to see, is arguably the emotion naturally *appropriate* to that deeply paradoxical state. For radical doubt is not, *pace* Descartes, something that can be merely intellectually contemplated as a curiosity. We must contemplate what it would be like to *live* it, to 'believe' it, if we are to know what radical doubt truly *is*. Anything else is merely going through the motions. Is unserious.

Mutual aversion[16] between self and world gives birth to a profoundly aversive state. Dread, is the consequence of – I am almost inclined to say, it *is* – the state of torture of not being at home *at all* in the social and natural world.

Dread is the emotion of the world's limits and not of its facts or things that can be expressed in language (not even of things that are absent, missing or doubtful).

6. Wittgenstein on schizophrenia

Now consider, in light of the above, the following sequence, from *Culture and Value* (p. 87), from 1948:

> The greatest happiness for a human being is love. Suppose you say of the schizophrenic: he does not love, he cannot love, he refuses to love – where is the difference?
>
> 'He refuses to...' means: it is in his power. And *who* wants to say that?!
> Well, of what do we say 'it is in his power'? – We say it in cases where we want to draw a distinction. I can lift *this* weight, but I will not lift it; *that* weight I cannot lift.

Wittgenstein captures the argument I have been essaying in this chapter. Profound psychic disturbance can deny its sufferer the resources to be open to us making, with respect to them, the distinctions which are the bread and butter of our basal socio-psychological competence with one another. Our concepts give out hereabouts – our conceptual faculties reach a limit, a limit *of sense*. Not because of a poverty of concepts on our part, nor on the part of the sufferer. (We are not dealing here with a situation like that of understanding an animal, whose concepts are different from and (roughly) more primitive than ours. Rather, we are dealing here with a systemic *unclarity*. The task of understanding is 'uncompletable', because there is nothing that would count as completing it, because even the kind of understanding perhaps achieved in a chapter like the present one is strictly *limited*. Limited in roughly the same kind of way as one's understanding of a nonsense-poem faces a hermeneutic limit which there is no such thing as transcending. (Roughly: There isn't anything that it is to understand a nonsense-poem. If one succeeds in 'understanding' it, then one has *ipso facto* failed to understand it.)

To return then to Wittgenstein's formulation: Any understanding will be profoundly difficult, to say the very least: How are we to understand their being unable to make the distinction between does not, cannot and refuses to, a distinction which we rely on as a resource and as a matter of routine?

The lifeworld of a person not subject to these elementary distinctions as we 'normals' are…Do we even recognize it as the/a world at all? The world of the unhappy and of the happy are very different, but they are at least both worlds…The kind of unhappiness involved in the total recession of love that is the case where does not = cannot = refuses to is profoundly another kind to that which we are used to trying to understand.[17]

In profound psychopathology, *the distinction between actions (voluntarily undertaken by a person) and afflictions (sufferings undergone) gives out*.[18] But this is itself a *limit* to our understanding, or at the very least a most severe impediment thereto.[19]

7. Summary: suffering from a loss of world

In this chapter, I have sketched the hazards incumbent upon insufficiently-radical attempts to comprehend the extreme aversive emotions. That is, attempts that would in one way or another assimilate what I am calling dread to 'mere' anxiety, or to fear. I have in particular tried to characterize the difficulty in comprehending true dread; *and,* ironically, I have *thereby* (I hope) started to make it easier to understand…As with the remark from *Culture and Value* earlier about the different world of the crying child; as with Winch's initial moves with the Azande, questioning the attempt to assimilate their beliefs to the category of science; as with Kuhn's making defunct science inaccessible ('incommensurable' – see Sharrock and Read (2002) for detail): the first move towards understanding truly the alien (insofar as we can understand it) is to emphasize just how distant from us it *is*, and to undo the attractions of 'false friends'. (Indeed, I think this is much of what makes Winch and Kuhn into profoundly Wittgensteinian thinkers: their active prevention of the premature rush to 'understand' (to assimilate – especially to the image of science, that always hangs over us!); their teaching of differences; their emphasis on the provision of new, less expected objects of comparison to free the mind.[20]) The felt unfreedom of the mind in the grip of psychopathology, like its analogue in philosophy – here, the pregnant parallel that Sass exploits so effectively – is yet stranger: for the surety of mind, and world, and others, and love, *at least as categories*, is just what is no longer securely present. And thus, dread: being afraid of *everything*, including crucially of 'things' that are not things at all (such as 'sense-data' in themselves);[21] or, *infinite* fear (bearing in mind here Wittgenstein's understanding of the infinite as *utterly* different to the finite[22]); or, at being unable not to bracket; or, profound *aversion to the state of not being able to distinguish at all between mind and world*. Terror not at this or that, nor even at nothing, but rather at [nothing], or at the alienation that this journey inevitably involves.

Not fear without object, but a torturing profoundly terrifying total and yet only partial *loss of objects*.[23] (Much the same loss, intriguingly, that rational philosophy (e.g. Rationalism and Empiricism) pretends to countenance or to insinuate.)

8. Some concluding reflexive remarks

Concepts end 'somewhere'. One such 'place' (or, rather, set of 'places'), is the non-place – the un-world – that is (are) the hell(s) of loss of objects and others. In attempting to avoid misunderstanding such a non-place(s), one is therefore naturally 'reduced' to reaching for literary-philosophical presentations of the phenomena. One is required, that is, to use terms that deliberately court paradox (e.g. 'non-place'), and to use terms in ways that bump right up against the 'limits' of our customary understanding and use of them. One needs, as I have done even in this short piece, to go around and around this (most unstable of) landscape(s), to try to learn one's way about. Indeed, to have a chance of *getting* dread, one has *in a certain sense* to *mimic* the systemic tendencies to delusion or confusion or loss that it involves.[24]

Therefore, I have offered no theory, in this piece. I have, however, offered some terms, some forms of words, some uses that (I hope) may make it at least *easier* to avoid misunderstanding the extreme aversive emotions. And to help one understand what the mind rebels at: their extremity; their (literal) unworldiness; something stranger perhaps than is dreamt of even in Heidegger's or Kierkegaard's philosophies.[25] I have inevitably bumped up repeatedly against the limits of our language: those bumps have been deliberate, and themselves offer what insight, if any, my writing here attains to.

And so then: if I have offered anything useful here, by extending and applying Wittgenstein's style of thinking and some gems of his thought, it is: the initial delineation of a conceptual possibility for the nature and understanding of extreme aversive emotion that has not ever previously been made clear ... A more useful verbal object of comparison for dread than has hitherto been offered.[26]

Notes

1. As will become clear, I submit that there is a qualitative change at some point in depression/anxiety; that these can become imbued with a more or less psychotic tinge or flavour or character, and that that is one point where it starts to make sense to talk of *dread*. As it were: The fear and trembling in the face of God is become at some point a dread in the face of existence itself, putting what existence *is* into some doubt. So long as the category 'God' is stable, there is a limit to *angst*; that limit can be breached, when (for instance) the possible *character* of God becomes entirely open (e.g. perhaps God is entirely malevolent). I will not be examining Heidegger or Kierkegaard here; but I will indicate very briefly why I take (my development of) Wittgenstein's philosophy to be better able to cope with more-than-neurotic conditions than they are. (In a fuller presentation, I would also dwell on what I mostly just pass over here: the deep *differences* between various psychopathological conditions, and the deep doubts, that I share, over whether such diagnostic categories as 'schizophrenia' are even well-defined; one certainly cannot as a philosopher have much faith in the DSM definitions thereof.)

2. Compare here this intriguing remark, on p. 62 of Wittgenstein (1998): ' "It is high time for us to compare this phenomenon with something *different*" – one may say. – I am thinking, e.g., of mental illness.'

3. Powerful examples discussed by Louis Sass (1992) are his remarks of de Chirico and of 'Renee', which are worthy of examination should the reader wish to take this aspect of my topic further. Compare, for instance, this passage from de Chirico (quoted on p. 43 of Sass's text): 'One bright winter afternoon I found myself in the courtyard of the palace at Versailles. Everything looked at me with a strange and questioning glance. I saw then that every angle of the palace, every column, every window had a soul that was an enigma ... '. This led to de Chirico's famous conclusion, that one had to 'live in the world as if in *an immense museum of strangeness*.' (italics added)
One can slightly taste such a remarkably alien(-ated) mood, in some of de Chirico's marvellous and disturbing paintings, such as his 'The enigma of a day'.

4. Non-Wittgensteinian philosophy is as rational as psychopathology is ... This, contrary to appearance, is, however, no insult. All these are human possibilities, *rational* possibilities ... For more on how I certainly do not mean to be 'othering' the mentally ill, see the latter portions of Read (In preparation). For detail on the crucialness of the question of mood to philosophical illusion, see the conclusion of Read (2007).

5. For explication and detail, see pp. 29–75 of Sass (1994). Read (2007) also sets out various worries about the limits of Sass's approach, about his sometime tendency to make it seem as if Wittgenstein's reading of solipsism and so on offers a *stable* comparator for schizophrenia, when actually it offers *'only'* something absurd, and a sense of how we are vulnerable to such absurdities.

6. This chapter is not the place for examining examples, which are detailed at length elsewhere in Sass's work, mine, and so on. This chapter is simply setting out a possible mode for thinking of extreme aversive emotions, not attempting to prove

that that mode is more fruitful than others. To get closer to such proof, I would recommend also, of course, reading memoirs by the mentally-afflicted themselves, some of which are discussed in Part II of Read (2007).

One recent memoir which would richly repay a thorough such reading is Jeff Cumberland's *To Schich and back* (2006). Though Cumberland clearly mis-self-diagnoses (Surprisingly for a professional (academic) psychologist, he does not seem to realise (e.g) that derealization and depersonalization are not uncommon symptoms of major affective disorder episodes), his unusual degree of philosophical, psychological and psychopathological knowledge makes his memoir of neurosis and near-psychosis peculiarly reflexively powerful and insightful. (See also the interview that Cumberland did for the Lulu.com magazine, which (for ease of public access) I have (with consent) uploaded to my website, under the title 'Cumberland interview', at www.rupertread.fastmail.co.uk.)

7. See also my work in progress, 'The fantasy of safety through power: the psycho-political philosophy of "The Lord of the Rings," at www.uea.ac.uk/~j339/ publications.htm ; and also cf. a relevant Book Review of mine (2005). I submit that *The Lord of the Rings* is best-read as an 'allegory' of the attraction and futility of retreat to a 'place' where one is omnipotent. Such attraction and such futility is, I believe, *experienced* in various different ways and to different degrees at the heart of various major psychopathologies.

8. I have in mind here Sass's excellent discussion, 'Act or affliction?' at the close of chapter 2 of *Madness and Modernism* (1992). Our concepts give out here: there *is* no good answer to the question whether the sufferer from schizophrenia merely involuntarily undergoes suffering ('affliction') or acts in ways that co-create her condition ('act'). (Compare n. 9, below; and the closing discussion (below) of Wittgenstein's important remark on acts and afflictions (1998).) Thus, the word 'retreat' is itself no more than an useful 'object of comparison'. 'Retreating' *is* a *way of seeing* the phenomenon I am after here, *not* any kind of straightforward action carried out by the patient/sufferer.

9. If you are put in mind of Moore's Paradox here, that is certainly no coincidence. I think that Moore's Paradox too can be lived by an individual. This doesn't make it any less of a genuine (rather than a 'merely pragmatic') *paradox*; it rather broadens our conception of what a human life can involve, of 'where' it can lead one, unstably, to 'be'. The *concept* of belief *starts to break down*. And that means simultaneously that *what we ought to say* about what is happening starts to break down, or multiply. (This is one reason why Sass looks to art to illuminate the nature of schizophrenia. A scientific approach sits uncomfortably in a situation where there are always multiple things one can say to illuminate what is happening, and not just one thing.) The concept of belief as it were best fits central cases of itself; there are cases that one can encounter in psychopathology that in the end make it moot whether one wants to call what is encountered a 'belief' or not. This can even be a genuinely reflexive realization: see my remarks about Schreber's own awareness of his own nonsenses (which he nonetheless does not give up), in Part II of my (2007).

10. See Read-and-Gregory 2007, for discussion. Therein, we lay out how, while Descartes explicitly states that only a madman would, as a matter of fact, be gripped and perhaps quite taken in by his kind of doubts (as in prolonged 'derealization'), he just does not give any sense of how terrifying those doubts would be. (Am I being unfair to Descartes in this chapter? I think not: Descartes acts as though the doubts he has in mind can be contemplated as merely an intellectual

curiosity; but that (e.g.) another being might actually have total control over my mind cannot be actually *contemplated* without dread.)

11. 'Objectless emotions' are generally seen as a problem for Cognitivist'/ existentialist/Wittgensteinian accounts of the emotions, and thus some see them as tacitly supportive of 'Jamesian'/Cog.Sci. accounts (e.g. see Griffiths 1997). But these emotions concern *ways* of world-taking; Hutchinson's 'World-taking cognitivism' (2008) – in which the world can be 'taken' in radically different ways – completely solves the alleged problem with 'objectless emotions', I think: see his chapter in this volume. And his approach is highly consonant with mine, as I hope is obvious. BUT whether all this is so or not, my approach to *the extreme aversive emotions* sidesteps the alleged problem altogether. For, I am suggesting that *these* are not properly construed as objectless emotions. They are emotions which are better characterized as internally related to a *loss* of objects/of world.

It might nonetheless be claimed that I am assuming (without giving any argument to support the assumption) that 'world-taking cognitivism' is broadly true, because I am *assuming* that persons take the world cognitively/emotionally, or fail to do so, in consequential ways set out herein.... There is probably some crude level of truth in this claim – that is, there is probably some trivial (non-) thesis along these lines that I don't see anyone being able to object to. Simply because I fail to be able to think about *human beings* at all, without making *some* such 'assumption'.

12. Laing brilliantly depicts this in the closing sections of *The divided self* (1965). Furthermore, much of my enterprise in the present chapter is clearly traceable back in intellectual lineage to Laing's (and Sass's) thoughts on 'ontological insecurity'. (Note that I use scare-quotes around the term 'strategem' because of concerns about whether what we are speaking of here is an act or an affliction. As set out elsewhere in this chapter, whether intentional descriptions are fully appropriate hereabouts is itself an important – and imponderable – issue.)

13. This claim is justified in Sass *The Paradoxes of Delusion* (1994): Sass uses the metaphor of 'double book-keeping' to try to gesture at the far stranger reality of schizophrenic delusion: that the delusions do *not* generally displace an accurate grasp both in theory and in practice of the physical and social world. The world is somehow present and yet lost simultaneously; and this simultaneity of contradictories is itself a source of distress or confusion, a push to think through one's life and mind further, a thinking through that is usually pathological, increasing rather than reducing the problematic.

14. In a fuller presentation, I would wish to examine in some detail the key nugget of insight in the generally (in my view) unilluminating presentation of neurosis and psychosis alike in cognitive science and 'cognitive psychology' (NOT to be confused with 'cognitivism' in Hutchinson's sense); that nugget of insight is the possibility of generating anxiety, including extreme anxiety, through the risk-averse strategy of considering even the slightest threat or potential threat as if it were a real and present danger. Such 'false positives' play for sure a major role in much anxiety. (See also notes 12 & 11, above).

15. *Perhaps* Heidegger can be read as meaning this when he refers to there being no 'where' from which anxiety or dread comes, such that a sense of uncanniness can pervade everything.

16. But what of a radical doubt of the world, such as at some moments in some forms of Buddhism, which is not aversive? Doesn't that indicate that my criticism of

Descartes *is* after all plainly unfair, excessive? No. Buddhist practice, if it really brackets the world, involves *meeting* the demons of terror, of dread. Whereas Descartes pretends that one can entertain radical doubt without being in the least emotionally disturbed or unsettled. That is just untrue. (See also n. 23, below.)

17. For largely like-minded orientation/understanding in the emotions more generally, see Heidegger's *Parmenides*, Agamben's (2004), and (especially) chapter 4 of Hutchinson's (2008). On p. 135, Hutchinson writes, 'emotional responses to the world are responses of an enculturated being to loci of significance in its meaningful world.' Precisely right; and I am writing about emotions consequent upon a gross loss or excess of significance, or indeed, as I put it below, upon a loss of world.

18. Some might argue that MOST human action is actually neither pure act nor pure affliction, and that it is simplifying grammar that forces us to choose and makes us think that things should always be described as one or the other. But I would respond: human *action* is more, or less, free. Then there are some things that we merely/simply undergo. What it means to say that in severe psychopathology this distinction between act and affliction 'gives out', is that there are no longer secure criteria, *for the sufferer themselves or for anyone else*, as to whether one is acting more or less freely or merely suffering/undergoing something. Any attribution of act or affliction as the relevant category becomes increasingly impositional, as the degree of severity of pathology increases (for further discussion, see part II of my *Applying Wittgenstein* (2007)). At some risk of overgeneralization, and awfully quickly, roughly: Is a depressed person – in his or her depression itself, in an automatic chain of negative thoughts – acting, or afflicted? Hard to say. Is a severely/radically depressed or a schizophrenic person – in his or her psychotical experiences themselves, in a 'worldless' state – acting, or afflicted? Impossible to say. In principle, not only in practice.

19. And this kind of thing is what 'neo-Jamesian' theorists of the emotions, such as Paul Griffiths, can *in no way* make sense of. Their analysis, best-suited (I submit) to emotions common to both human and non-human animals (although in the end pretty hopeless and vapid even there, as Hutchinson demonstrates), just has no bearing at all, where our conceptual faculties reach a limit, and a quasi-artistic presentation – in which we test our language and our facility with words to the limit – becomes essential. The neo-Jamesians *have nothing to say* about the emotion that fits a true felt '*loss* of objects/world'.

20. For detail on what I have in mind here, see the compilation of the later Gordon Baker's excellent work *Wittgenstein's Method* (2004).

21. Being afraid of everything might awfully sound like being afraid *sans object*; but that is why my qualification above is crucial. One is afraid of 'non-things' too; one's entire mode of experiencing the world has shifted, such that it is misleading to talk of 'the world' any more, for fear of reminding us too much of what that term is freighted with, for us. For detail, see, for example, chapters 8–10 of Sass's (1992), on 'phantom concreteness', 'world catastrophe', and so on.

22. See part III of Read (2007) for some discussion; I have particularly in mind remarks of Wittgenstein's such as 'It isn't just impossible "for us men" to run through the natural numbers one by one; it's *impossible*; it means nothing.' (1975, p. 146); and 'Where the nonsense starts is with our habit of thinking of a large number as closer to infinity than a small one' (1975, p. 157).

23. Not, that is to say, objectless fear, but a state where even the *issue* of objects (of fear) or their absence is no longer assured, is no longer central. Where having

nothing to fear is no longer the main problem, because the environment in which it makes sense for one to 'have' *objects* at all is no longer assured, no longer present (Cf. my discussion of 'Renee' in Read (2007)).

A further question naturally raises itself at this point, a difficult question which would take another chapter at least to answer, but that it would be remiss of me not at least to mention: what makes the difference between psychopathology and mysticism? Don't some mystics too 'lose the world', but in a way that is not experienced by them as painful, and which does not incapacitate them?

In very brief: I think the essence of the difference lies in *confidence*, and *non-attachment*. I explain the former in my [In preparation]. The latter is examined with dexterity in Mark Epstein's work, especially his *Going to Pieces without Falling Apart* (1999).

But what Epstein and a number of key Buddhist thinkers have also pointed out is the absolutely crucial point that actually most successful mysticism does NOT in fact involve a loss of world (nor even a loss of self). It involves no *loss;* in a particular and oft-misunderstood sense, it involves finding self, world and so on to be 'empty', but this 'emptiness' is itself empty (rather than being felt as, as I believe it is in psychopathology, the one full thing). It involves only a loss of a fantasy of self, an *affirmative* realization of the 'emptiness' of self – and an *opening* to the world. Whereas in one way or another, as in my four psychopathological 'scenarios' outlined above (in section 3), most (though admittedly of course not all) psychopathology involves a kind of 'drowning' in self, and in fact a *substantiality* of self that delivers the *opposite* of what its constructor hopes for.

In Buddhist terms, in fact: fear is a form of suffering; anxiety is the predominant form of suffering from that suffering, or at least an extended form of that suffering even when its 'conditioning' object is not present; and what I am calling dread is a kind of suffering felt as if beyond any suffering, because no objects at all are securely present any more (and nor in the ordinary sense is there any security in categories such as 'mind' or 'suffering') and this is felt as a terrifying and unworlding lack, not as an insight or simply an experience.

24. For details on what my use of the term 'mimicry' here amounts to, see part II of Read (2007), especially my discussion there of 'creative mimicry'.

25. Though that (e.g.) both objects and the nothing themselves noth is, as intimated at the opening of this piece, a pretty good place to start in getting 'someplace' in comprehending this unworldiness.

26. Thanks for suggestive ideas and helpful comments to Alun Davies, Jeff Cumberland, Louis Sass, Laura Cook, Eugen Fischer and (especially) to Anne J. Jacobson and to this volume's editors. Grateful acknowledgements to Phil Hutchinson for a very fine detailed set of comments on an earlier draft of this chapter, comments which I doubt I have done justice to. All remaining flaws are of course in any case mine alone.

Bibliography

Agamben, G. (2004), *The Open: Man and Animal*. Trans. Attell, K. (Stanford: Stanford University).

Baker, G. (2004), *Wittgenstein's Method*, Morris K. (ed.) (Oxford: Blackwell).

Cumberland, J. (2006), *To Schiz and Back: A Philosophical Memoir of Hell* Lulu books [Lulu.com].

Epstein, M. (1999), *Going to Pieces Without Falling Apart* (New York: Random House).

Griffiths, P. (1997), *What Emotions Really Are*. (Chicago, I.L.: Chicago University Press).

Hutchinson, P. (2008), *Shame and Philosophy: An Investigation in the Philosophy of Emotions and Ethics* (Basingstoke: Palgrave).

Laing, R.D. (1965), *The Divided Self* (London: Penguin).

Read, R. and Sharrock, W. (2002), *Kuhn: The Philosopher of Scientific Revolution* (Oxford: Polity).

Read, R. (2005), Book Review: *The Lord of the Rings and Philosophy Philosophical Psychology* 18(3), 383–397.

——. and Gregory, M. (2007), Book Review: *Persons and Passions: Essays in Honour of Annette Baier Mind* 116, 173–176.

——. (2007), *Applying Wittgenstein* (edited by Cook, L.) (London: Continuum)

——, Hutchinson, P. and Sharrock, W. (2008), *There Is No Such Thing as Social Science: In Defence of Peter Winch* (London: Ashgate).

——. 'Can "schizophrenic language" be interpreted?', work in progress at www.uea.ac.uk/~j339/publications.htm

——. [In preparation] *The Lord of the Rings: A Philosophical Reading* (edited by Davies, A.).

Sass, L. (1992), *Madness and Modernism*. (Cambridge: Harvard).

——. (1994), *The Paradoxes of Delusion: Wittgenstein, Schreber, and the Schizophrenic Mind* (Ithaca, N.Y.: Cornell).

—— (2007), 'Contradictions of Emotion in Schizophrenia', *Cognition & Emotion* 21(2), 351–390.

Wittgenstein, L. (1975), *Philosophical Remarks* (Chicago, I.L.: University of Chicago Press).

——. (1998), *Culture and Value* (revised edition) (Oxford: Blackwell).

Index

Printed in Great Britain
by Amazon